MW01258501

ROCK CLIMBING
MINNESOTA

Third Edition

Katie Berg
and Angie Jacobsen

ESSEX, CONNECTICUT

An imprint of The Rowman & Littlefield Publishing Group, Inc.
4501 Forbes Blvd., Ste. 200
Lanham, MD 20706
www.rowman.com
Falcon and FalconGuides are registered trademarks and Make Adventure Your Story is a
trademark of The Rowman & Littlefield Publishing Group, Inc.

Distributed by NATIONAL BOOK NETWORK

Copyright © 2000, 2012, 2022 by The Rowman & Littlefield Publishing Group, Inc.
Unless otherwise noted, photos © Angie Jacobsen
Maps by The Rowman & Littlefield Publishing Group, Inc.
Photos edited by Patrick Maun
Technical editor: Hillary Waters

All rights reserved. No part of this book may be reproduced in any form or by any electronic
or mechanical means, including information storage and retrieval systems, without written
permission from the publisher, except by a reviewer who may quote passages in a review.

British Library Cataloguing in Publication Information available

Library of Congress Cataloging-in-Publication Data

Names: Berg, Katie, 1985- author. | Jacobsen, Angie, author.
Title: Rock climbing Minnesota / Katie Berg, Angie Jacobsen.
Description: Third edition. | Guilford, Connecticut : FalconGuides, 2022. |
    Previous editions of this guide were the combined Rock climbing
    Minnesota and Wisconsin. | Includes bibliographical references. |
    Summary: "This updated edition contains three brand-new areas and describes over 1,100
    routes at 14 major areas, offering a lifetime of cragging for beginners and experts alike"—
    Provided by publisher.
    Identifiers: LCCN 2021047757 (print) | LCCN 2021047758 (ebook) | ISBN
    9781493047598 (paperback) | ISBN 9781493047604 (epub)
    Subjects: LCSH: Rock climbing—Minnesota—Guidebooks. | Minnesota—Guidebooks
Classification: LCC GV199.42.M6 B474 2022 (print) | LCC GV199.42.M6 (ebook) | DDC
796.522/309776—dc23
LC record available at https://lccn.loc.gov/2021047757
LC ebook record available at https://lccn.loc.gov/2021047758

♾️™ The paper used in this publication meets the minimum requirements of American
National Standard for Information Sciences—Permanence of Paper for Printed Library
Materials, ANSI/NISO Z39.48-1992.

The authors and The Rowman & Littlefield Publishing Group, Inc., assume no liability for
accidents happening to, or injuries sustained by, readers who engage in the activities described
in this book.

WARNING:

Climbing is a sport where you may be seriously injured or die. Read this before you use this book.

This guidebook is a compilation of unverified information gathered from many different climbers. The author cannot assure the accuracy of any of the information in this book, including the topos and route descriptions, the difficulty ratings, and the protection ratings. These may be incorrect or misleading, as ratings of climbing difficulty and danger are always subjective and depend on the physical characteristics (for example, height), experience, technical ability, confidence, and physical fitness of the climber who supplied the rating. Additionally, climbers who achieve first ascents sometimes underrate the difficulty or danger of the climbing route. Therefore, be warned that you must exercise your own judgment on where a climbing route goes, its difficulty, and your ability to safely protect yourself from the risks of rock climbing. Examples of some of these risks are: falling due to technical difficulty or due to natural hazards such as holds breaking, falling rock, climbing equipment dropped by other climbers, hazards of weather and lightning, your own equipment failure, and failure or absence of fixed protection.

You should not depend on any information gleaned from this book for your personal safety; your safety depends on your own good judgment, based on experience and a realistic assessment of your climbing ability. If you have any doubt as to your ability to safely climb a route described in this book, do not attempt it.

The following are some ways to make your use of this book safer:

1. Consultation: You should consult with other climbers about the difficulty and danger of a particular climb prior to attempting it. Most local climbers are glad to give advice on routes in their area; we suggest that you contact locals to confirm ratings and safety of particular routes and to obtain first-hand information about a route chosen from this book.

2. Instruction: Most climbing areas have local climbing instructors and guides available. We recommend that you engage an instructor or guide to learn safety techniques and to become familiar with the routes and hazards of the areas described in this book. Even after you are proficient in climbing safely, occasional use of a guide is a safe way to raise your climbing standard and learn advanced techniques.

3. Fixed Protection: Some of the routes in this book may use bolts and pitons that are permanently placed in the rock. Because of variances in the manner of placement, weathering, metal fatigue, the quality of the metal used, and many other factors, these fixed protection pieces should always be considered suspect and should always be backed up by equipment that you place yourself. Never depend on a single piece of fixed protection for your safety, because you never can tell whether it will hold weight. In some cases, fixed protection may have been removed or is now missing. However, climbers should not always add new pieces of protection unless existing protection is faulty. Existing protection can be tested by an experienced climber and its strength determined. Climbers are strongly encouraged not to add bolts and drilled pitons to a route. They need to climb the route in the style of the first ascent party (or better) or choose a route within their ability—a route to which they do not have to add additional fixed anchors.

Be aware of the following specific potential hazards that could arise in using this book:

1. Incorrect Descriptions of Routes: If you climb a route and you have a doubt as to where it goes, you should not continue unless you are sure that you can go that way safely. Route descriptions and topos in this book could be inaccurate or misleading.

2. Incorrect Difficulty Rating: A route might be more difficult than the rating indicates. Do not be lulled into a false sense of security by the difficulty rating.

3. Incorrect Protection Rating: If you climb a route and you are unable to arrange adequate protection from the risk of falling through the use of fixed pitons or bolts and by placing your own protection devices, do not assume that there is adequate protection available higher just because the route protection rating indicates the route does not have an X or an R rating. Every route is potentially an X (a fall may be deadly) due to the inherent hazards of climbing— including, for example, failure or absence of fixed protection, your own equipment's failure, or improper use of climbing equipment.

There are no warranties, whether expressed or implied, that this guidebook is accurate or that the information contained in it is reliable. There are no warranties of fitness for a particular purpose or that this guide is merchantable. Your use of this book indicates your assumption of the risk that it may contain errors and is an acknowledgment of your own sole responsibility for your climbing safety.

CONTENTS

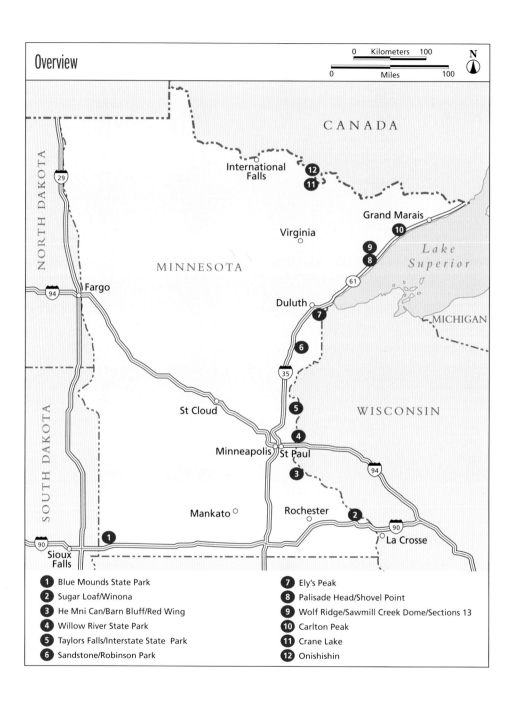

Overview

| 0 Kilometers 100 |
| 0 Miles 100 |

N

CANADA

International Falls

⑫

⑪

NORTH DAKOTA

⑳ 29

Grand Marais

⑩

Virginia ○

MINNESOTA

⑨
⑧

Lake Superior

⑳ 94 Fargo

61

Duluth

⑦

MICHIGAN

⑥

35

St Cloud

⑤

WISCONSIN

④

SOUTH DAKOTA

Minneapolis) St Paul

③

94

Mankato ○

Rochester ○

② 90

⑳ 94

⑳ 90

①

Sioux Falls

La Crosse

① Blue Mounds State Park
② Sugar Loaf/Winona
③ He Mni Can/Barn Bluff/Red Wing
④ Willow River State Park
⑤ Taylors Falls/Interstate State Park
⑥ Sandstone/Robinson Park

⑦ Ely's Peak
⑧ Palisade Head/Shovel Point
⑨ Wolf Ridge/Sawmill Creek Dome/Sections 13
⑩ Carlton Peak
⑪ Crane Lake
⑫ Onishishin

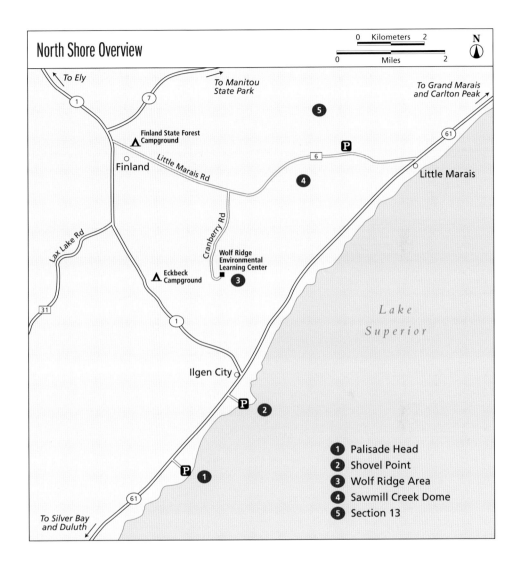

North Shore Overview

To Ely

To Manitou
State Park

To Grand Marais
and Carlton Peak

N

0   Kilometers   2

0   Miles   2

1

7

61

5

Finland State Forest
Campground

P

6

Finland

Little Marais Rd

4

Little Marais

Lax Lake Rd

Cranberry Rd

Wolf Ridge
Environmental
Learning Center

Eckbeck
Campground

3

31

1

Lake

Superior

Ilgen City

P

2

61

1   Palisade Head
2   Shovel Point
3   Wolf Ridge Area
4   Sawmill Creek Dome
5   Section 13

P

1

To Silver Bay
and Duluth

PREFACE TO THE THIRD EDITION

This book could not have been made without the incredible support of the Minnesota climbing community and their willingness to share their knowledge, passion, and expertise to help us make this the best guidebook we possibly could create.

If we were to list everyone who answered a question here or there, gave us their thoughts on an idea or photo, or reached out with suggestions to make this book better, well, we wouldn't have room for much else. However, we do want to recognize a handful of folks who donated significant amounts of time and talents to this project.

For all the tireless proofreading of numerous editions of the manuscript, editing of topos and maps, fact-checking, answering our incessant questions, and endless encouragement throughout the entirety of the project, we'd like to thank Eric Barnard, Randall Baum, David Butcher, Michael Endrizzi, Jeff Engel, Sean Foster, Peter Graupner, Jess Griffith, Kurt Hager, Josh Helke, Tyler Hoffart, Steve Johnson, Bryan Karban, Rick Kollath, Paul Kralovec, Lucas Kramer, Karina Krosbakken, Taylor Krosbakken, Eldon Krosch Jr., Peter Lenz, Jeremiah LeTourneau, James Loveridge, Bobby Omann, Jerry and Brenda Pohlman, Kelly Randall, Peter Smerud, Taylor Stewart, Ray Theiler, Slavomír Tkáč, Al Wiberg, and Mark Wright.

Thank you to the following photographers whose images grace the pages of this edition: Rich Anthony, Randall Baum, Dan Brazil, Adrian Danciu, Chris Deal, Sean Foster, Kris Gorny, William Hopkins, Craig Huang, Seth Iverson, Anthony Johnson, Taylor Krosbakken, Peter Lenz, Patrick Maun, Pi, Tony Mansourian, Crysten Nesseth, Sheila Novak, Bobby Omann, Brenda Piekarski, Sevve Stember, Slavomír Tkáč, Rutger Van Huber, and Andy Wickstrom.

To those—way too numerous to list—who came out to climb (wearing bright colors!), who sat for interviews about the crags in this book, who filled out surveys about your favorite climbs in the state, and to those who supported us with hugs and encouragement, coffee, cookies, and scotch, we never would have finished this project without you. Thank you.

Thanks to the Minnesota Climbers Association and the Duluth Climbers Coalition for all of their support in the creation of this book, and for all their ongoing stewardship within the state.

Special thanks to Hillary Waters for being our technical editor, and to Patrick Maun for being our photo editor. Your help in the final stages of editing cannot be overstated and has only made this guidebook better.

And finally, thanks to Mike Farris, who wrote the first two editions of this guidebook. We also were greatly helped by the multitude of previous Minnesota climbing guidebooks and their authors; find this list in "Additional Resources" at the end of the book.

Katie's personal thanks: There is no way that I could have written this book without the constant love, support, and outright cheerleading from my friends and family. From supportive messages, cards in the mail, flowers and care packages, to even deadline-week lunch deliveries—you all kept me going and kept me happy, and I am so incredibly grateful for each and every one of you. I could not have done it without you. A big thank-you to my partner in this crazy endeavor, Angie. If it wasn't for her, I wouldn't have even thought about taking on this project.

Thank you to my husband Paul. While he wasn't psyched that I spent so many hours, nights, and weekends at the computer, he supported me throughout the process with love, taking on more of the home load, and food. Love you, dear.

And, of course, a giant thank-you to my core supporters: Kyle, Kendra, Olin, and Mom and Dad. Our adventures together are the stuff of legends. I love you and appreciate you all so much. Let's go on another epic family trip soon so we can laugh when things go massively wrong.

Angie's personal thanks and dedication: Thanks to my writing partner Katie for agreeing to take on this enormous project and providing so much enthusiasm and stoke along the way. Shout out to the folks at Arc'teryx MSP for all your support, and for keeping me warm on all those frosty days up north. To the following dear friends: Bridget for always listening to my joys and frustrations and casually throwing out brilliant insight into my psyche; Sean for being my climbing partner all these years (#TeamSlowestAscent), for gently pushing me out of my comfort zone and teaching me there is always time for one more climb; Mark for his mentorship, always being game to support my objectives, and for reminding me when climbs get hard, "we're just exploring!"; and Rachelle, who not only inspires me with her strength, compassion, and brutal honesty, but gently pushes me to be a better climber and human—I appreciate you all and love you a ton. To my favorite kids Aaron and Kylie: You're the best, and I'm honored you're still willing to hang out and even climb with me once in a while. Finally, this book is dedicated to my dad for tirelessly supporting every crazy endeavor I've ever done and inviting me and all my climber friends to use the cabin as a basecamp and refuge during the creation of this book. I love you! Now let's go fishing.

Shovel Point Aerial photo: Brenda Piekarski

INTRODUCTION

Minnesota is not particularly well known for its climbing. But we have a secret.

Minnesota has a rich tapestry of different rock types and locations scattered across the state and everything from roadside crags to backcountry adventures only accessible via boat.

Buttresses rise out of the flat prairie at Blue Mounds State Park. The Sioux quartzite makes for some of the oldest climbable formations in Minnesota and gives the cliffs a signature blue tint at sunset.

Interstate State Park climbers get in a full-value day on cliffs bordering the St. Croix River, then can celebrate sends with an evening float. Its basalt rock is black-to-gray, and the fine-grained igneous rock can feel slippery when wet or even humid. The many potholes sprinkled throughout the park are a reminder of the park's glacial history. Willow River gives climbers an overhung world of burly moves above a raging waterfall. It's not uncommon to see climbers midroute resting on a kneebar with spray in their face.

Three Minnesota crags were former quarries, currently redeveloped for sport climbing. Sugar Loaf's Oneota dolomite, a sedimentary limestone, interrupts the rolling hills in Winona and is a great place for beginning outdoor sport leaders. He Mni Can's unrelenting vertical test pieces hone technique, finger strength, and grit on limestone faces marked by its past. Sandstone is a multifaceted year-round playground where one can boulder, sport, trad, and ice climb—sometimes all in the same day.

Going farther north, a day at Ely's Peak could start with climbing and end with mountain biking on a wedge of basalt that indicates that the rocks are among the oldest of the North Shore lavas. Northern inland climbing at Carlton Peak, Wolf Ridge, Sawmill Dome, and

Section 13 boasts rare anorthosite rock, and while it can tear apart fingertips, it helps new trad climbers stick to the wall as they practice their skills.

On Lake Superior, Shovel Point is approachable and fun, with some routes lowering to the water and spectators (hopefully) crawling on their stomachs to peer over the edge.

The sheer cliffs of Palisade Head beckon the brave to scale, with long routes overhanging the big lake. Both Shovel and Palisade boast 200-foot-thick flows of red, porphyritic rhyolite, which contains an abundance of quartz, alkali feldspar, and plagioclase minerals. The rhyolite forms such spectacular cliffs because it is more resistant to weathering than the surrounding basalts. It's a good thing they are, as the waves of Lake Superior boast an epic background soundtrack for climbers, sometimes supplemented with wind, chilling fog, and intense storms.

At Crane Lake, a day of climbing could mean paddling to the crag. And in the far north at Onishishin, escape by boating just across the border into Canada for a true backcountry climbing experience in the Northwoods on bomber granite, complete with bear and moose sightings, fishing for dinner, belaying off of a raft, and staying up to see the northern lights.

We are excited to share the information needed so you can find, navigate, and fully experience every single one of these amazing places.

Climb on, friends.

OUTDOOR ETHICS, ETIQUETTE, AND SAFETY

The information in this book is as accurate as possible at the time of publication. Over time things change, holds break, access changes, roads close, pillars collapse, folks will free climb old aid routes, and pandemics might close borders again. A handful of small crags were not included because either access is in flux or there was not enough information for a fully developed chapter.

If you have minimal or no outdoor climbing experience, there are a few things to be aware of:

- Climbing indoors and climbing outdoors on real rock are completely different experiences. Unlike in the gym, where the space has been designed to keep you as safe as possible, when you are outdoors, you are taking your safety into your own hands. **If you've never climbed outdoors, seek out qualified instruction,** whether from a course, an experienced mentor, or a professional guide.
- It is the responsibility of every climber to preserve the climbing environment for future users. Check out the "Access and Environmental Concerns" section below on how you can do this.
- Learn about the Access Fund, the national nonprofit dedicated to stewardship, keeping climbing areas open and accessible, and promoting "The Climber's Pact" so we can be the best stewards possible for our sport.
- Learn about local nonprofits, such as the Minnesota Climbers Association, the Duluth Climbers Coalition, and the local chapter of the American Alpine Club, and how you can support their work for climbing access and education in Minnesota.
- Check out local Adopt-a-Crag events to build trails, clean crags, and give back.

Some **outdoor statewide climbing ethics** to consider:

- Pay park entry fees and park in designated areas.
- Register for a climbing permit if required.
- Follow all regulations and ethics listed for a specific area.
- Do not toprope through fixed anchors (except Sugar Loaf). General ethic is for the last climber to lower off of sport routes in Minnesota as opposed to rappelling. It's faster and safer.
- Please replace worn or unsafe anchor carabiners with one of your own, or report the location and route to the Minnesota Climbers Association.
- Minimize the use of chalk, and use natural-colored chalk if available.
- Do not place pitons; do not chip or glue rock holds.
- If you are considering bolting new routes, check with the MCA about access.
- Avoid unnecessary "cleaning" (destroying vegetation, including lichen).
- Avoid slinging trees or bushes that are close to cliff edges, small, or unsturdy (for your sake and the tree's).

Some **outdoor climbing etiquette** to consider:

- If you must bring your dog, tie them up away from others and clean up their poop and dispose of it properly. If they bark, leave them home. If access is difficult, leave them home.
- Leave your Bluetooth speakers at home. Most outdoor users prefer nature sounds or peace and quiet over your favorite band.
- Don't smoke at the base of crags. Walk a good distance away so the smoke does not affect others while they're climbing or belaying. Pack out your butts.
- Learn how to use a WAG bag, or how to poop outdoors appropriately, or don't poop at the crag. Pack out your TP.
- Drones are illegal to fly in state parks without a permit from the DNR. They also have strict regulations to follow at many of the other crags in Minnesota. In addition, most climbers find them extremely annoying. Follow the rules and be considerate.

The future of climbing in most areas in this guide depends on climbers, as a group, cooperating with landowners and managers to keep access open.

Access and Environmental Concerns

Access to the public and private lands we climb on is a privilege many have spent years working for. Local and national nonprofit organizations such as the Minnesota Climbers Association, the Duluth Climbing Coalition, and the Access Fund (among others) work with landowners and government agencies to ensure that climbers have continued access to the crags we love so much. In addition, these organizations work toward educating climbers on land access and Leave No Trace principles, maintaining the integrity of fixed hardware on bolted routes, and hosting events like cleanups and community gatherings.

While there is a history of some climbers simply doing what they want, often under the radar, the tide has shifted to the climbing community having a working and open relationship with landowners and government agencies. Instead of quietly bolting a route on state land and possibly getting the entire crag closed to climbing, climbers have shifted to being responsible stewards of the sport. To make sure that these positive relationships remain intact and crags remain open, climbers must be sensitive to their impact at every crag, educate themselves on the places that they're climbing, and adhere to locally established principles. A great place to start is by following the Seven Principles of Leave No Trace.

The Leave No Trace Center for Outdoor Ethics has compiled seven principles for not only climbers but all outdoorists to adopt in order to keep impact low and access open. These principles were created in conjunction with scientists, land owners and managers, and outdoor education leaders, and are supported by extensive research. They are revisited often to reflect the latest data on how the outdoor community can minimize our impact on these special places.

The Seven Principles of Leave No Trace are:

- Plan Ahead & Prepare
- Travel & Camp on Durable Surfaces
- Dispose of Waste Properly
- Leave What You Find
- Minimize Campfire Impacts
- Respect Wildlife
- Be Considerate of Other Visitors

The wording of these is broad for a reason, allowing them to be adapted to all outdoor activities, including mountain biking, kayaking, hiking, and climbing. Some of the ways these principles can apply specifically to climbers are:

- **Plan Ahead & Prepare**
  - Get permits, learn about and respect route closures, and follow all regulations at the crag you'll be visiting.
- **Travel & Camp on Durable Surfaces**
  - Stay on approach and descent trails and avoid causing extra erosion by taking short cuts.
  - Avoid spreading your gear all over the base of the area you're climbing. Do not crush any plants or create a tripping hazard on the trail.
- **Dispose of Waste Properly**
  - Pick. Up. Your. Trash. All of it. Pack out what you packed in.
  - There is a right way and a wrong way to go to the bathroom outdoors. Learn before you go.
- **Leave What You Find**
  - Do not chop down trees or prune limbs that might interfere with a route.
  - Do not remove or disturb any artifacts you encounter.
- **Minimize Campfire Impacts**

- Build a fire only inside of an existing fire ring. Rock outcrops can often show black fire scars for years.
- **Respect Wildlife**
  - Keep your distance from all wildlife and never feed them. If you are affecting their behavior, you are too close. Do not disturb bats, for both their health and your own.
  - Respect areas closed due to wildlife.
- **Be Considerate of Other Visitors**
  - Be respectful of all other user groups. You represent the climbing community when you interact with them.
  - Many areas in Minnesota have multiuser trails. Yield to other users when appropriate and remember those traveling uphill have the right of way on narrow paths.
  - Don't play music or allow your dogs to bark incessantly. Many users, not just climbers, come outdoors for peace and quiet.

These are only some of the many ways that the Seven Principles can be interpreted by the climbing community, and as the sport adapts and climber advocacy evolves, so should the community. By following Leave No Trace ethics, climbers can help ensure continued use of our favorite crags by being responsible stewards of the land.

The North Shore Climbers Chalk Ethic

The short version: The vast majority of climbers on the North Shore use chalk. Climbers should do their best to know and practice Leave No Trace principles.

The long version: The original North Shore Climbers "No-chalk Ethic" is only part of the story.

Chalk use on the North Shore of Minnesota is often misrepresented as to the original intent and purpose of the ethic. Historically, there have always been two schools of thought, but only one has seen any attention in print. Some climbers, working with the DNR and state parks to establish climbing management plans, promoted the idea that there should be no chalk use along the North Shore. And yet there were as many, if not more, climbers that continued to use chalk—including many first ascensionists—putting up routes at the same time or earlier as those who began the no-chalk ethic.

There is no policy prohibiting the use of chalk when climbing in the designated climbing areas in Minnesota state parks. Representatives at the DNR and state parks have said chalk use will not impede access, and there is no time in the history of Minnesota climbing that chalk has not been used on the North Shore. Only on the private land of Wolf Ridge do the landowners prohibit climbers from using chalk as part of their land use policy.

The over-focused attention to the no-chalk ethic has been an unfortunate distraction and disservice to the larger discussion of climbers practicing Leave No Trace principles at the crag. This is not to say chalk is not part of that conversation, but overall climber impacts are far greater than chalk use. While it's appreciated that chalk use is part of the LNT conversation, arguments about chalk overtake the opportunities to learn about so many other behaviors that are far more problematic than chalk, like cutting down or destroying trees, blaring music, not picking up dog poop, stepping on and killing cryptobiotic soil, not respecting route closures, and the like. Each causes far more damage to the climbing areas and to relationships with land managers than chalk on any route.

The main point has been missed. The big-picture focus for climbers as stewards should be practicing LNT principles at all times. As climbers, we should always evaluate and critically analyze our own practices as well as revisit and question past ideals so that we can best care for the resources that we love.

Safety at Minnesota Crags

- Loose rock is abundant at almost all of the crags across the state, though it's arguably worse at He Mni Can, Sugar Loaf, Interstate State Park, and Palisade Head. All cliffs have erosion, and the freeze/thaw cycle that's a normal part of the harsh Minnesota winters means that rock that was great for anchors one season is unsafe the next. Be diligent with gear and anchor placements, wear helmets when climbing and belaying, and keep in mind that the cliff is constantly changing every season.

- Many of the climbing areas are in tourist areas, next to hiking trails, or even smack in the middle of a city. People and kids of all ages feel compelled to throw things over the edge, even if you are clearly visible below. They also are fascinated by climbing gear and may not understand that tampering with anchoring gear could be catastrophic. Constantly check your systems, and know you may have to answer questions from curious bystanders.

- There are numerous pieces of old fixed protection at multiple crags across the state. Just because it's fixed doesn't mean it's still reliable. Pitons should always be considered unreliable due to their age. There is no guaranteed way to test a bolt's integrity once placed. Even the most carefully placed bolt is only as strong as the rock in which it is found. For example, chunks of rock with bolts attached to them have fallen off at He Mni Can and Willow River, especially in the spring. Please be cautious.

HOW TO USE THIS GUIDEBOOK

Each chapter is divided into sections at the beginning to give you important information. Here's what to expect:

Name of an Area: The character of an area, rock type, fun local specifics, and any weather info or crag orientation opens each area.

Types of Climbing and Gear: Is it slab, face, overhanging, crack, or something else? Here's what to expect, as well as any details about anchors or belays.

- **Standard Single Rack:** Throughout the book the term "single rack" is used. This refers to a traditional climbing rack that would consist of a full set of nuts or stoppers, a full set of camalots from 0.3 to 3 inches, and eight to ten quickdraws supplemented with three to five long slings. Routes that need longer rope lengths beyond a standard 60-meter rope are noted.

- **Note on Gear Recommendations:** They are just that—recommendations. Use your own personal judgment and experience to decide what to bring to suit your own comfort level.

- Bolt counts are given when known and do not include the anchors. Bolt counts are estimates, as bolts are occasionally added or removed from routes.
- Trad and mixed routes in a predominantly sport climbing area are noted in the route description, and vice versa.

Land Acknowledgment: The climbing crags throughout the state of Minnesota are located on traditional, ancestral, and contemporary lands of indigenous people. We acknowledge that this is a complex and layered history, and a land acknowledgment is one of the ways in which climbers can begin a conversation about this land and our relationships with it and each other. We encourage the climbing community to learn more about the history, treaties, communities, nonprofits, and people of these lands as part of our stewardship. Resources like the Native Governance Center of Minnesota or local tribes are a great place to start.

Permits, Local Ethics, and Regulations: To maintain access to all of the crags in this book and keep relationships positive with land owners and managers, please learn about and follow the information in this section, which includes:

- Vehicle permits (*All* Minnesota state parks require a vehicle permit.)
- Climbing permits (*All* Minnesota state parks require a free climbing permit specific to each state park, and some areas require a specific check-in.)
- Seasonal route closures (Many areas have closures for peregrine falcons.)
- Rules related to dogs

Getting There and Parking: Driving directions and parking information, and occasionally GPS coordinates.

Approach: How to get to the climbs, usually with both top and bottom access as needed.

Camping and Amenities: Where the nearest campground(s) are and restroom availability.

Hazards: Besides realizing that you are out in the wilderness and may encounter animals, old gear that isn't trustworthy, and ticks, this section points out hazards that are specific to that particular area, such as poison ivy, wasps, and the like.

Routes Not to Miss: These are a variety of high-quality and fun routes, often popular, but also some hidden gems.

Grades

- This guidebook uses the standard American Yosemite Decimal System (YDS).
- Some grades have been changed from the previous editions due to rockfall, polished elements, or current general consensus gleaned from the authors' personal experience, interviews with multiple locals from each crag, and input from mountainproject.com.
- Grades generally are unique to that particular area, though related overall to YDS. A 5.11 130-foot crack at Palisade Head will feel different than a 60-foot 5.11 crimpy face at He Mni Can. Take grades with a grain of salt, as they depend on technique, experience, height, finger strength, fitness level, and all the other factors that make grading very subjective.

Names

- Routes are traditionally named by the first ascensionist and renamed when climbed in a "better" style (for example, an aid climb going free).
- Some route names have been changed by the first ascensionists in response to the ongoing national conversation regarding route names. A few have been changed by the authors when the first ascensionist was not known.

Quality Ratings

Quality ratings are indicated using a system of zero to four stars. Quality ratings were based on input from other climbers, personal experience, previous guidebooks, community input from mountainproject.com, and by inspection. Just like difficulty ratings, these quality ratings can change through time and are absolutely and completely subjective.

★★★★: One of the best climbs in the area; a must-do.

★★★: A great climb that is well worth doing, especially if you don't get to this crag often.

★★: A good route worth climbing.

★: An OK route that may have some redeeming qualities, but probably doesn't need to be climbed more than once.

No stars: The route may be mossy, have poor rock, is uninteresting, have awkward or not great movement, is misbolted, or there is little to no information.

FA Info and How It's Displayed in This Book

This is not a history book. There was not enough space to chronicle the story behind the development and naming of every route. To stay consistent with modern guidebook standards, if a free ascent is known, that is what is listed. Previous guidebooks for the area(s) chronicle those who put up a route on aid, or first toprope, etc. If a route was led from start to finish in the style of the area, the climber who did that is the one listed as the FA. In some cases (especially on the North Shore), it's not even known if the first ascent was on toprope or lead. For more information, check out "Additional Resources" at the end of the book for a list of previous guidebooks and other references.

For the first ascent information that is included with some climbs, acronyms are used (when the information is known) and defined as follows: FA—first ascent (either lead or aid); FTR—first toprope ascent.

Topo Legend

Red = fully bolted sport route

Yellow = trad or toprope. Could have an occasional bolt or old fixed pin or piton.

Orange = mixed. The following standard was used to determine if a route should be orange:

- Two or more bolts on a trad route
- One or more areas or runouts on a bolted sport route that most climbers would want to protect with gear

Map Legend

Transportation

═⟨5⟩═	Interstate Highway
═⟨8⟩═	US Highway
═⟨3⟩═	State Highway
═[CR 23]═	Local Road
= = = =	Unpaved Road
├———┤	Railroad Tracks
———	Paved Trail
- - - - - -	Trail

Water Features

⬭	Body of Water
	Marsh/Swamp
	River/Creek

Land Management

- - - - - -	State Line
▭	Park

Symbols

🛶	Boat Launch
‿	Bridge
▲	Campground
⊥⊥⊥⊥⊥	Cliff
❶	Climbing location
⬭	Crag/Boulder
▲	Mountain Peak/Summit
🅿	Parking
🛖	Picnic Area
■	Point of Interest/Structure
🚻	Restroom
○	Town
❓	Visitor Information/Fee Station

Topo Legend

××	Fixed belay station	▬▬▬▬▬	Mixed Route
———	Trad Route	▬▬▬▬▬	Bolted Sport Route

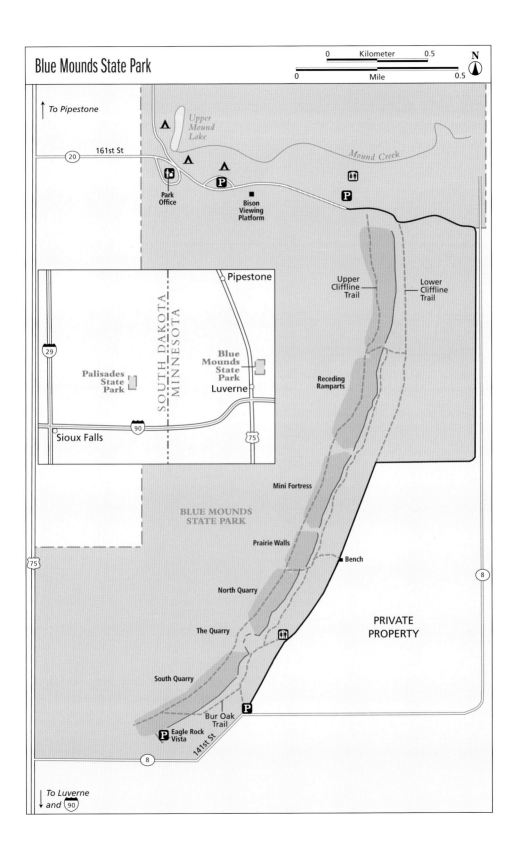

Blue Mounds State Park

0   Kilometer   0.5

0   Mile   0.5

N

To Pipestone

Upper Mound Lake

Mound Creek

161st St

20

Park Office

Bison Viewing Platform

P

P

Pipestone

Upper Cliffline Trail

Lower Cliffline Trail

SOUTH DAKOTA

MINNESOTA

29

Palisades State Park

Blue Mounds State Park

Luverne

90

Sioux Falls

75

Receding Ramparts

BLUE MOUNDS STATE PARK

Mini Fortress

Prairie Walls

Bench

75

North Quarry

8

The Quarry

PRIVATE PROPERTY

South Quarry

Bur Oak Trail

P

P Eagle Rock Vista

141st St

8

To Luverne and 90

Kelly Randall rope-soloing *Black Wall* (5.9)

BLUE MOUNDS STATE PARK

With 1.5 miles of picturesque cliff line rupturing the surrounding prairie, Blue Mounds hosts some truly incredible crack and face climbing with folklore and mysterious history to boot. For climbing, the quality of the quartzite here matches that of Devil's Lake and is completely different from all the other climbing in the state.

There are excellent moderate topropes and trad leads without a giant approach, and the face climbing is thought-provoking and fun. Hone your trad skills with lots of passive pro here. Fewer climbers also means a more adventurous feel to the climbs—you won't be able to rely on obvious chalk lines, and you may have to do some minor "gardening" up top to clear out cracks for setting anchors. The approach, flat land, and sparse crowds also make Blue Mounds a great place to bring kids and still get an adventure feel. Biking and hiking paths, a bison herd, bird watching, and a nearby river with a collapsed dam make for good rest day adventures.

Types of Climbing and Gear

Blue Mounds is primarily toprope climbing on natural anchors with some trad. A single rack (nuts, hexes, tricams, cams up to 4 inches), a lot of long anchor line (three different 30- to 60-foot webbing or static rope pieces), and a carpet to pad your edges will be helpful. Totems are fantastic for the flaring cracks if you have them. A 60-meter rope will leave you plenty to spare.

Many of the routes are seldom or never led. The local ethic is to note FTRs because few routes have solid pro. Although there are a handful of good leads, it is far from common, and leaders should be aware of the potential for cams to pop or walk on slick, flaring cracks. This is a good place to use passive pro (nuts, hexes) and to be cautious. The rock itself is solid and high quality—so you don't need to worry when toproping with stationary anchors.

Land Acknowledgment

We acknowledge with respect and gratitude that this climbing area is on the traditional lands of the Kiikaapoi, Sauk and Meskwaki, Myaamia, Waaziji (Ho-Chunk/Winnebago), and Očhéthi Šakówiŋ people.

Permits, Local Ethics, and Regulations

You need a Minnesota state park vehicle permit for your car (daily or yearly) and to register for your free climbing permit for the park in the self-registration box in the parking lot.

Dogs must stay on a 6-foot leash and be under control, and you must clean up after them.

Climbing at the Quarry is not recommended.

Try to stay on trails to prevent erosion. Some light "gardening" at the top to set anchors is acceptable.

Getting There and Parking

To get to the park entrance for vehicle and climbing permits, head for "Blue Mounds State Park Campground" (see map p. 1). There's parking at the end of the road, where you can hike to the climbs from the north, hitting the Receding Ramparts first.

You can also park at the south lot ("Blue Mounds State Park Rock Climbing Area"), which has a kiosk for vehicle and climbing permits. A mile north of Luverne on US 75, go east on Rock County 8. Or, you can park at the Eagle Rock Vista to hike to the South Quarry. If these parking lots are full, head to the north parking lot as described above. Do not park along 141st Street, where you can get ticketed.

Approach

The cliff faces generally east, and the routes are described from south to north (left to right from the base), and for description simplicity, buttresses are assumed to face east. The rock is naturally divided into a series of buttresses 20 to 100 feet wide and are relatively easy to spot from below.

The climbs in this section are found in five distinct areas: the South Quarry Area, the North Quarry Area, the Prairie Walls Area, the Mini Fortress Area, and the Receding Ramparts Area. The Quarry itself is loose and is avoided by most climbers.

Top access information will be found in area or buttress descriptions.

Camping and Amenities

Camping is available in Blue Mounds State Park. There are restrooms available throughout the park at trailheads and even along the trail, as seen on the map. Luverne has many restaurants, coffee shops, and a brewery for some post-send celebrations.

Hazards

Loose and slippery rock, poison ivy, and cactus.

In the spring, temporary pools form in shallow depressions in the rock and support a number of rare plant species that are found nowhere else in Minnesota. If you encounter a muddy basin in the rock, avoid walking through it for this reason. In addition, a rare species of prickly pear cactus inhabits the cracks of Blue Mounds.

Routes Not to Miss

Ivy Right (5.5), Kanaranzi Corner (5.7), Jasper's Dihedral (5.8), Debauchery (5.8),

South Quarry—Routes 1-20

Super Slab 1 | Picnic Buttress 2-3 | Cobblestone Buttress 4 | WS Buttress 5-7 | Mirage Boulder 8-10 | Great Roof Buttress 11-15 | The Watchtower 16-19 | Jungle Gym Buttress 20

Balcony Center (5.10b), Oath of Fealty (5.10b), Avoiding the Bat (5.10+), Purgatory (5.11a), Gravitron (5.11+)

South Quarry Area

This is the closest area to the south parking lot and can be reached in a few minutes.

Access: Take the trail from the back of the parking lot. Fork left toward two enormous boulders.

Top access: Arriving at the cliff line, take a hidden gully to the top.

Route 1: Micro Chip

Super Slab

A boulder 150 yards left of Cobblestone Buttress.

1. Micro Chip (5.11a) ★★ The face up the middle of a large boulder.

Picnic Buttress

Look for the huge tiers with a roof a few feet off the ground, between Super Slab and Cobblestone.

2. Keep a Beer in Your Hand (5.10b) The face to the left of *Cactus Crack*, follow just to the right of the black streak in the middle of the wall. **FTR:** Jeremiah LeTourneau.

3. Cactus Crack (aka False First Ascent, 5.8) The obvious corner.

Picnic Buttress

Photo: Jeremiah LeTourneau

Route 4: Cobblestone

WS Buttress

Cobblestone Buttress

This buttress is topped by a large, rounded rock.

4. Cobblestone (5.10d) ★★ Climb the south face of this buttress, left of the large inset. **FTR:** Craig Lais and Gary Johnson.

WS Buttress

The taller buttress just left of Mirage Boulder.

5. Cruise Control (5.7) Fifteen feet left of *Short Hop*. Up a left-facing dihedral, then move right around the overhang. **FTR:** Craig Lais and Gary Johnson.

6. Short Hop (5.8) ★★ Straight up over the initials "W.S.," a bit right of the arête. **FTR:** Mark Strege.

7. Knee High (5.7) Through the weakness in the overhang a few feet right of *Short Hop*. **FTR:** Mark Strege.

Mirage Boulder

The short buttress left of the triangular overhang.

8. Boulderdash (5.8) ★ On the south face, just left of the southeast arête. **FTR:** Gary Johnson.

9. Brianna (5.9) ★ On the east face, just right of the southeast arête.

10. Jumpin' Jack Flash (5.10c) ★★★ Five feet right of *Brianna*. A boulder problem often climbed on toprope. **FA:** Craig Lais.

Mirage Boulder

Great Roof Buttress

All routes are to the right of the roof.

11. Off Your Rocker (5.8) Off-width on the right-facing inside corner of the big roof. **FA:** Jeremiah LeTourneau.

12. Stick It (5.9) Follow the crack line that begins in the middle of two black patches on the rock, and head to the right of the triangle mini-roof at the top. **FTR:** Jeremiah LeTourneau.

13. Slab It (5.9+) ★ This is the crack to the right of the black patches on the bottom, following the face to the left of the arête to the top. **FTR:** Jeremiah LeTourneau.

Great Roof Buttress-Left

PHOTO: JEREMIAH LETOURNEAU

14. Roof or Woof? (5.9) Around the corner find the start in a small corner as it heads up through the V created by mini-roofs around it. **FTR:** Jeremiah LeTourneau.

15. Up Up and Away (5.9) The dihedral just to the right of *Roof or Woof?* that doesn't have greenery in it. Head up through a series of small roofs before enjoying the dihedral to the top. **FTR:** Jeremiah LeTourneau.

Great Roof Buttress-Right

PHOTO: JEREMIAH LETOURNEAU

The Watchtower

Route 20: Vanishing Point

Jungle Gym Buttress

About 30 feet right of *The Watchtower* is a small buttress with overhangs on the left side and a black streak beneath.

20. Vanishing Point (5.10b) ★★ Up the thin seam a few feet right of the overhangs. **FTR:** Craig Lais and Gary Johnson.

The Watchtower

16. You da Man (5.7) Southwest corner. **FTR:** Craig Lais and Gary Johnson.

17. Rube Goldberg (5.7) Southeast corner. **FTR:** Craig Lais and Gary Johnson.

18. Shake 'n Bake (5.6) Up the obvious crack on the east face. **FTR:** Craig Lais and Gary Johnson.

19. Twisted Sister (5.10b) ★★ No topo. The right edge of the north face through a tiny overhang. **FTR:** Craig Lais and Gary Johnson.

Red Rock Buttress

Access: Take the first trail to your left from the parking lot, walking toward the quarry past the Red Rock Buttress (you probably won't be able to see it because it's well hidden in the trees). Cut left just before the quarry on a path (it may be overgrown; try to stick to the path to help maintain it) and walk in a slot between two boulders. To get to the base of the cliff, cut left just below the cliff line.

Red Rock Buttress

24. Face Value (aka Hollow Mr. Flake, 5.8) ★ A few feet left of *Off-Width*. **FTR:** Craig Lais and Gary Johnson.

25. Off Width (5.7) ★ A crack becomes puzzling above the horizontal ledge.

26. Hard Right (5.8) ★★ The crack between the *Off-Width* and the awkward ledge. Begin in the crack as it heads to the ledge before becoming a thin seam at the top.

Top access: To get to the top of these climbs, take the path up right just after you've passed through the slotted boulder. It'll take you to the top of the quarry, where you then turn back south toward the cliff. This will get you to the top of climbs from here through Hidden Buttress.

21. Hanging by a Thread (5.7) No topo. Just south of *One Move Wonder*, find this crack to the left of a cluster of three trees as it heads past the left side of a roof. **FA:** Jeremiah LeTourneau.

22. One Move Wonder (5.10) ★ On the left edge of the south face, to the left of *Coyote Blues*. **FTR:** Craig Lais and Gary Johnson.

23. Coyote Blues (5.10b) ★ Start just around the corner left from *Off-Width* on the south face. Bounce up a couple of moves and over the overhang, then move up and left to a more moderate finish.

27. Deception Ledge (5.9) ★★★ The bottom starts to the right in the dihedral before heading up a tricky face above the horizontal ledge. Make sure your anchor is set above the sidepull.

28. Six Footer (5.8) ★ A long reach will stymie the vertically challenged.

Wasp Haven Buttress

29. Inside Corner (5.4) ★ A right-facing corner on the south face.

30. Bushwhacker (5.9) ★ Climb straight up the outside corner. **FTR:** Craig Lais and Gary Johnson.

31. The Wanderer (5.9) ★ Start below the roof left of *EZ Chimney* and traverse beneath the roof to join *Bushwhacker*.

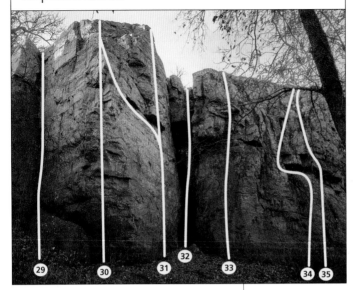

Wasp Haven Buttress

29 30 31 32 33 34 35

35. Stinger (5.11+) ★★★ Head up the slab to the roof and find the magic left side-pull to get over the roof. Once up, you can either head left to make it easier, or head right to get up to the top of the buttress. **FA:** Al Provorse.

Variation: The Wanderer Direct (5.10b) ★★ Goes straight up the face 2 feet left of *EZ Chimney* instead of traversing left. **FTR:** Craig Lais and Gary Johnson.

32. EZ Chimney (5.4) ★ The chimney in the middle.

33. Double Trouble (5.10d) ★★★ Spectacular route through the right side of the over-hang a few feet right of *EZ Chimney*. Climb some cool slab moves before a bomber hand jam in a crack on the roof. Use a directional at the top for the anchor to help keep it from sliding into the chimney. **FTR:** Craig Lais and Gary Johnson.

34. Grassroots Movement (5.8) Look to the left of *Stinger* for a left-facing sidepull. Climb the slab to the roof, traversing left until you can pull around the left side of the roof before enjoying easier terrain at the top. **FTR:** Brett McGraw.

Sun Drop II Tower

This tower has a few short, easy lead options. Bring small hexes or medium stoppers for top anchors. Routes are described going clockwise around the tower, starting in the northwest corner.

36. Junior Varsity (5.10a) ★ The northwest arête, nearest the main cliff. Start up the arête on large holds, then lurch right over a bulge.

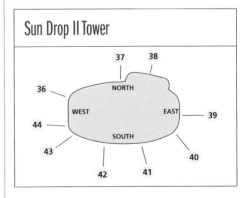

Sun Drop II Tower

37 38 36 NORTH 44 WEST EAST 39 SOUTH 43 40 42 41

Sun Drop II Tower

42. Into the Sun (5.11+) No topo. Head up the face on the full gambit of climbing moves with only one rest.

43. Who's Kenny? (5.10c) No topo. To climber's right of the crimps of *Tryout*, enjoy easier crimps. **FTR:** Jeremiah LeTourneau.

44. The Tryout (5.11+) ★★ No topo. Enjoy the crimps up the west face of the tower. **FA:** Doug Lintz.

45. Short and Sweet (5.7) ★★ No topo. This crack is *not* on the Sundrop II Tower; rather, look at the west wall just north of the tower to find this climb splitting the face.

Hidden Buttress

Directly south of Quarry Corner Buttress. Loose rock is an issue on some routes.

46. It's Finally Over (5.9) No topo. Around the corner to the left of *It Ain't Over*, this is on the south face. To the left of the arête, hug the dark streak heading through cracks before pulling the roof all the way to the point at the top. **FTR:** Jeremiah LeTourneau.

47. It Ain't Over til It's Over (5.9) ★★ No topo. On the south face, start between the overhangs and trend slightly left at the top. **FTR:** Craig Lais and Gary Johnson.

48. Park Bench (5.7) ★ A chimney with an overhang partway up marks the left edge of the south face. Take the chimney and face just to the right.

49. Clingon (5.10) ★★ Straight up the face between *Park Bench* and *Elm Tree Pinch*. **FTR:** Mark Strege.

50. Elm Tree Pinch (5.7) ★ Up the dihedral on the outside corner, then keep following corners to the top.

37. Burnt-Out Candle (5.5) ★★ The route closest to the wall on the north face with a lot of ledges and cracks. Climb the right-facing corner.

38. Piece o' Cake (5.6) ★ Just climber's left of *Burnt-Out Candle* is a splitter crack leading to a ledge.

39. Esterify Me Again! (5.6) No topo. A goofy-looking crack on the east face.

40. Who Killed Kenny? (aka Southeast Arête, 5.7) ★ No topo. From the southeast corner gain a ledge below a square-cut roof, then turn the roof to the left. **FTR:** Craig Lais and Gary Johnson.

41. Sun Drop (5.9-) ★★ No topo. Climb the podium on the south face before heading up the face and arête.

51. Thin Line (5.7) ★★ Start beneath a corner above the overhangs high on the face. Work up the face and cut left into a shallow corner.

52. Hidden Direct (5.9) ★★ Forge boldly over the roof and up the corner rather than chickening out on *Thin Line*.

53. Handy Capp (5.9) ★★ Climb up flakes under the right side of the overhang. Make a delicate traverse right around the roof, then up. Don't use the wall behind you.

Quarry Corner Buttress

Top access: Follow directions for Red Rock Buttress. Instead of turning south after you've reached the top of the cliff, turn right (north) toward the Quarry.

54. The Corner (5.5) ★ Chimney up a few feet to a corner on the arête. Follow corners to the top.

55. Wish Song (aka Leg Jam, 5.10X) ★★ Ascend the black streak a few feet left of *Headbanger*. Poor pro that might not hold in a fall. **FA:** Cheryl Strege.

Quarry Corner Buttress-East

56. Headbanger (5.7) A spooky, wide crack/chimney with lots of loose junk. Keep your belayer and others well uphill out of the fall line.

57. Acute Face (5.11a) This sustained climb heads up the dihedral 6 feet left of *Acute Corner* before finishing on the face. **FA:** Ben Ingman.

58. Acute Corner (5.10d) ★★★ Start on the prow under the roof. Muscle up to the triangular roof, then make a move or two in the black crack on the left.

59. Static Cling (5.10b) ★★ A few feet right of *Acute Corner*, just right of the black streak. Aim for the shallow depression in the white rock. **FTR:** Mark Strege.

60. Inca Roads (5.11) ★★ Go over the small overhang and up the smooth face just right of *Static Cling*. **FTR:** Jeff Peterson and Steve Peterson.

61. Thriller Pillar (5.8+) ★★ Up the left side of the prow. **FTR:** Jeff Peterson and Steve Peterson.

62. Killa Piller (5.9+) Head straight up the prow in the crack through the mini-roofs to the top.

63. Piton (5.9) Up the right side of the prow.

64. Flake it 'til You Make It (5.8) Follow the obvious crack through the face toward the little roof and up the left side of it to the top. **FTR:** Jacob Walker.

The Quarry

Climbing here is not a good idea. There is lots of loose stuff, some of which is very, very big.

North Quarry Area

This area contains a good selection of hard face, crack, and roof problems, with a few nice moderate routes sprinkled in for good measure. On hot days, the trees provide comforting shade for belayers and spectators.

The approach for all buttresses in this area begins at the outhouse about 5 minutes in on a bike path and heads west (directly uphill) down a mowed path called the Bur Oak Trail. Pass straight through trees to get to the cliff at the base of ORC. There's an attempt to maintain trails up to the cliff line but they often get overgrown, so do your best to find them.

You may find some 10-foot-high boulders and should be very near Two Boulders Buttress.

ORC Wall

Top access: To the right (north) of the ORC (Old Rock Climbers) Wall, there's a gully between *A Rock and a Hard Spot* and *Dirty Dog*. Take this gully to the top of ORC and Two Boulders Buttress.

This small rock is two outcrops south of Two Boulders Buttress and north of the quarry.

1. Burn Gage (5.11) ★★★ Three feet left of *Shoshin*, use the crack until you head up the black streak. **FTR:** Jeff Peterson and Steve Peterson.

2. Shoshin (5.10b) ★★★ Directly up the black streak; finish either left or right.

3. First Blood (5.6) Over two chockstones in a "big hollow crack" on the left side.

4. Twinkle Toes (5.10b) ★★★ Snake left and then right while going up all the time. **FTR:** Craig Lais and Gary Johnson.

5. Lumberjack Crack (5.5) A crack angling up and right.

6. Death's Door (5.11) ★★ Head up just past the roof, traverse left to the arête, then climb up the arête.

7. Squeeze Play (5.7) About 20 feet right of *Lumberjack Crack*, you'll find two off-width cracks in the chimney—this one is on the left. **FTR:** Craig Lais and Gary Johnson.

8. Between A Rock and a Hard Spot (5.7) The off-width crack to the right of *Squeeze Play*. **FTR:** Craig Lais and Gary Johnson.

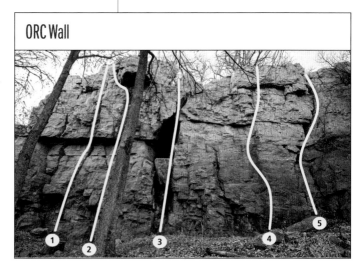

ORC Wall

ORC Wall-Right

Two Boulders Buttress

Two Boulders Buttress

9. Dirty Dawg (5.8) ★ On the right edge of the south face is a shallow, right-facing corner. Paw your way up this, or go up the left side of the outside corner (*Dirty Dawg Direct*, 5.9).

10. Mad Dawg (5.9) ★ 20/20 vision will help you spot the handholds needed to make this route go. Take a direct line up the left corner of the east face of Two Boulders Buttress, right of *Dirty Dawg Direct*.

11. Rabbit Dawg (5.10-) ★★ No topo. On the north side of the boulder, follow the crack to the arête before crimping to the top.

Primitive Buttress

Access: As you come up the trail for ORC, pass the gully you use to access ORC and Two Boulders Buttress. Instead, hike another 100+ feet toward a stack of big boulders and another gully just after *Primitive Man*.

Top access: Turn left (south) at the top of the gully to get to the top of Primitive Buttress and right (north) to the top of Kanaranzi through to Little Ranzi.

Primitive Buttress

12. The Lean Years (5.9+) ★★ The arête left of *Death Scream*. Follow a crack up and left of the roof, then move straight up. Cool moves with great flow. **FTR:** Craig Lais and Gary Johnson.

13. Death Scream (5.10c) ★★ Go up the crack leading to the right edge of the main roof, try to rest, then swing out left and pull the roof while letting your death scream loose. If this is too tame, do a harder variation to the left.

14. Old World Monkey (5.10c) ★★★ Three feet right of *Death Scream*. Ascend directly to the hanging corner. Cool high feet with some big committing moves. **FTR:** Mark Strege.

15. Evolution (5.11) ★★★ Directly up the arête, avoiding *Old World Monkey*. Great exposure. **FTR:** Mark Strege.

16. Missing Link (5.9) ★ On the north face, 4 feet right of *Evolution*. You might find an undercling and a corner. **FTR:** Craig Lais and Gary Johnson.

17. Barbarian (5.9+) ★ A few feet right of *Missing Link*. Turn the little roof at the top on the left. **FTR:** Craig Lais and Gary Johnson.

18. Robin's Nest (5.6) The left-facing corner. **FTR:** Craig Lais and Gary Johnson.

19. Cam Shaft (5.6) A wide crack passes a triangular overhang on the left. **FTR:** Craig Lais and Gary Johnson.

20. Huff and Puff (5.9) ★★ Up the middle of the face just right of the triangular overhang. **FTR:** Mark Strege.

21. Hot Flash (5.5) The dihedral/chimney. **FTR:** Craig Lais and Gary Johnson.

22. Failing Fingers (aka Raspberry Roof, 5.9+) ★ Begin in the dihedral at the right edge of the overhangs, then traverse left and up through the nest of overhangs. **FTR:** Mark Strege.

23. Primitive Man (aka Mild Yet Tasty, 5.10b) ★★ Start on the bulging corner 4 feet right of *Failing Fingers*; go straight up. **FTR:** Mark Strege.

Kanaranzi Buttress

This buttress, one of the taller ones in the park, has something for almost everyone. The routes are found on both the south and east faces. The south face has three large dihedrals, while the east face is characterized by a band of roofs near the top.

24. Bumbly Bee Crack (5.5) The chimney just left of *Plumb Line*. **FTR:** Craig Lais and Gary Johnson.

25. Plumb Line (5.9+) ★★ Straight up just to the left of the arête, avoiding the little roof. **FTR:** Craig Lais and Gary Johnson.

26. Pillar Start (5.9+) ★ Climb the little pillar at the base of *Triple Chockstone* and wander up the face above. **FTR:** Craig Lais and Gary Johnson.

27. Triple Chockstone (5.5) The leftmost of the three chimneys with—you guessed it—three (or so) chockstones.

28. The Gambler (5.10) ★★ Stay just left of the black streak just right of *Triple Chockstone*. **FTR:** Craig Lais and Gary Johnson.

29. On a Roll (5.9+) ★★ The arête right of *The Gambler*. **FTR:** Jeff Peterson and Steve Peterson.

30. 5/8 (5.9) ★ No topo. Take the east face to the left of the middle chimney, just right of a triangular overhang. Climb up flakes and skirt the overhang at the top to the left.

31. The Squeeze (5.7) ★ The middle chimney is best climbed by avoiding chimney techniques as much as possible. You'll see what we mean.

32. The Natural (5.10b) ★★ The narrow face right of *The Squeeze*. Trend right at the top. **FTR:** Craig Lais and Gary Johnson.

33. Hidden Line Trois (5.10d) ★★ Start a couple of feet left of *The Layback*. Surmount the roof and follow the arête above. **FTR:** Jeff Peterson and Steve Peterson.

34. The Layback (5.11b) ★★★ Left of the rightmost chimney is a large roof about 12 feet up. Plod up the corner above.

35. Chimney Sweeper (5.7) This is the big and obvious chimney to shimmy up, using both walls. **FTR:** Jeremiah LeTourneau.

36. K-1 (5.9+) ★★ On the right margin of the right-hand chimney (the one with a huge block at its top) is a flake. When the flake ends, improvise straight up, staying on the right side of the chimney. The left side is off-limits.

37. Kanaranzi Left (5.11a) ★★ Just left of *Kanaranzi Corner* is a very thin black crack. Proceed straight up until you're about even with the roof, then bail up and right (but stay off the arête).

38. Kanaranzi Roof (5.11) ★★★ Start in the same corner as *Kanaranzi Corner*, but at the roof, pull through and then stay just left of the arête to the top.

Kanaranzi Buttress-South Face

39. Kanaranzi Corner (5.7) ★★★ The roofs and arête add more exposure than you usually find here. There is a dihedral at the junction of the south and east faces. Climb the corner up to the first roof, go right, then up the east-facing crack to the upper roof.

40. Run and Gun (5.10c) ★★ Straight up from the short corner just left of *Crazy Crack*. **FTR:** Craig Lais and Gary Johnson.

41. Crazy Crack (5.7) ★★★ Start in a crack about 5 feet right of the notch and go up, zig left, and end at the slight notch at the top left side of the *Purgatory* wall. A great 5.7 lead; also good first lead that will teach you to extend your pro and give you some rests. Hard anchor set up; you need long webbing (100 feet) to use the great placements across the gully.

42. Stairway to Heaven (5.11) ★★★ Start about 6 feet right of *Crazy Crack* and keep that distance until you are squeezed left by the big roof at the top. Fantastic varied movement. You could go over the roof (5.11b).

43. Purgatory (5.11a) ★★★ Maybe the classic spectacular crack route (with the occasional face hold) at Blue Mounds. It starts in a little square black niche about 15 feet right of *Crazy Crack*. Work upward, possibly moving left to take advantage of vertical cracks/flakes. Three roofs at the top may represent eternal damnation for some.

44. Stairway to Hell (5.11) ★★ If the previous two routes leave you with some extra energy, start about 6 feet right of *Purgatory* and go straight up. Expect horizontal ledges and a thin, hairline crack, which forms the line but provides few holds.

45. The Crack (5.7) ★ An off-width chimney that's often dirty, an overhanging jam crack,

and a bit of a stem provide a photographer's delight for the harder climbs on both sides. Seldom led.

46. Gravitron (5.11+) ★★★ Levitate up the narrow face just right of *The Crack* without straying onto the routes on either side. Enjoy the great refrigerator moves on a photogenic climb.

47. Kanaranzi Right (5.9+) ★★★ Excellent, varied climbing that continually makes you think. If you miss the secret handhold, it will be 5.10. Start just left of some talus boulders on redder rock with large holds. Work up and right to white rock, then cut to the left side of the large overhang and pull it. Scamper to the top.

48. The Guillotine (5.9) ★★ Just around the corner from *Kanaranzi Right* is a north-facing climb that is a cut above many routes here. Start up the crack in the middle of the face.

Little Ranzi Buttress

A few feet north of Kanaranzi Buttress.

49. Left Cheek (5.6) Climb 6 feet left of *Little Ranzi Crack*.

50. Little Ranzi Crack (5.7+) ★★ Climb up the shallow indentation in the center of the face. A tricky start and a balance move at the top shatter any delusions of the former 5.6 rating.

51. Right Cheek (5.8+) Climb 4 feet right of *Little Ranzi Crack*.

52. Round Off (5.10c) Start on the north face, just right of the arête, climb up a few feet, cut left to the east face, then up to the top.

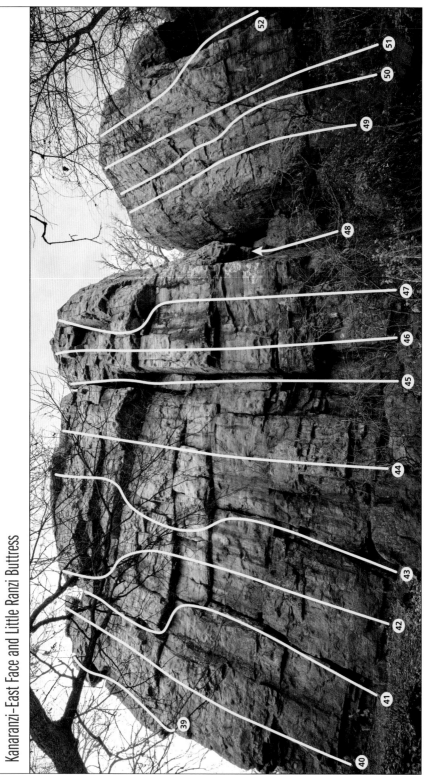

Kanaranzi–East Face and Little Ranzi Buttress

Flattop Buttress

This buttress is characterized by a huge block in the chimney to its left and a big red roof about 15 feet up.

Top access: Continue north after accessing Kanaranzi, go around Little Ranzi, and walk down a hill. By some trees you'll see the flat top—it's spooky to jump across to the top of Flattop. There may be a rope lovingly placed there by local climbers to help protect the jump. To set up anchors, you will want big hexes (10 and 11), and/or #4 and #5 cams.

53. Cactus Jam (5.10b) ★★ On the south side of the rock is a thin crack about 4 feet left of a black streak above the roof. Starting from a vertical fin of rock, climb up to this crack.

54. Dave's Dangle (5.11a) ★★★ Just to the right of the prow, this strenuous route goes over the roof to a thin crack right of some red rock. Start just right of the large boulder and look for a crucial block under the roof.

Flattop Buttress

55. Diagonal Crack (5.6) ★★ On the east face a crack leads to a hanging corner and a roof. Large gear if you lead it.

Tyrannosaurus

Go north from the base of Kanaranzi past Flatop Buttress at the bottom of the cliff. You'll know you're there when you see three mega roofs and a thin flake. You'll hopefully get a laugh recognizing the T-Rex looming over you.

Top access: Climb the gully between Tyrannosaurus and Thanksgiving Day (going left up top for T-rex and right for Thanksgiving).

56. Tyrannosaurus Rex (5.12d X) ★★★★ Start in the corner under the roofs. Head straight up the trunk of the T-Rex. Not

Tyrannosaurus

leadable (hence the X), but even on toprope you'll swing hard into a tree if you don't use the piton that serves as a directional (clip on rappel with a double-length sling). Great exposure and quality movement. **FTR:** Rob Pilaczynski.

57. Tyrannosaurus Flex (5.10a) ★★ Follow the crack to the right of the arête before heading straight up. **Variation:** Follow the crack about 2 to 3 feet left, but if you go to the arête, you've gone too far. **FTR:** Jeremiah LeTourneau.

58. Tyrannosaurus Hex (5.9) ★ Follow the middle crack system. **FTR:** Jacob Walker.

59. Tyrannosaurus Sex (5.8) This is the crack farthest right near the back side of the "dinosaur." **FTR:** Jacob Walker.

Thanksgiving Day Buttress (aka Bison Buttress)

Just north of the Tyrannosaurus is another detached block, this one with an inset on the east face and a prominent crack running through an overhang on the right.

60. Going to Granny's (aka Buffalo Hand Puppet, 5.7) About 15 feet left of *Celtis Crack* on the far left side of the buttress, climb the left-facing corner that starts from a ledge 15 feet up. **FTR:** Craig Lais and Gary Johnson.

61. No Time for Turkey (5.9) ★ The crack and rounded prow a few feet left of *Celtis Crack*. **FTR:** Craig Lais and Gary Johnson.

62. Celtis Crack (5.6) ★ A wall leads to a large ledge (the inset). Climb the left-hand crack.

63. Out and In (aka Buffalo Burr, 5.6) ★ The right-hand crack from the large ledge.

Thanksgiving Day Buttress

64. Relish This (aka Destination Unknown, 5.10) ★★ Climb the black water streak through the weakness in the roofs a few feet left of *Oath of Fealty*. **FTR:** Craig Lais and Gary Johnson.

65. Buffalo's Bulge (5.10b) ★★ Head up straight to the double bulge to the left of the *Fealty* crack, and stay on the face.

66. Oath of Fealty (aka Repeat Offender, 5.10b) ★★ This crack is about 40 feet tall and overhangs 8 feet. A surprising and unusual route for this area in that it's actually easier than it looks. Take a #4 cam or two if you lead it. **FTR:** Craig Lais and Gary Johnson.

67. Lightning Buzz Kill (5.6) ★ Ten feet right of *Oath of Fealty*, head up the crack into a slot-like dihedral.

68. Overbite (5.9-) ★★ Fifty feet right of Thanksgiving Day Buttress. Start beneath a large overhang, surmount it on the right and finish to the right of a large roof. **FTR:** Craig Lais and Gary Johnson.

69. Spectacular Hand Crack (5.8) ★★★ No topo. About 100 feet right of *Overbite* is an obvious crack with a black patch at the bottom. It's located left of the approach to the top of the Tree Ledge Buttress. **FA:** Jeremiah LeTourneau.

Prairie Walls Area

This area is home to the highest concentration of good routes in the park. Walk along the bike path and go about half a mile past the outhouse until you see an extended area of cliffs not shaded by trees. Look for a climber's path near a bench leading toward the cliffs. This will take you to Saturday Buttress at the base of Jasper's Dihedral.

The best summit access from the left end of this area is the marked 2 Mile Trail, which attains the top a few dozen yards south of Yellow Lichen Buttress, just past Berry Brothers. On the right end the large chimney between Everyday and Chimney Buttresses can be scrambled to the top. Intervening gullies can be passed with various degrees of difficulty as noted below.

Route 68: Overbite

Tree Ledge Buttress

Just right of the marked trail.

1. Berry Brothers (5.6) Start below a squat, flat-topped boulder just right of the trail leading to the top.

Boke's Buttress

A short buttress left of Yellow Lichen Buttress.

2. Last Grasp (5.7) ★ Climb up to the third ledge on the left side of the buttress, then step right to the nose.

3. Read Between the Lines (5.8) ★ A face climb 4 feet right of *Last Grasp*. **FTR:** Craig Lais and Gary Johnson.

4. Last Day's Misery (5.6) ★ Up the middle of the face toward a small depression at the top.

Yellow Lichen Buttress

The south wall is the namesake of Yellow Lichen Buttress. There are some kid-friendly climbs on the east face.

5. Projectile Vomit (5.10c) ★★ Five feet left of Yellow Lichen Crack. Straight up to a tiny roof on the rounded corner. **FTR:** Greg Fossom.

6. Yellow Lichen Crack (aka Gold Line, 5.9) ★★ The south wall has a short but trying intermittent crack. **FTR:** Craig Lais and Gary Johnson.

Yellow Lichen Buttress-South Face

11. Pedestal Right (5.5) ★★ A slightly more difficult route than its counterpart to the left. From the ledge you may climb left and up the face of the pedestal (5.8+).

12. Cactus Platform Face (5.7) ★ From the ledge, forge right to the upper right corner of the face.

13. Behind the Trees (5.6) No topo. Find a nose of rock (the trees are gone). Climb the nose to a corner.

Bottom Boulders Buttress

Just right of Yellow Lichen Buttress. You can access the top from the gully on Many Cracks Buttress, but it's not as easy or clean.

14. Layback Crack (5.7) ★★ Find a reddish, triangular overhang near the bottom of the left side. Start up the large flake to the left of

7. Likin' Lichen (5.9) ★ Just right of Yellow Lichen Crack is a thinner but taller crack. **FTR:** Craig Lais and Gary Johnson.

8. Paul's A-Version (5.5) Cut left to a left-facing corner after climbing 10 feet of *Pedestal Left*.

9. Pedestal Left (5.4) ★★★ A nice crack with good stemming for the beginner. Climb the dihedral to the left of the obvious nose, or pedestal.

10. Up on a Pedestal (5.9) ★★ Wrap yourself around the pedestal as you figure out how to compression-climb around the bulge.

Yellow Lichen Buttress-East Face

Bottom Boulders Buttress

that overhang, up to the top of a block, then keep going up the corner.

15. Bulge Across (5.8) ★ Angle right from the top of the block. A direct start (5.10c) goes directly through the big overhang.

16. Piernas Borrachas (5.10c) ★★ A thin seam starts halfway up the center of the face. Get to it and climb it. **FTR:** Mark Strege.

17. Pumpitude (5.10b) ★★ The face just left of *Save-Me-Tree*. **FTR:** Craig Lais and Gary Johnson.

18. Save-Me-Tree (5.8) ★ The tree is pretty much gone. Find a crack on the right side of Bottom Boulders Buttress with a twig partway up.

Many Cracks Buttress

Just left of Saturday Buttress.

Access: If you don't want to walk all the way to the maintained trail, you can take the gully just after *Harmless Old Neutered Dogs*. The gully is shared with *Dirty, Hard*. There's a chockstone wedged between the gully about halfway up. Beware of poison ivy.

19. Third Time's a Charm (5.8) Up the pedestal, trend left.

20. Cussin' Crack (5.8+) Up the pedestal, trend right.

21. Wrestle You for the Dry Spot (aka Stairway to Pizza Ranch, 5.9+) ★★★ Start at the base of *Noseprick*, but stay only on the face to the left. Even in rain, one spot stays dry. **FTR:** Greg Fossom and Gary Johnson.

22. Noseprick (5.8) ★★ The big obvious crack heading right up the middle of the wall.

23. The Klinger (5.9) ★★ Face climbing to a crack that starts halfway up the wall.

Many Cracks Buttress

19 20   28
                                          27
                                      26
                21 22   23 24   25

24. Incapacitation (5.8) ★★ The crack to the right of *Klinger.*

25. Harmless Old Neutered Dogs (aka Abby's Bulge, 5.10a) ★★★ Up the rounded prow just right of *Incapacitation* and just left of the large block in the gully. **FTR:** Greg Fossom and Gary Johnson.

26. Dirty, Hard, and Worth Doing (5.11a) ★★★ Start on the easy ledges in the access gully before heading straight up the steepest part of the bulge on tiny edges.

Saturday Buttress

Saturday Buttress has a large left-facing corner in its middle (*Jasper's Dihedral*) and is one of the most popular destinations in the park. The chimney behind the buttress has loose rock.

27. Angle of the Dangle (5.10c) ★★ Start at the base of the large block near the bottom of the access chimney. Up the crack on the right edge of the black wall and trend left at the top. **FTR:** Mark Strege.

28. Black and Blue Bulge (5.8+) ★★ There are three routes to the left of *Jasper's Dihedral.* Find a short, thin seam at ground level about 13 feet left of the corner. Start a few inches left of this seam and climb up to a short finger crack. From the left end of the overhang, power up a red bulge.

29. Black Wall (5.9) ★★ Start in the seam mentioned above or to the right (harder). Stay about 6 feet right of *Black and Blue Bulge.* Clear the overhang to the left of two black streaks (crux).

30. Gulliver's Travels (5.8) ★★ Start 6 feet left of *Jasper's Dihedral* and climb directly up to a short corner at the top of the wall.

31. Jasper's Dihedral (5.8) ★★★★ This excellent route is often led (large hexes/cams), but be prepared for the crux near the top. Climb the large left-facing corner.

32. Becky's Arête (5.8) ★★ Up the face between the cracks.

33. Ivy Right (5.5) ★★★ Just right of the top of *Jasper's Dihedral* is a small notch. Climb the crack leading to it. Many Blue Mounds first

Erik Peterson on *Old Stump* (5.7-)

Saturday Buttress

trad lead.

34. Hard Rock Café (5.9) ★★ Up the face between the cracks. **FTR:** Craig Lais and Gary Johnson.

35. Old Stump (5.7-) ★★ Follow a smaller, left-facing corner on the right side of the buttress. **Variation:** Move left at the finish.

36. Alexandra David Néel (5.8) ★ Slide up the face and corner about 10 feet right of *Old Stump*.

37. Revenge of the Nerds (5.9) ★ The face just right of *Alexandra David Néel*. **FTR:** Craig Lais and Gary Johnson.

Midnight Buttress

Top access: Use the chimney behind Saturday Buttress.

38. Mean Streak (5.9++) ★★★ Start in the corner on the face, zip up the chimney, and traverse right under an overhang. The fun begins after you pull over the roof for a really cool route. **Variation:** Straight over both roofs, using only the face (*Don't Let Your Meat Loaf*, 5.10d).

39. Easy Street (5.6) ★ Climb the broken corner to the left of *Prow-ess* and zip up to a platform and a south-facing crack. You'll

Midnight Buttress

head up the face a few feet left of *Obvious Crack*.

40. The Obvious Crack (5.7) ★★ Head up the bottom of *Easy Street* before following the hand crack in the back of the dihedral.

41. Prow-ess (5.10c) ★ Easier after you've done it once. Climb dark rock just left of *Midnight Chimney*. Take the overhang on a thin bracket to the left, then move right and head up as the route bulges outward. A 5.9 version exists if you stick to the chimney on the right.

42. Midnight Chimney (5.4) ★★ An excellent chimney for climbers new to that technique.

Sunday Buttress

If you only have a few hours to climb, come here—you'll blow yourself out with time to spare. The large balcony, or window, is the easiest landmark to spot.

Top access: After you are at the top of the cliff via either the nice trail at the southern end or via the gully on Bottom Boulders, you will have to scramble across some boulders and make an exposed step around the southeast corner of the buttress (Class 3) to set up. You can walk from here all the way across to *Debauchery*.

Brenda Piekarski on *Balcony Right* (5.9+)

43. Avoiding the Bat (5.10+) ★★★★ Start 12 feet left of *Balcony Center* as you move through the roof, finishing on the right-facing corner without using the arête. Dyno off some tiny crimps.

44. No Go Crack (5.12b) ★★ Look for the huge balcony—you'll start on the black face before you follow an overhanging thin crack below the left side of the balcony. Exit the balcony at its left edge as well. Not a great lead (PG13)—you only have one piece of good pro.

45. Balcony Center (5.10b) ★★★★ Mega-classic for the area. Start up the crack under the very center of the balcony. Grab the jugs, flow up to the balcony, and try to climb over the center of the balcony roof. A 9+ route with one move of 10b at the end.

46. Balcony Right (5.9+) ★★★ Start just right of the crack and pass through the right side of the balcony. Stout for 5.9 leaders.

47. Cactus Capers (5.10c) ★★★ The large protruding block on top is directly above

Sunday Buttress

a jog in the main roof about halfway up. Smooth, difficult to rest, a reachy crux—just another route at Blue Mounds. Find a hidden hold shoulder deep.

48. Warrior's Waltz (5.11) ★★★★ Climb within a few feet of the right edge of the buttress and subdue the overhang at a thin crack. **FTR:** Mark Strege.

49. Everyday Chimney (5.4) ★ This is the big chimney between Sunday Buttress and Everyday Buttress.

Everyday Buttress

This is the buttress that begins just left of the access chimney and contains several steep and popular routes.

Access: Get to the top of Sunday Buttress and walk to the far north end. There's a second, wider step across with a sloping

foothold on the very corner of the buttress. This is a textbook example of alpine Class 3. Please do not climb in the isolated grotto behind this buttress, as the vegetation is too delicate to withstand trampling. You can also lead *Jammer* to the top.

50. Jammer (5.9) ★★★★ Near the left edge of the buttress is a black crack and corner system to jam your way up, leading to a vexing little roof about two-thirds of the way up. The best trad lead at Blue Mounds—might feel stout on gear.

51. Lechery (5.10b) ★★★ Home of one of the world's sharpest finger locks. About 8 feet right of *Jammer* is an overhang halfway up with a right-facing corner below. Climb to the corner, then trend right and into the upper crack.

52. Sudden Sweat (5.11b) ★★★ Between *Lechery* and *Treachery*. Climb the face and go over the roof. **FTR:** Mark Strege.

53. Treachery (5.9+) ★★★ The treachery is the bad feet and the old-school rating. On the right side of the buttress is a left-facing corner that matches the right-facing corner on *Lechery*. Climb directly up to this and on to the top.

54. Debauchery (5.8) ★★★ Just left of the access chimney is a shallow corner on the north face of the buttress. Follow this corner to the top.

Everyday Buttress

The following climbs are in the access chimney between Everyday and Chimney Buttresses. Do not climb in the isolated grotto behind Everyday Buttress, and make sure that others can pass through safely while you are climbing.

55. Fun Bags (5.9+) ★ No topo. On the right wall, just before you turn right when ascending the access chimney. **FTR:** Greg Fossom and Vern Olson.

56. Air Conditioned Bars (5.9+) No topo. On the right wall, 5 feet after you turn right. **FTR:** Greg Fossom and Vern Olson.

57. Ass Cannon (5.5) No topo. If you do not turn right, you will bump your nose on this crack. **FTR:** Greg Fossom and Vern Olson.

Chimney Buttress

This is just right of the chimney that provides access to the top and has some shrubs and trees at the base.

Approach: Follow the bottom of the cliff past Everyday Buttress.

Top access: Look for a 6-foot-wide gully just to the right of *Debauchery* and right of *Jugs of Whine* to access Chimney Buttress through Clandestine.

58. Jugs of Whine (aka Magic Carpet Ride, 5.9) ★★★ Start just right of the chimney and improvise up a shallow corner. Skirt the upper overhang either left or right (harder), depending on your setup. Don't use the blocks at the base of the chimney. **FTR:** Craig Lais and Gary Johnson.

59. Roofs (5.9+) ★★★ Climb directly up to the overhang and left-facing corner about 15 feet right of the buttress's corner.

60. Poika (5.11a) ★★ Climb directly up to the roof and forge through. Very sequential. *Poika* is Swedish for "little boy."

61. X (5.7) ★★★ Ascend the crack at the right-hand edge of the roof to a right-facing corner.

62. Y (5.8+) ★★ Climb straight up, 6 feet right of *X.* The route gets more obvious the higher you go.

Chimney Buttress

63. Z (5.9) ★ Climb straight up to the hanging wide crack right of *Y* and undercling around the roof to gain the left-facing corner. **Variation:** *Cowboy Todd's Rodeo Roll* (5.10+ ★★) goes straight over the roof.

64. The Abyss (5.7) No topo. Go into the little cave to the right of *Z* and look for the off-width on your left.

65. Wormhole (5.8) No topo. This is also in the chimney, following the left wall. Head through the tight hole between the chockstone and the left side of the wall. Named after *Regular Route* with the wormhole in the Black Hills. The crux may be choosing which way to face. **FTR:** Jeremiah LeTourneau.

66. Weasel Exit (5.7) No topo. This is in the chimney on the right side. Follow the wide crack going up the flake side of the chimney.

67. Bushmaster (5.8) ★ The east face of the cave block has a right-facing corner starting near the ground. Climb up this to the center of the top block.

68. Seduction and Rejection (5.9) ★★ The roof has jugs before joining *Bushmaster* at the top.

69. The Horizontal Tango (5.10) ★ Up the roof 12 feet right of *Seduction and Rejection*, then up on the face.

70. In and Out (5.6) ★ Head up the dihedral toward the off-width crack before jumping in and enjoying it.

71. Boy Howdy (5.7) ★★ Climb directly under the corner before it turns into a crack above the roof.

Clandestine Buttress

Clandestine Buttress

Right of Chimney Buttress and across a shallow gully is a short buttress.

72. Mums the Word (5.7) ★ Around the corner from *Balancing Act*, enjoy some chill face climbing. **FTR:** Craig Lais and Gary Johnson.

73. Balancing Act (5.10) ★★ Enjoy face climbing with a small roof halfway up. **FTR:** Craig Lais and Gary Johnson.

74. Killroy was Here (5.9) ★★ To the right of *Balancing Act*, head up to the small roof and exit on the right side of it before heading straight up the face. **FTR:** Craig Lais and Gary Johnson.

75. Mighty (5.9) ★ Start on the corner on the right edge of the buttress before heading over a tiny left arc and straight up the face. **FTR:** Craig Lais and Gary Johnson.

Mini Fortress Area

These rocks are smaller and generally in the shade. Describing the approach is tricky because of the ever-changing tree line. In general, there are a series of grassy slopes and tree-filled depressions north of Chimney Buttress. From the Prairie Walls area, walk north. Lonesome Stepchild is 20 yards north of Clandestine and the Peteza Tower is about a hundred yards farther through trees.

Lonesome Stepchild Buttress

Top access: Take the gully just to the right of Clandestine.

1. Humble Pie (5.11) ★★ Start in the middle of this small buttress up the crack, then arc to the left and then to the right. **FTR:** Greg Fossom and Vern Olson.

2. American Pie (5.10b) ★★ Same start, then go right to a shallow dihedral and crack system. **FTR:** Craig Lais and Gary Johnson.

Lonesome Stepchild Buttress

Peteza Tower

Walk north of the Lonesome Stepchild buttress through the woods until you're almost at the clearing.

Top access: Before the clearing, a trail going south, then west will bring you to the top of First Fortress. *Peteza* is the free-standing tower—no top access without climbing it.

3. Peteza (5.4) ★ Find an obvious crack on the back of this tower.

First Fortress

First Fortress

4. Pete's Face (5.8) ★ Head up the face a few feet right of the right-most arête as it turns into a mini-corner before the top. **FTR:** Jasper Hunt and Pete Hunt.

5. Jasper's Face (5.8+) ★ Look for the bulging overhang at the top—you'll head directly up the face toward the right side of that bulge. **FTR:** Jasper Hunt and Pete Hunt.

6. Surprise Ending (5.7) ★ On the left side of the higher buttress is a prominent nose with an overhang at the top. Start where you must to get into the crack.

7. Dusty Problem (5.7+) There is an alcove to the right of *Surprise Ending*. On the right side is a corner with a roof partway up. Climb a crack in that corner, then move right onto the nose.

8. We Came, We Saw, We Kicked Ass (aka A Fool and Their Beer Are Soon Parted, 5.10c) ★★★ Five feet right of the *Dusty Problem* crack, follow the dihedral through a series of roofs as you head straight up. **FTR:** Craig Lais and Gary Johnson.

9. Chainsaw (5.9) ★★ Five feet right of *We Came, We Saw* is this dihedral. Crimps guard the opening before it gets easier as you head up. **FTR:** Craig Lais and Gary Johnson.

10. Finger Games (5.7+) ★★★ Ascend the blunt arête just right of the red corners.

11. 5.3 Lead (aka Unnamed Scramble, 5.3) ★ This is the crack to the left of *Fortress Chimney*.

12. Fortress Chimney (5.4) ★ Find the wide crack/chimney and simply enjoy it.

L-Buttress

About 100 feet north of First Fortress.

Access: Between *Grasshopper* and *Bend Over*, there's a system of grassy ledges you can take to the top.

13. Desperado (5.9+) ★ The southernmost face of the buttress overlooks the south access gully. The roof at the top is split by a crack. Climb the crack up before trending left to blast through the crack in the roof. **FTR:** Craig Lais and Gary Johnson.

The south-facing wall just left of *Hammer* is home to the following four routes.

Route 13: Desperado

L-Buttress-South Face

14. Power Booster (5.5) At the far-left side of this face is an off-width crack in a corner.

15. Fate of a Fool (aka I Don't Remember, 5.9) ★★ A couple of feet right of *Power Booster*, enjoy face climbing without using the cracks on either side. **FTR:** Craig Lais and Gary Johnson.

16. Poison Vines (5.7) ★★ About 6 feet right of *Power Booster*, this beautiful crack cuts through the entire face.

17. Nuances (5.10c) ★★★ Start just left of the big roof below the corner. Move right as you pull through the roof, then stay between the corner and the crack system to the left. **FTR:** Craig Lais and Gary Johnson.

L-Buttress

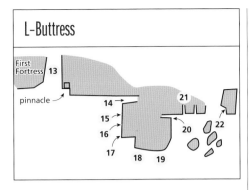

18. Hammer (5.8+) ★★ Around the corner from *Nuances* on the east face, head up the corner to the big roof and keep going straight up the crack.

19. Loose Rock (5.8) ★★ Get up to a ledge about 10 feet right of *Hammer* before following the natural fault line straight up. Aptly named.

L-Buttress-East Face

L-Buttress-North Side

20. I'll Be Home for Christmas (5.6) ★ Around the corner from *Loose Rock* is this fun corner hand crack. **FTR:** Craig Lais and Gary Johnson.

21. Grasshopper (5.4) Big, beautiful crack that heads up, then right, then up. **FTR:** Craig Lais and Gary Johnson.

22. Ben Dover (5.7) ★ No topo. It is basically its own rock, not part of the buttress. A huge right-leaning crack that begs for you to lieback. **FTR:** Craig Lais and Gary Johnson.

23. Full Tilt (5.10+) ★★ No topo. Ten feet right and around the corner from *Ben Dover*.

Twin Block, Spiderbush, and Square Block Buttresses

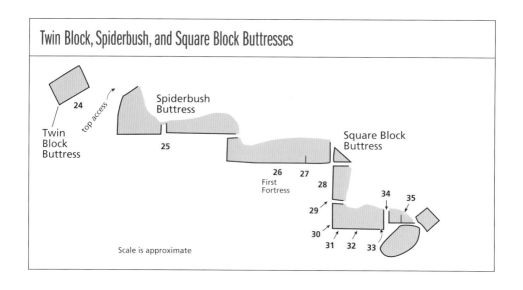

Twin Block Buttress

24

top access →

Spiderbush Buttress

25

26   27

First Fortress

28

29

30

31   32   33

34   35

Square Block Buttress

Scale is approximate

Route 24: In Yer Face

24

Route 25: Ding Dong

25

Twin Block Buttress

The next three buttresses are close together. About 50 to 100 feet past Ben Dover, you'll see a block on your left (*In Yer Face*) and an off-width (*Ding Dong*).

Top access: Climb the obvious gully before Twin Block Buttress to access the top of these through Fortress Wall Buttress.

24. In Yer Face (5.9) ★ Look for the big crack splitting the face. Head straight up the black streak into the crack at the top. **FTR:** Craig Lais and Gary Johnson.

Spiderbush Buttress

25. Ding Dong (5.5) This off-width cuts straight up through some red rocks before it fades to white as the crack trends left and up. **Variation:** Near the top, go into the off-width on the right.

Square Block Buttress

26. Watch My Monkey (5.11) ★★ A nice-looking route 8 feet left of *George of the Jungle*, this heads to the left in the top half, following the crack. Would be three stars if clean (the moss takes over quickly). **FTR:** Greg Fossom and Vern Olson.

27. George of the Jungle (5.8) ★★ Fun thin crack straight up the face. **FTR:** Craig Lais and Gary Johnson.

28. Arachnophobia (5.10c) ★★ Six feet left of *Season's Opener*. **FTR:** Roy Reichle.

29. Season's Opener (5.6) ★ A wide crack on the south side that moves into a smaller crack on the right before finishing on the face at the top.

30. Plant Manager (5.9+) ★★ Just left of the arête on the south face. **FTR:** Craig Lais and Gary Johnson.

31. Nemesis (5.10b) ★★★ Six feet right of the arête on the east face. **FTR:** Craig Lais and Gary Johnson.

32. Pojama People (5.10b) ★★ Up the east face through a blackish area with fun movement that requires a touch of technique.

33. Blockhead (5.9) ★★ Ten feet to the right of *Pojama People*. Start just right of the outside corner and pass the overhang at the top on the left. **Variation:** Pull the roof (5.10). **FTR:** Craig Lais and Gary Johnson.

Square Block Buttress

34. Inch Worm (5.9) ★ No topo. Off-width goodness. **FTR:** Craig Lais and Gary Johnson.

35. Grape Vine (5.8) No topo. Look for the finger crack behind the boulder, 10 feet left of *Inch Worm*. **FTR:** Greg Fossom, Vern Olson, and Gary Johnson.

Fortress Wall Buttress

This buttress has an obvious inset and some huge roofs down low on the right side. There is a cement foundation about 100 feet below the wall.

36. Glacier Calf Moo (5.9) ★★ Left of the inset, start on the left edge of a platform. Up the overhanging black crack before face climbing at the top.

37. Crack Lovers Delight (5.9) Up the left side of the inset, following the big crack on the left side of the roof.

38. Fancy Feet (5.7) Up the right side of the inset and in the crack on the right side of the roof.

Fortress Wall Buttress

39. Owl Wisdom (5.11d) ★★ No topo. Find the corner and roof system just north of *Fancy Feet* for a hard start into easier fun climbing up the corner. **FA:** Jesse Littleton.

Receding Ramparts

The start of this formation is about 1,000 feet north of Fortress Wall Buttress following the cliff. If heading here from the south parking lot, walk down the bike path and where it makes a sharp right, go straight on the grassy trail instead. A short way down, a small metal sign says "Receding Ramparts." Turn left here and go due west to reach Behind Balancing Rock.

You can also access from the north parking lot for a shorter approach (in case you want to boulder and then come south for ropes).

Behind Balancing Rock

Top access: South of the Balancing Rock area, there is an easy approach up a hill. This gets you top access through Potpourri Pieces.

1. Beavis (5.8+) ★ Head up the corner of the buttress to the left of the big gully, pulling through two mini-roofs. **FTR:** Craig Lais and Gary Johnson.

2. Butthead (5.10a) ★ Head up the corner on the buttress to the right of the big gully, trending left at the overhang and up the face. **FTR:** Craig Lais and Gary Johnson.

Balancing Rock

3. Laughter's Echo (5.10b) ★ No topo. On the west side, head up the face. **FTR:** Mark Strege.

Behind Balancing Rock and Balancing Rock

4. Stonecutter (5.9+) ★★ On the south face, up a leaning corner just right of the tree in the photo. **FTR:** Mark Strege.

5. Double Bucket (5.6) On the east face start just right of the left-hand roof, then move left to the arête.

6. Forget-Me-Not (5.6) No topo. Up the right side of the east face.

Skinny Buttress

Thrash north of the small buttress just north of Balancing Rock.

7. Obtuse Corner (5.8+) ★★ Go straight up the southeast corner of the buttress. A patient climb with great exposure and some long reaches. **FTR:** Jeremiah LeTourneau.

8. In the Slime (5.7+) ★ An obvious crack 5 feet right of *Obtuse* that oozes up the buttress. Good lead.

Skinny Buttress

9. Reach Me (5.9) ★★★ Start in the crack under the roof, heading straight up through the roof. Roof pull is a cool feet-cutting dyno. **FTR:** Jacob Walker.

10. The Hardest 5.4 in the Park (5.10) ★★ Head up to the right of the roof and up the crack through the face. **FTR:** Jeremiah LeTourneau.

C-Buttress

Approach as for Balancing Rock or take the chimney on the left side (Class 3).

11. Hard Start (5.7+) ★ Follow the face of the mini-buttress on the left side of the main face to the overhang and the crack slot on top. **FTR:** Mark Strege.

12. Mulberry Drive (5.4) Enjoy this fun crack/corner/roof just right of *Hard Start*. **FTR:** Craig Lais and Gary Johnson.

13. The C Direct (5.6) ★★ Climb directly up past the right edge of the long overhang and follow the dihedral to the top (5.6). **Variation:** The C (5.9, no stars) curves in from the left.

C-Buttress

Domestic Pillar

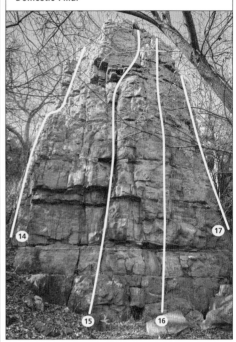

Domestic Pillar

These are lead routes with no top access. Rappel "needles style."

14. Couch Potato (5.4) ★ Pick an easy way up the south face of the tower. You'll enjoy a nice ledge about halfway up.

15. Two Kids and a Honda (5.8) ★ Up the crack/overhang on the left side of the east face, trending right at the top to follow the crack system.

16. Shady Lady (5.9+) ★★ Two feet right of *Two Kids and a Honda*, this route heads straight up. **FTR:** Craig Lais and Gary Johnson.

17. Watching Monday Night Football . . . (5.5) ★ A crack on the northeast corner leads to easier climbing on the north face.

Potpourri Pieces

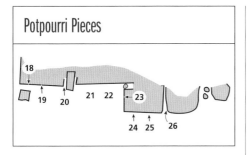

Potpourri Pieces

This rock is well defended by vegetation at its base.

Top access: Climb *Chockstone Chimney* if you're comfortable free-soloing 5.4, or access from Balancing Rock.

18. Dancin' Fool (5.9) ★ There is a large overhang not far off the ground left of *Chockstone Chimney*. At its left edge, climb a crack to a jutting block and up the corner.

Potpourri Pieces–Left

Potpourri Pieces–Center

19. Take Your Clothes Off When You Dance (5.10+) ★★★ Big roof to a crack, just right of *Dancin' Fool*.

20. Chockstone Chimney (5.4) Climb the prominent chimney that looks like you'll definitely drop huge blocks down on top of your belayer.

21. Disco Boy (5.5) ★ Up the clean face between *Chockstone Chimney* and *Mini Overhang*.

22. Mini Overhang (5.6) ★ Up to a triangular mini overhang and step right.

23. Off Balance (5.8+) ★★ Go straight up the left edge of a black-streaked wall just right of a corner chimney. Lieback up to a ledge and go up a shallow groove, or step in from the chimney (a bit easier).

Potpourri Pieces-Right

24. Gomer's Pile (5.9+) ★ The left side of the face on the jutting-out buttress. **FTR:** Craig Lais and Gary Johnson.

25. Mono Mania (5.10) ★★ The right side of the face. **FTR:** Craig Lais and Gary Johnson.

26. Big Crack Attack (5.7) ★ The big, deep crack/chimney. **FTR:** Craig Lais and Gary Johnson.

Table Rock Buttress

A large flat rock sits about 50 feet from the cliff, providing a nice picnic table and landmark. A couple of harder climbs make this a more popular destination than most of the buttresses at this end.

Top approach: Take the gully right after *The Sicle.*

27. Quick Draw McGraw (5.7) ★ A crack 12 feet left of *Opposing Forces.* **FTR:** Craig Lais and Gary Johnson.

28. Don't Give Up (5.7) ★ Start on the left crack under the left of the roof described for *Opposing Forces.*

29. Opposing Forces (5.8) ★ Muscles and gravity. On the left side of the buttress is a small overhang about halfway up. Take the line to the right of the overhang, then up the east face to the top. **Variation:** Go straight over the roof (10a). **FTR:** Mark Strege.

30. Double Chimney (5.4) ★ No topo. The right side of the inset on the left side of the east face.

31. Bald Eagle (5.8) ★★ No topo. The south-facing wall just right of *Double Chimney.* **FTR:** Craig Lais and Gary Johnson.

32. Easy Rider (5.9+) ★ Up the arête, staying right of the roof. **FTR:** Craig Lais and Gary Johnson.

Table Rock Buttress-Left

Table Rock Buttress

33. Tricky Dick's Galactic Trip (5.10c) ★★ Up the face between the cracks on either side.

34. Prehension (5.7) ★ Looks like a big, wide off-width crack but doesn't climb like one as much as you'd think.

35. Puzzle Foot (5.10b) ★★ Three feet right of *Prehension*, avoiding surrounding routes and cracks. **FTR:** Mark Strege.

36. Thumbnail Direct (5.9+) ★★ A thin crack right of *Prehension* doesn't quite reach the ground. Lever up the bottom section, then crunch your bones on the second crux. To avoid the first crux of getting off the ground, traverse into the crack from the right.

37. No Rest 4 the Wicked (5.10b) ★★★ Enjoy some crack climbing at the bottom before heading up the face a few feet right of *Thumbnail Direct*. **FTR:** Craig Lais and Gary Johnson.

38. Whiskey-a-Go-Go (5.9+) ★ Start on the broken, blocky northeast corner. Follow the right-angling crack. **FTR:** Vern Olson and Craig Lais.

39. The Sicle (5.8) ★ No topo. Thirty feet north of *Whiskey-a-Go-Go* on the next buttress, surrounded by vegetation. Start at cracks if you can get that close. **FTR:** Vern Olson and Craig Lais.

Proceeding Buttress

Proceeding Buttress

You could continue along the grass path (going straight from the bike path) and spot another metal sign for Proceeding Buttress or follow the cliff edge north from Table Rock.

Top access: Just to the south of *Two Way*, you'll find an easy, adventurous gully.

40. Short but Thin (5.7) ★ No topo. In the chimney behind the left side of the buttress is a slightly overhanging crack. Start low, gain a ledge, and climb the crack. The nicest climb on the buttress.

41. Cheater's Paradise (5.7) No topo. Thrash up the face just left of a large oak, avoiding the tree and vegetation.

42. Two Way (5.7) ★ Climb the crack just left of the large overhang on the left side of the main face. Start on some blocks under an overhang.

43. Belly Flop Overhang (5.7-) ★ A hanging, left-facing corner is capped by an overhang. Up the corner, flop over the roof on the right side.

44. G-Spot Tornado (5.9+) ★★ Four feet right of *Belly Flop Overhang*, follow a crack through the roof. **FTR:** Jeff Peterson and Steve Peterson.

45. Overhang and Face (5.7) A short overhanging slot is fun to overcome before heading up the face, trending right near the top.

46. Falling Crack (5.4) ★ On the right side of the buttress is a pointed overhang. A wide crack lies just to the right. Climb it through loose chockstones at the top.

47. Falling (5.8) ★ No topo. A variation on *Falling Crack*, start 5 feet right and go up to the ledge below the top.

Beginner's Buttress

Beginner's Buttress

The northernmost buttress that is worth climbing with a rope. Trees on top for anchors, trees on the bottom for shade, and relatively short and easy routes make this a decent place for kids and those wanting to learn (it is a bit dirty and has a small amount of loose rock though).

Top access: As for Proceeding Buttress.

48. Not a Beginner's Roof (5.10) ★★ Below the big roof, enjoy easier climbing before cranking through two roofs, aiming for a thin crack on the right side of the roof at the top.

49. Beginner's Dihedral (5.5) ★ While sometimes dirty, this is a fun and straightforward crack.

50. Beginner's Stairsteps (5.4) ★ One tricky move at the start leads to 5.0 higher up. **Variation:** (5.8-) Go up the face between this route and *The Knees Ledge*.

51. The Knees Ledge (5.6) ★ Start under the left edge of the big roof and traverse underneath it to the right, around the corner to the top.

52. Beginner's Chimney (5.4) Mostly face, with back and foot for a couple of moves.

53. Beginner's Overhang (5.5) A bit of a misnomer, head up the crack to the overhang, then find a fist jam and stem near the top.

Eric Barnard on *Running Scared* (5.10-)

SUGAR LOAF/WINONA

Sugar Loaf is a new mecca in Minnesota for sport climbers, both those looking for picturesque moderates on an exposed face high above the river and new leaders learning to clip draws on well-bolted easier climbs. The West Face in particular has a kid-friendly base hangout and some kid-friendly climbs. While the history of it includes a quarry, old bolts, and excursions from local climbers, it wasn't until 2015 that local outdoor educator Eric Barnard began cleaning and bolting the area extensively. He developed an incredible southern crag with beautiful views and easy access to the city. This is the place for those learning to sport-climb who are looking to get a lot of mileage to work on their leading skills. With some routes needing a tie-in at the belay and others passing a set of anchors before reaching a second set at the top, it is also a great place to practice multipitch skills.

Not only did Barnard bolt the majority of sport climbing on Sugar Loaf, he has been instrumental in creating the Winona Ice Park and advocating for the community to get out and appreciate the incredible offerings around the city of Winona. Year-round fun runs abound in this special corner of Minnesota.

Types of Climbing and Gear

Sport climbing is the only thing you'll find at this crag. Bring a 60-meter rope, at least eight draws, and helmets. The tallest route tops out at 80 feet, with the majority of them around 50 feet.

If you plan on climbing the North Face, bring a way to clip into the belay bolts at the bottom of the routes.

Land Acknowledgment

We acknowledge with respect and gratitude that this climbing area is on the traditional lands of the Saux and Meskwaki, Wahpeton, and Očhéthi Šakówiŋ people.

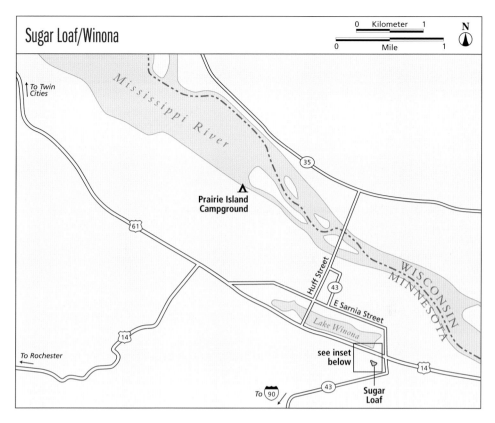

Sugar Loaf/Winona

To Twin Cities

Mississippi River

Prairie Island Campground

35

61

Huff Street

43

E Sarnia Street

Lake Winona

14

To Rochester

see inset below

To 90

43

Sugar Loaf

14

WISCONSIN

MINNESOTA

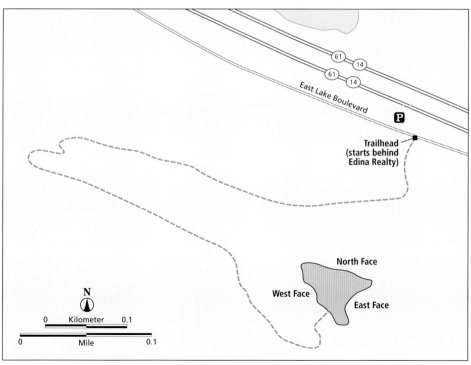

61 14

61 14

East Lake Boulevard

P

Trailhead (starts behind Edina Realty)

North Face

West Face

East Face

Permits, Local Ethics, and Regulations

No permits are needed to park or climb here. Guided groups must get a permit from the city of Winona prior to running trips.

Toproping directly on the fixed gear—stainless-steel wire-gate carabiners—is allowed and encouraged.

Dogs must be kept on a leash and under control, and please clean up after them.

Getting There and Parking

From SH 61 in Winona, head south on SH 43 before a quick right turn to East Lake Boulevard, where you'll see signs for "Sugar Loaf Trailhead" parking. Parking is on gravel at the side of the road only; do not park in the lot for Edina Realty.

Approach

The Sugar Loaf trail leaves from Edina Realty's parking lot. Follow the trail as it climbs steadily uphill. At the fork, take a left. Continue to climb, passing a sandcastle (don't worry, it's not your crag!) before emerging at the cliff between the west and east face. Turn left and continue on the trail to get to an overlook and the farthest end of the west face (or go straight to the sets of practice anchors on the East Face). Climbs are described left-to-right, starting on the end of the West face, heading counterclockwise around the bluff.

Camping and Amenities

The city of Winona is visible as you climb, offering anything you could need after a day (or more) of climbing.

There are a few campgrounds in the city such as the Prairie Island Campground, which welcomes climbers and often has live music, food trucks, a swimming beach, and a disc golf course. Others are the Pla-Mor Campground and the Great River Bluffs State Park, which is about 15 miles southeast along the river.

Hazards

This is a newer-established area, so rockfall is common and should be expected by climbers and belayers. Wear helmets everywhere (climbing and belaying) but especially on the North Face.

Routes Not to Miss

Six Pack (5.7), Franklin's Direct (5.8), The Saga (5.8), Running Scared (5.10-), The Deputy (5.10), Rope Thief (5.10)

West Face

1. NW Corner (5.3) ★ The route to the farthest left on the West Face. Easy climbing with good exposure. Good access to set up the route *Northwest Toprope* on the North Face. 3 bolts.

2. Beginners Delight (5.3) ★★★ Brand-new sport climbers will love this well-bolted lead with two big ledges and a tiny runout at the top. You might feel you're climbing one of the pyramids. 5 bolts.

3. Amoeba Route (5.4) ★★ Look for the white amoeba spot halfway up—that's the crux for yet another great beginner lead. Has a high first bolt and good ledges. Near the end it trends right to share the anchor with *First Lead*. 4 bolts.

4. First Lead (5.4) ★ Grab some high feet and crystal pockets for a heady first lead. Leans left and shares anchors with *Amoeba*. 4 bolts.

5. Back in the Saddle (5.6) ★★ Head up the middle of the wall over the bump and follow the steep corner system before moving to the right. Has a short fun crux in the "saddle." There's some rope management around a bulge if you're toproping. Shares an anchor with *Time Bandits*. **FA:** Sean Davidson. 4 bolts.

6. Time Bandits (5.4) ★★★ Just left of the *Ramp Route*, head up a vertical section to an inside corner system. 5 bolts.

7. Ramp Route (5.6) ★★ Start just right of the major corner climbing to ledges, then follow up low-angle climbing as it trends left to the chains. 6 bolts.

8. Leftover Salmon (5.9+) ★ This super-short yet sweet route heads straight up, avoiding the crack to the right and the ledges to the left to achieve a tougher grade for the wall. **Variation:** Climb to the left of the first two bolts or directly over them for a harder eliminate in the mid-5.11 range. 3 bolts.

9. Green Room (5.7) ★★ All the business is at the bottom on one of the longest routes at Sugar Loaf. Start in a short crack and trend left at a mini arête halfway up, then finish high over Salmon near the top. 6 bolts.

10. Six Pack (5.7) ★★★★ A tricky slab start at the bottom as you head up and through a dark patch of rock and trend right as you climb. See if you can find the hold near the top that the route is named after. 6 bolts.

West Face-Left Side

11. Keystone Light (5.9-) ★★★★ A route that tops out for full value, start on a bouldery few moves on the face before climbing through a subtle corner and then trending right to another crux in the face midway up. Be sure to climb past the chains for *Six Pack* to top-out. This route can be done in two pitches if you wish to practice multi-pitch. 8 bolts.

12. West Face Overhang (5.9-) ★★ Starting below a small jut-out in the rock and sharing the first few bolts with either *Keystone Light* or *Franklin's Tower*, head up a steep nose to a slab before a well-protected overhang. Finish on easier climbing. 7 bolts.

13. Franklin's Tower (5.7) ★★ Another route you can do in two pitches, start up the left side of a seam to a ledge before heading straight up using the corner and the arête to stem to easier terrain. This shares the anchor with *Franklin's Direct*. **FA:** Franklin Hessler. 5 bolts.

14. Franklin's Direct (5.8) ★★★★ After sharing the first bolt with *Franklin's Tower*, head right for tougher terrain and truly stellar climbing before returning left to share anchors with *Franklin's Tower*. This was the first route bolted at Sugar Loaf. 6 bolts.

15. Winona Alpine Club (5.10-) ★★★ Head up the bottom big two steps for a blocky start to gain the ledge, then climb crimps and pockets while trying to find the old star drive bolt from the 1930s–'40s, placed by the Winona Alpine Club. **Variation:** Start to the right of the blocks for a tougher opening. 5 bolts.

West Face-Right Side

East Face

On a lofted belay area, you'll see three bolted practice anchors for teaching new climbers.

16. Photogenic (5.3) ★ The easiest route on the wall if you want a good photo stance to capture climbers out to the right. You can access the summit on this route. 3 bolts.

17. Runnin' Late (5.8+) ★★ Start below the leftmost of the three practice anchors. Thin climbing leads to big pockets. Avoid the ledge to the right before things ease up to the anchors. 4 bolts.

18. E-Walks (5.4) ★★ Head up the obvious inside corner, where you'll stem and gain bigger and bigger ledges. **FA:** Ethann Piekarski. 4 bolts.

Ethann Piekarski (age 11) on the FA of *E-Walks* (5.4) Photo: Peter Lenz

East Face

Katie Berg on *Tiny Hammer* (5.6)

19. Tiny Hammer (5.6) ★ Just to the right of the *E-Walks* corner, start in the middle of the large belay area and follow ledges on slab climbing, trending slightly left before a final mantel at the top. 4 bolts.

20. The Exterminator (5.7+) ★★ This starts directly under the rightmost practice anchor and continues to steeper but easier climbing. 5 bolts.

The next three climbs share an anchor.

21. Buzz (5.8) ★★ Start at the small fin to the right of the set of practice anchors. After two bolts, use the remaining bolts of *Saga* but stay on the left side of the bolts for some great movement. 7 bolts.

22. The Saga (5.8) ★★ At the climber's right end of the belay area there is a waist–shoulder height block and a very subtle arête bolted on both sides. Start in a finger crack on the left side of this arête, heading over a bulge before stemming the inside of a corner. Ends in a steep layback to clip the chains. 7 bolts.

23. The Pillar (5.8) ★★ The right side of the subtle arête (with a less-than-finger crack) has great climbing on ledges with some sidepulls and stemmy moves. There's a funky bulge with some blind footwork. Make sure you get to the third bolt so you don't deck. The anchor is less heady to reach from this side. 6 bolts.

The next three climbs start down from the large belay area.

24. East Face (5.6) ★★ Start down from the ledge to the right of *The Pillar*, looking for two bolts at the opening of this short route. 4 bolts.

25. The Lamp (5.7) ★ Ten feet right of *East Face*, head up a short steep face with a fun rockover move before following a flake through the middle of the face, getting over a lip to reach the anchor. 4 bolts.

26. NE Corner (5.3) This is a great access route for setting up topropes on *Matador/Air Pig* and *The Sheriff/The Deputy*. New leaders will enjoy good climbing and easy clips with a great perch for taking pictures of the North Face climbs. 4 bolts.

North Face

Belaying is from a narrow ledge that can be precarious. To help this, there are bolted anchors for belayers to clip to at the bottom of the climbs, and the center of the wall has been expanded for a more comfortable staging area.

27. Matador (5.10-) The route farthest to the left, climb to the top of a hollow pillar before enjoying a concave to big holds. Shares an anchor with *Air Pig*. 5 bolts.

28. Air Pig (5.9+) ★★ Just above the first belay bolt, climb through a small overhang to a baby arête before moving left through a bulge. Avoid the ledge to the left at the bottom. 5 bolts.

29. The Deputy (5.10) ★★★★ Enjoy larger bouldery moves with stellar holds heading toward an inside corner. End on the same anchors as *The Sheriff*. 5 bolts.

30. The Sheriff (5.9+) ★★★ This might seem intimidating from the ground, but great flakes and edges make for excellent larger moves before heading into a steep concave section. This was the first route bolted on the North Face at Sugar Loaf. Either bail left or work hard side-pulling for full value. 5 bolts.

31. One Eyed Lady (5.10-) ★★ Named after the quartz-filled pocket in the opening moves of the route. Enjoy finger locks and hand jams after some big ledges. 4 bolts.

32. Fear and Loafing (5.9) ★★★ Start by pulling a small overhang into a corner with a black streak before heading up a flake into the final corner. Big bouldery moves on fantastic

North Face

AERIAL PHOTO: RICH ANTHONY/LANDMARK SERVICES

ledges, sidepulls, and pockets. **Variation:** At the high horizontal break, go straight up the face to the right of the flake to a second set of anchors (5.11). **FA:** Rich Anthony. 6 bolts.

33. Rope Thief (5.10 PG13) ★★★ Open with big ledges into steep edges and eventually sidepulls and laybacks off of a large flake. Careful between the second and third clip—there's the possibility of decking. 6 bolts.

34. Running Scared (5.10-) ★★★ Climb on the left side of the bolt line enjoying big flakes and a big jug to an even bigger jug before the end. 5 bolts.

35. Running Scared Direct (5.11-) ★★ This route shares all bolts with *Running Scared* but climbs on the right side of the bolt line. Tiny crimps and slopers that require a good amount of balance end with a big huck before ending on *Running Scared*. 5 bolts.

36. The Beekeeper (5.11-) ★★★ Buzz up the overhanging face on big holds toward an overhanging notch. Use the horizontal ledges to climb through the notch to finish. 6 bolts.

37. Lonely Arête (5.10-) ★★ Head up the leftmost route on the face of the obvious pillar before barreling up the steep, bulgy wall on the arête above. 7 bolts.

38. Shakedown Street (5.10-) ★★ Climb the right face of the pillar, then head up really fun pockets to get to the top. This is the best route of the three on the right side and can also be used to set the *Northwest Toprope*. 5 bolts.

39. Northwest Toprope (5.10) ★ This is a TR only due to the multiple ledges, but climbers can climb the *NW Corner* (route #1) on the West Face to reach out and clip the anchors to set up the rope.

Maggie Shafer on *Mississippi* (5.12c) Photo: Chris Deal

HE MNI CAN/
RED WING/BARN BLUFF

Rising 350 feet above ground level, He Mni Can is home to over 150 sport-routes only an hour's drive from the Twin Cities. This old quarry site saw an explosion of bolting in the 1990s and is one of the more popular sport-climbing crags in the state. The Oneota dolomite rock houses some fun, mostly vertical climbs, has an easy and accessible approach, has free parking, and no permits are required.

That said, it can be a bit crowded during peak times, you'll share the area with hikers, and you may have to dodge rocks (either dislodged or thrown from the top) and choss. While it's not necessarily world-class, this year-round climbing area has a large variety of routes that will test your fingers, strength, and technical skills.

Types of Climbing and Gear

This is primarily a sport-climbing crag with a handful of trad routes. It can be climbed with a set of ten draws (a few require more) and a 60-meter rope. Stick clips are helpful here since the bottom of many routes are often slick. Bolt counts do not include anchors—bring two extra draws if your party will be following or toproping.

All routes must be led to set up topropes as there is no access to the top. The moderate routes are quite polished, so they may feel sandbagged, and it's not the best place for brand-new leaders. Generally, the harder a route, the better the quality.

He Mni Can/Barn Bluff/Red Wing

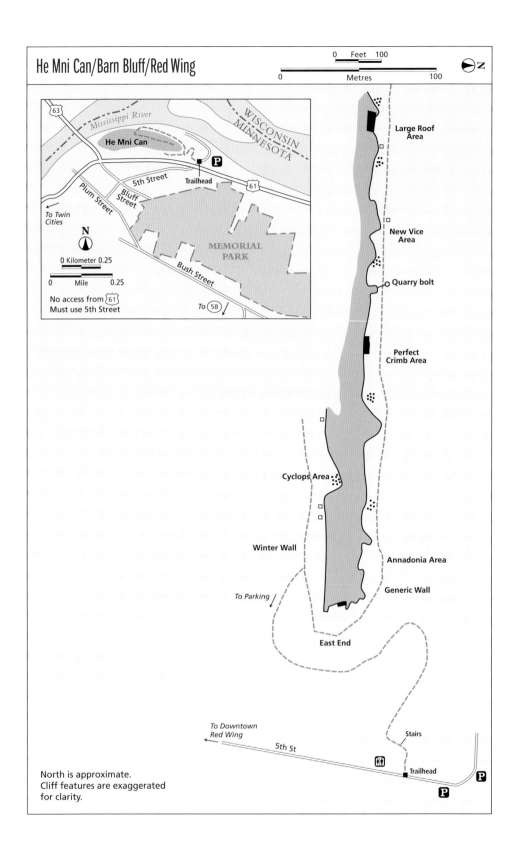

0   Feet   100

0   Metres   100

N

63

Mississippi River

He Mni Can

WISCONSIN
MINNESOTA

P

5th Street

Trailhead

Plum Street

Bluff Street

61

To Twin
Cities

N

MEMORIAL
PARK

0 Kilometer 0.25

0   Mile   0.25

Bush Street

No access from 61
Must use 5th Street

To 58

Large Roof
Area

New Vice
Area

Quarry bolt

Perfect
Crimb Area

Cyclops Area

Winter Wall

Annadonia Area

Generic Wall

To Parking

East End

To Downtown
Red Wing

Stairs

5th St

Trailhead

P

P

North is approximate.
Cliff features are exaggerated
for clarity.

Land Acknowledgment

We acknowledge with respect and gratitude that this climbing area is on the traditional lands of the Očhéthi Šakówiŋ people.

Permits, Local Ethics, and Regulations

Use your own gear for toprope setups but lower on fixed gear while cleaning. If you see any hardware that needs replacing, please let the Minnesota Climbers Association (MCA) know through their website.

He Mni Can is managed by the city of Red Wing. The assessment, replacement, and maintenance of all of the bolts and anchors is done by the MCA. If you climb here on any sort of regular basis, consider becoming a member or making a donation.

Dogs must be kept on a leash and under control, and please clean up after them.

Getting There and Parking

He Mni Can is located near downtown Red Wing, just east of the bridge over the Mississippi River. Get to the "Barn Bluff Trailhead" and park in the big new lot just past the trailhead.

Approach

Trailhead GPS: N44.5679' / W92.5192'

Go up the stone stairs, then switchback left and up. You'll reach the cliff with the recognizable crack of *Barnburner*, between the Winter Wall and the East End.

The cliff is divided into south and north faces, with the East End in between. The routes are described in a counterclockwise (left to right) direction, starting with the westernmost climbs on the south face. The climbs are located in eight distinct areas on these faces. For route-finding purposes, the trails are presumed to run due east and west.

Camping and Amenities

There's a biffy at the base near the stairs. Camping is available at Frontenac State Park, just over 10 miles away. The town of Red Wing has an abundance of places to stay, eat, hydrate, and shop.

Hazards

Wear. A. Helmet. *Especially* when belaying but even when climbing or watching below. The biggest hazard here is rockfall, which happens year-round but is most prolific during the spring thaw when entire routes or giant blocks with bolts still attached have been lost. There are hiking paths at the top of the cliff, so loose gravel will come down if a tourist is getting close to the edge. Kids *love* throwing rocks off the top, despite the potential bloodshed. Belayers should never stand directly below a route line while belaying. And wear a helmet.

Trails during the spring and winter can be muddy, icy, and slippery.

Wasps love to make nests around or directly on the climbs. There are rumors of timber rattlesnakes.

Routes Not to Miss

The Future (5.8), Two-Tone Zephyr (5.9), Sleeping Bat in a Ziplock Bag (5.10b), Frequent Flatulence (5.10b), Roof Burner (5.11a), Chinese Freedom (5.12a), Annadonia (5.12a), Work Ethic (5.12a), Femme Fatale (5.12b), Mississippi (5.12c), Paradigm Shift (5.13a)

The Cyclops Area

This is the area the farthest south and west with the large "Cyclops Eye" staring at you. Direct sun and little wind means great climbing for cooler, winter days.

1. Sobriety (5.10+) The farthest left bolted route starts on the pedestal. While having a reputation as kitty litter, when the route is clean, there are some fun moves that require thinking and a high crux. 4 bolts. **FA:** Nate Postma.

2. User Friendly (5.12b) ★ Start a few feet left of *Wasp Mentality*. Super-crimpy and sequency down low, it eases up tremendously after the first few bolts. The choss

Slavomír Tkáč on *Work Ethic* (5.12a) PHOTO: RUTGER VAN HUBER

up top simply adds adventure. 5 bolts. **FA:** Mike Dahlberg.

3. The Girl with the Dragon Tattoo (5.12a) ★★★ A link-up that begins on the first two bolts of *User Friendly* for the crimpy sequence early on, then traverses right across two bolts. Clip the third bolt of *Wasp Mentality* and finish on that route. 7 bolts. **FA:** Jack Powers & Peter Graupner.

4. Wasp Mentality (5.11d) ★★★ Tricky and fun. Start about 3 feet left of *Forearm Smash* through some crimps down low to the huge undercling (that occasionally has a family of wasps living in it) before the route eases up. 5 bolts. **FA:** Mike Dahlberg.

Cyclops Area-Left

Cyclops Area-Center

8. Cyclops (5.12a) ★★★
Look for a line of bolts leading to a cyclops eye straight out of the Greek myths. A combination of a brief crux and the eye makes for fun, balancey climbing that can be height-dependent. 6 bolts. **FA:** Mike Dahlberg.

9. Sleeping Bat in a Ziplock Bag (5.10b) ★★
Start just left of a whitish face. The bottom of this route has become incredibly polished but once past the second clip, it's fun climbing. Goes left at the ledge before heading back right on the final slabby section. The top feels exposed, but the holds are all there. **Variation:** A direct finish (*End Play*, 5.11+) is possible if you head straight up from the ledge instead of moving left. 8 bolts. **FA:** Mike Dahlberg.

5. Forearm Smash (aka Cooler Crack, 5.8)
TRAD ★★ A 4- to 5-inch crack at the bottom. Solid pro for competent leaders, enjoy wide hands and fist climbing to bolted anchors.

6. Work Ethic (5.12a) ★★★
This is often the 5.12 breakthrough route for local climbers. It's all about technique and sequence through the first five bolts before letting up to a completely different climb to the anchors. 6 bolts. **FA:** Mike Dahlberg.

7. Suicide Squeeze (5.11c) ★★★
This route is similar in style to *Work Ethic* in the balance, technique, and crimps for the bottom part. 4 bolts. **FA:** Dan Meyer.

10. Urban Chunks (5.11b) ★★
Start just left of the outside corner arête. Interesting pockets and knobs guard a sequency and technical crux, and the giant body-sized satellite dishes are not gimmes. 5 bolts. **FA:** Mike Dahlberg and Jeff Engel.

11. Big Rocks Remembered (5.11d) ★★
Six feet right and around the corner from *Urban Chunks*. The opening is crimpy and doesn't let up. Traverse left after the second bolt to huecos that aren't as good as you want them to be. Runout at the top. Shares anchors with *Piranha*. 5 bolts. **FA:** Pam Postma and Nate Postma.

Cyclops Area-Right

12. Piranha (5.12b) ★★ In the middle of the face, a technical boulder problem at the bottom moves around before trending left. For full value, go straight up over the bulge (escaping left is easier). It eases up after the bulge and shares anchors with *Big Rocks*. 5 bolts. **FA:** Mike Dahlberg.

13. Piranha Blues Direct (5.12b) ★★ This big link-up starts on the opening moves of *Piranha*, heads over through *Pigeon Paranoia*, and finishes on *Coronation Blues* on a bad sidepull and a shallow pocket before clipping the chains from the left at the lip. Use long runners to prevent rope drag. The meandering nature adds intrigue, and there are different ways to traverse for variety. **FA:** Jack Powers.

14. Pigeon Paranoia (5.10+) ★★ 4 feet left of the large block against the wall is this route that climbers either love or loathe. Start up in the corner next to the block, stemming to the first bolt between the block and the corner. There are more pocket holes than crimps, and the top turns into a slab that's a touch run out and slopey. Can be scary with the potential for bad falls. Be confident. 5 bolts. **FA:** Jeff Engel.

15. Coronation Blues (5.10c PG13) ★★ Scramble up a small approach gully until on the second pedestal above and to the right of *Pigeon Paranoia*. Bolts start here and go straight up. After clipping the last bolt, go more to the right for the easier 10c. **Variation:** *Coronation Blues Direct* goes straight after the last bolt, avoiding easier holds on the right, through a bad sidepull and shallow pocket (11c). 3 bolts. **FA:** Peter Graupner and Jack Powers.

The Winter Wall

Right of the scree pile, the wall faces south-west for about 25 yards, then curves around to face almost directly south for about 80 yards to *Barnburner*. The three major cracks in the right half of this area and some talus blocks at the base of the climbs provide land-marks for locating the routes.

This area gets a lot of sun and can be climbed on some of those warmer winter days.

16. Orange Marmalade (5.13a) ★★ Climb up an easy left-trending ramp until reaching a ledge. Chill, then traverse right on two huecos of bouldery climbing, then head up as it keeps getting harder toward a ledgy jug. After that, celebrate your way to the top with choss. 6 bolts. **FA:** Josh Helke.

17. Skooter Rash (5.11b) Start on the first two bolts of *Orange Marmalade* before cutting straight right on small holds for the crux. Finish on *Longing*. 6 bolts. **FA:** Nate Postma.

18. Longing for Miss Adonis (5.12b) ★★ This route has some tough sequences following three bolts up to a hueco, then heads up the left side of the upper dihedral. Using the crack and ledge on the left makes this closer to 5.11+/12-. 8 bolts. **FA:** Josh Helke, Jeremy Mariette, and Mike Helke.

19. Relentless (5.11b) TRAD ★★ Around the corner from *Jump Start* and to the right of the scree pile, find a thin crack that goes up, angles left, and then goes up again. A great crack with a nice variety of jams, laybacks, seams, and the added fun of possible loose rock, wasps, or a bat or two. **Variation:** A direct finish heading straight up is 5.12+. At the top of the thin crack, head right to a sloped-out crack and then up into crimps. There's a fixed pin on the direct—use with caution. **FA:** Mike Dahlberg (direct).

Winter Wall–Far Left

20. Gravity Heroes (5.13a) Begin in the *Relentless* crack and the first bolt of *NSP*. (Stick-clip that first bolt to avoid bringing trad gear for the crack). Traverse right and then climb up through lock-offs before heading through a technical and crimpy crux with some big moves. Stay focused until you clip the anchors. 6 bolts. **FA:** Kurt Hager.

21. Meet the Feebles (Open Project) The direct start to *Gravity Heroes* not using the *Relentless* crack hasn't been completed yet. Will you be the first?

22. NSP (5.13a) ★★★ The first bolt is above a small crescent in the rock for this powerhouse of a climb. Fun crimping before a tough crux followed by awesome jugs. Watch out for the red point crux guarding the chains. 6 bolts. **FA:** Keith Anderson.

23. OSS (5.14-) This route requires focus and control, as well as being able to stick one big move to a sloping edge. **FA:** Jim Merli and Pi Vonsavanthong.

24. Paul's Boutique (5.13c) ★★ Begin on the rounded arête before heading up and to the left through a mini-roof. 6 bolts. **FA:** Andy Raether.

25. PTC (Present Time Consciousness) (5.13b) ★★ Start on *Paul's Boutique* before finishing on *Soft Touch*. **FA:** Scott Hahn.

26. Soft Touch (5.12b) ★★ A line of bolts drops down from the dihedral right on the corner between the two faces. This route has had significant rockfall and now climbs the arête left of the bolt line. **FA:** Nate Postma.

27. Right Touch (5.12b) ★★ This linkup starts on *Soft Touch* before heading over to *New Kids* after the crux to avoid a lot of the looser rock at the top. **FA:** Mike Dahlberg.

Winter Wall-Far Left

About 75 feet right of *Relentless*, the wall curves east and there is a 6-foot-tall block next to the wall.

29. Jump Start

(5.10a/b) ★★ Flailing the bottom section is a rite of passage for new He Mni Can climbers. Start left of the block before making a big right move to a pocket. Once you get that move, it's just fun climbing with some crimps to the top. 6 bolts.

30. Jump Start to Something Good

(5.11c) ★★★ Do the "jump" of *Jump Start* and clip the first bolt, then navigate the tricky traverse to the right past a bolt before joining up with *The Start of Something Good*. 8 bolts.

28. New Kids on the Rock (5.10d) ★★ Starts left of a nose before heading straight up the face. The nose is awkward, but once you're past it, it's fun climbing to the top. Stay right of the arête at the top for a pure ascent. Lots of known rockfall here. 5 bolts.

31. The Start of Something Good (5.12c) ★★ If you can start it, you're good. Consistent 5.11 huecos and edges to the finish; it's long and pumpy. This route starts from the block, angles right, and ends right of the woody bushes at the top. 7 bolts. **FA:** Mike Dahlberg.

Winter Wall-Left

32. Squeeze Play (5.12) Climb the initial tough moves of *The Start of Something Good* before taking a hard right to the hueco through some small slopers. Breathe at a slot jug, then head up. 7 bolts. **FA:** Mike Dahlberg.

33. A Drilling Experience (5.11b) ★★ A low crux (still above the third bolt) as you figure out where your holds are in the overhang leads to a spooky 5.9 left-trending runout traverse before ending on fun moves and good holds. 7 bolts. **FA:** Mike Dahlberg.

34. Preemptive Strike (5.12a/b) ★★★ A long and fantastic route. Hit a bouldery lower crux about 20 feet up, or trend left toward a seam. Either way, get to a big hole before another crux and trending right to the top. There are good jugs to clip the anchors if you can hold on. 7 bolts. **FA:** Mike Dahlberg.

35. Barney Rubble (aka The Birch Tree Crack, 5.9) TRAD ★★ The leftmost of the three continuous cracks on the south face. Fun fingers and hand cracks with good feet before opening up at the top into off-width and slopers. Has enough of an overhang to put butterflies in your stomach.

36. Pretty in Pink (5.10b) MIXED Start in the *Barney Rubble* crack for 20 to 25 feet until the crack splits about halfway, then work right, following the bolts. Bring gear for the crack down low. 4 bolts + gear. **FA:** Pam Postma and Nate Postma.

37. Toxic Art (5.11a) This route somehow uses the crack, then breaks out right below where *Pretty in Pink* does to head over and finish on *Vias*. **FA:** Nate Postma.

Winter Wall-Center

39. Last Dance of the Fat Man (5.13b) ★★
Start at the rounded hueco and go straight up. The hard moves right off the deck can be tougher for shorter folks. Sustained crimping throughout. Only one bolt at the anchor. 7 bolts. **FA:** Jeremy Mariette and Keith Anderson.

40. Rock Pigs (5.13a) ★★★
Right of the hueco for *Vias* and *Last Dance*. Climb uncomfortable and truly tough moves off the ground that make you think before heading up. Chossy, and seems to get harder every season with rock breakage. 8 bolts. **FA:** Nate Postma.

41. Light My Fire (5.12d) ★★★
A two-finger pocket starts the route before heading to a seam and undercling. 5 bolts. **FA:** Jeff Engel.

42. Super High-Tech Jet Fighter (5.12d) ★
Just left of *Kelly's Arête*, beginning under a small roof. After the second bolt, stay to the left on the undercling and pocket holds. Things ease off after the fourth bolt. 5 bolts.

38. Vias (aka Godzilla, 5.12c) ★ This has great movement for shorter climbers. Begin on the hueco for *Last Dance of the Fat Man*, then take the left-hand line after the second bolt for big moves and fun crimps. It eases up after the fourth bolt. 6 bolts.

Winter Wall-Center

43. Kelly's Arête (5.12c) ★★★ Start in *Jam and Jelly*, using the crack to the first bolt. Move up then pull left onto the arête for delicate climbing up. *Note:* The second bolt came off with rockfall and as of this writing has not yet been replaced. **FA:** Kelly Gorder.

44. Jam and Jelly (5.7) TRAD ★★ The center of the three obvious cracks in this face. Good pro, though the first moves in the crack are getting more polished and difficult. At the ledge, angle up and left to the fixed anchor.

45. The Go Between (5.11c) ★★★ This route has a little bit of everything—crack, face climbing, then an overhang—full value! Start in the crack (on gear) or use the optional face start just to the right (runout to first bolt) on some technical crimpy face. Head up to the roof for some good holds before pulling over to the anchors. **FA:** Mike Dahlberg.

Near the top of *Jam and Jelly*, a large ledge runs out to the right. The next three routes end just below this ledge and share a common start below a 3-inch pocket about 15 feet up. This pocket is directly above the highest point of ground right of *Jam and Jelly*.

46. Foreign Affairs (5.11a) ★★★ Climb the shared start with *Chinese Freedom* before making a slippery traverse up and left from the hueco about 15 feet up. From there, head straight up through technical terrain with crimps, open-handed holds, and some big physical moves. 6 bolts. **FA:** Mike Dahlberg.

47. Chinese Freedom (5.12a) ★★★★ Classic He Mni Can technical climbing dialed to 11 with the fun of a polished crux, two hueco jugs, and a steep finish. After the shared start, go straight up toward the very distinct double huecos and head for the chains. 6 bolts. **FA:** Nate Postma.

48. Do the Right Thing (5.12a) ★★Follow *Chinese Freedom* to the double huecos, then traverse right on tricky moves before going up and ending just left of an inside corner. **FA:** Mike Dahlberg.

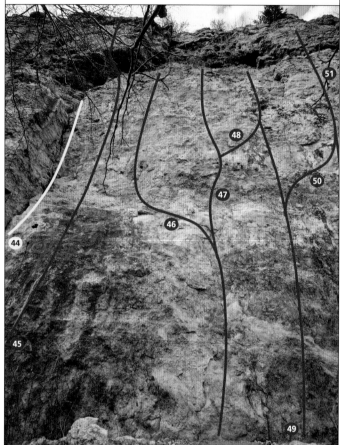

Winter Wall-Right

50. Cooler Than Paradigm (5.13a) Start on *Cooler Than Ice* and traverse to *Paradigm Shift* above its third bolt. Both routes may be underrated due to missing holds. This linkup combines the toughest parts of each route. **FA:** Matt Tschol.

51. Paradigm Shift (5.13a) ★★★★ This gem is technical, crimpy, and ready to unceremoniously kick you off anywhere below the sixth bolt. A powerful boulder problem leads to a thin seam, followed by another boulder problem, bigger moves, and crimps. Don't fall off the 5.10 choss before the anchors. 7 bolts. **FA:** Mike Dahlberg.

Between the hueco on the previous climbs and the thin crack of *Barnburner* lie four lines of bolts.

49. Cooler Than Ice (5.13a) ★ The line about 6 feet right of the *Chinese Freedom* huecos at a black bolt climbs straight up on invisible holds to a ledge where it gets easier. It will probably get harder as more crimps break off. **FA:** Darin Limvere.

52. Blankman (5.13b/c) Start on *Paradigm Shift*, then traverse right after the second bolt to *Insectaphobe*. At the hueco, head right to finish on the last three bolts of *Mississippi*. 7 bolts. **FA:** Andy Raether.

53. Insectaphobe (5.14a) ★★ This route will turn your face red and allow you to see all the veins in your arms by the time you reach the top. Head through a boulder problem to the second bolt, then continue through four more bolts before merging with *Mississippi*. 6 bolts. **FA:** Andy Raether.

Winter Wall-Far Right

56. Living All Over Me (5.12c) ★★★ Another gem that epitomizes the powerful climbing required at He Mni Can. Follow the flat edges to a nasty gaston, then after a brief rest, head into a big reach and undercling before bumping up. Now just stay on the route and clip the chains, which is no small feat. **FA:** Tom Ramier.

57. The Itch (5.11+) Climb the left side of the arête but avoid reaching too far around to the right face. A bit contrived but fun movement. **FA:** Josh Helke.

54. Mississippi (5.12c) ★★★★ One of the ★best★ 5.12s at He Mni Can. Three hard boulder problems in between functional rests. The first crux is a huge move left. After a few moves to a rest, enjoy some tough laybacks before traversing left for a rail, the crux for most. Pretend to rest, then navigate one more boulder problem before 10 feet of moderate climbing. 6 bolts. **FA:** Keith Anderson.

55. Barnburner (5.10d) TRAD ★★★ At the right end of the Winter Wall is an obvious, thin crack that eats gear. The original route starts in the right-hand crack, then traverses left on a ledge into another crack up and left. Pull over the flake on to the face and clip the chains. **Variation:** The right-hand finish (up the face from the ledge) is 5.11c. **FA:** Jim Blakley.

Brian Bos on *Blankman* (5.13c) Photo: Chris Deal

The East End

Right of *Barnburner* and around the corner is a 6-foot-wide buttress (home of *The Prow Left* and *Dead Dog Arête*). The 20-foot face to the right of that buttress ends in a left-facing dihedral (*Barnie's Corner*).

58. The Prow Left (aka Pietro Loves Iris, 5.9) ★ The Prow has two routes that share the initial first bolt. Start in the middle of the face, then go straight up the left line on the prow for a one-and-a-half-move wonder. 3 bolts. **FA:** Michael Endrizzi.

59. Dead Dog Arête (aka Prow Right aka Gene Machine, 5.9) ★ Go right after the first shared bolt with *Prow Left*. Head around the corner to one more bolt. Shares anchors with *Barn Dance*. **FA:** Michael Endrizzi.

60. Dead Dog Face (5.11a or 5.11c) ★★★ Between a pedestal and the major roof 15 feet up. Fun and technical with pockets. The eliminate version (11c) avoids the crack at the left edge of the roof. Shares anchors with *Barn Dance*. 4 bolts.

61. Barn Dance (5.9) ★★ Toprope or use bolts on *Dead Dog Face*. This climb is left of *Roof Burner's* bolted line, going up to the corner left of the roof.

62. Roof Burner (5.11a) ★★★ This is an excellent sustained and pumpy route over two roofs. Head up the slab, move left, and pull the first roof. Head up, then right to the second roof and gun for the chains. 6 bolts. **FA:** Nate Postma.

63. Barnie's Corner (5.10a) TRAD ★ The big corner and crack to the right of *Roof Burner*. Enjoy big steps before heading in to a fun (at times awkward) hand crack before it eases off. Traverse left onto good rock at the top to clip *Roof Burner's* anchors. **FFA:** Jim Craighead and Mark Wehde.

East End

64. Thief of Wives (5.12d/V6) On the dark wall right of *Barnie's Corner* is a bolted boulder problem. Use only the face on the lower part; the arête is on route after the tiny triangular roof. 2 bolts. **FA:** Jeremy Mariette.

Generic Wall

This area begins at the front face of the protruding gray Sunburst Buttress and continues right to the large, ugly corner of *Cookie Crumble*. The trail is slightly elevated here and is separated from the rock by a small talus area.

This area is popular with a lot of moderates, but the routes are getting polished and slick due to the high traffic. Several require meandering.

65. Left Lane (5.10a) ★★ Start on the flat face of the buttress up white rock, keeping left of the round nose above. The first bolt is about 15 feet off the deck. 5 bolts. **FA:** Nate Postma.

Generic Wall-Left

Dag Riseng on *Micro Balls* (5.9+)

66. Sunburst (5.8 R) ★ On the face of the buttress, find a bolt about 8 feet up on gray rock. This route, especially the bottom, has become incredibly polished as you head up the arête and face. Stay in a shallow corner, just right of the rounded nose. 5 bolts. **FA:** Nate Postma.

67. Cardiac Standstill (5.10c) ★ A shallow inside corner with a 6-foot block as its base. Stay several feet left of this dihedral and weave up through some pockets to chains. If you weave a lot, you can make it easier. 5 bolts.

Generic Wall-Right

71. Too Low for Zero

(5.8+) ★★ Beginning at a right-facing crack, start up a face leading to a bolt at 10 feet. Stay left as you head up toward the anchors, then finish just right of the big hole. 5 bolts.

72. Year of the Ankle

(5.9) ★★ Just left of the right edge of the face. A bouldery start in a shallow corner gets you to a ledge on the arête and finally to the first bolt about 15 feet up. The crux is pulling left into a big hole near the top. 5 bolts. **FA:** Nate Postma.

73. Micro Balls (5.9+)

★★ Around the corner from *Year of the Ankle*, climb the dihedral before following the bolts left through a small overhang. The bottom half is nice and clean, and it's one of the better routes on this wall. 5 bolts. **FA:** Dan Meyer.

68. Freebase (5.9-) TRAD ★ The corner

crack. Be sure you feel good about inventive gear placements before starting up this route, but it's got a great variety of corner and crack movements.

69. Rock-a-holics (5.8 PG13) ★ Just left of

a little buttress, this route has a low committing crux that will test your head game high above the first bolt. You will deck if you fall. 4 bolts. **FA:** Nate Postma.

70. Danger High Boltage (5.9-) ★★ Start at

a thin crack and enjoy edging and mantling while moving back and forth with a crux after the third bolt. 5 bolts.

74. Cinq Jour d'Affille (5.7) ★ Eight feet

left of the *Cookie Crumble* corner. Stay right of the bolts while going straight up toward a small roof. 4 bolts. **FA:** Nate Postma and Penny Sperlak.

75. Cookie Crumble (5.7) TRAD The obvi-

ous corner has a wide variety of crack sizes that could be enjoyable for the right person.

Annadonia Area-Left

Annadonia Area

These routes run right of *Cookie Crumble* to the buttress right of the lieback flake (*Looking for Lust*).

76. Femme Fatale (5.12c) ★★★★ Should you be tempted by this route, be ready for painful crimps, power moves, and a crux on slab. Start on the block at the base of *Cookie Crumble* and move up and right. A direct start takes the bolts just right of the pedestal. A great 12 at He Mni Can when it is not moist, though it often is. 6 bolts. **FA:** Nate Postma.

77. Quiet Desperation (5.13a) ★ Work up the blunt arête that quietly squashes egos left and right. Enjoy hard unique movement, painful crimps, and a high redpoint crux before jugs to the anchors. 5 bolts. **FA:** Jeff Engel.

78. Campinini (5.12a PG13) Up the left wall of the shallow dihedral of *Geriatric Sex Maniacs* beginning off a 2-foot-tall boulder. The crux is getting off the ground to the second bolt. It's not popular so expect dirt and poor rock quality high up. 6 bolts. **FA:** Tom Ramier.

79. Geriatric Sex Maniacs from Mars (5.10c) ★★ Start on a crack leading to a small overhang. Up to and over the bulge is your crux. Head left after the ledge toward the corner above. Expect grit. 6 bolts. **FA:** Nate Postma.

80. Out of Control (5.11a) ★★ Start on *Geriatric*. When you get to the ledge, head up the middle line of bolts for less sand. Steep huecos at the top provide the crux, then stretch to the anchors about 6 feet right of *Geriatric*. 6 bolts. **FA:** Nate Postma.

81. Stylin' (5.11a) ★★ Start on *Geriatric*, then at the ledge head to the right line of bolts as you dance across some thin horizontal face moves to overhanging jugs. Finish about 6 feet right of *Out of Control*. 7 bolts. **FA:** Nate Postma.

82. Shower the People You Love with Bolts (5.10b) ★★ Start as for *Geriatric*, wander right and get to the shelf 20 feet above the *Annadonia* start. Traverse back left about 6 feet to get the small hueco before heading straight up, staying on the face and avoiding the big pockets to your right into the final overhang. **FA:** Michael Endrizzi.

83. The Future (5.8) ★★★★ Start on *Geriatric*, then cross over *Annadonia* at the ledge before heading into the upper part of *Looking for Lust*. This route is super-tall and one of the best warm-ups at the Bluff. It's long, fun, and varied and moves you around, gives you different types of climbing, makes you think, and the crimps don't destroy your fingers. Clean by following to avoid a huge swing. 9 bolts. **FA:** Chris Hirsch, B. Busch, and J. Williams.

84. Annadonia (5.12a) ★★★ Start under a thin crack that peters out before it reaches the ground. A technical start that's both bouldery and sequency to a ledge. After that it's bigger holds and bigger moves, and the big bulge at the top feels like a roof when you're on it. Go straight up and over the bulge for the 12a, or finish left up the dihedral corner for an 11b variation. Goes on gear if you're ambitious. 8 bolts. **FA:** Nate Postma.

85. Looking for Lust (5.9) ★★ This is the longest line at He Mni Can, clocking in at just under 100 feet. A 60-meter rope will *just* make it. The first 20 feet is a lieback on a flake that is so polished and slippery that you'll be cursing the rating, but once you get past that, it's far more fun. 8 bolts. **FA:** Nate Postma.

86. Dirty Corner (5.9+) TRAD Look for the corner crack. Not recommended, but if you decide to try it, wear goggles as you snorkel through sand and dust, breaking holds and not trusting any of your higher-placed gear. Closed for nesting owls February through June.

From the large gray buttress (right of *Looking for Lust*) to the scree pile 75 feet west is an area in which owls used to roost. If you see or hear any, stay away.

87. Cool for Cats (5.10b) ★ Start on a dark face with two bolts, then up the arête through a tricky overhang. Chains below the first grassy ledge. 7 bolts. **FA:** Jeff Engel.

88. Vertical Willies (5.11b) A TR from the anchors of *Cool for Cats*. Has some interesting moves and odd holds.

89. A Salami for Your Boy in the Army (5.10a/b) ★ Climb the crack clipping the bolts until meeting up with the final two bolts and anchors for *Rude Awakening*. **FA:** Peter Graupner.

90. Rude Awakening (5.11a) ★★ Immediately right of the talus is a line of six bolts. Fun moves right off the ground. **FA:** Kelly Gorder and Scott Wright.

Annadonia Area–Right

91. Last Call for Alcohol (5.10a) ★★ Thirty feet right of *Rude Awakening*, just right of a very straight tree next to the wall. The opening is tough but the movement flows, and you'll wish it went on longer. Often gritty. **FA:** Kelly Gorder and Scott Wright.

Perfect Crimb Area

Halfway between the Annadonia area and the New Vice Area, look for two large roofs marking the center of the routes and some large boulders on a dirt slope. This area is about 100 feet off of the main trail.

92. Two Hand Edge (5.9) TR ★ Climb the face to the left of the crack. Toprope only, setting from *One Hand*.

93. One Hand Jam (5.6) ★★ A bolted crack/face that's the farthest left bolted route in the area. Unfortunately short, as it's the nicest easy climb here. Awkward belay. **FA:** Jeff Engel.

Perfect Crimb Area-Left

94. Demystification (5.12a) ★★★ Hard patina slab with balancey moves on great rock. Start on top of a large pedestal, where you can also belay if you stick clip the first bolt for safety. **FA:** Liz Hajek.

95. Don't Mean Nothin' (5.10b) TRAD ★★★ A good trad lead but a little harder than it looks, find the thin crack in a dark face leading to a lowering station. You'll want smaller gear. **FA:** Nate Postma.

96. Technical Difficulties (5.12a/b) ★★ Hug the arête to the top. The bottom 10 feet is the crux, with easier climbing at the top. **FA:** Mike Dahlberg.

97. Vice Squad (5.12d) ★★ A crimpfest. Technical and powerful moves on ridiculously hard slab. **FA:** Mike Dahlberg.

98. Perfect Crimb (5.9) ★★ Start on the small pedestal underneath the main roof. Stem the shallow dihedral going just left of the large roof. Can be led on gear. 5 bolts. **FA:** Nate Postma.

99. Pulldown Menu (5.12d) ★★ Go up to the left side of the main roof. Have fun on the bouldery moves pulling the roof before moving right to the chains. **FA:** Mike Dahlberg.

100. Fallout (aka Perfect Sex, 5.12b) ★★ Start up the face toward a small roof below a larger one. Be ready for big moves and a lot of try-hard. After pulling the first roof, head left around the hanging flake before pulling the next roof. Careful with your rope—the flake is sharp when lowering. **FA:** Mike Dahlberg.

101. Advanced Birding (5.12a) ★★★★ Up an easier face on crimps and through two small roofs that have a hueco between them. Some big moves and power pulls. **FA:** Mike Dahlberg.

102. Hateful Pleasures (5.9-) MIXED ★★
The dihedral crack to the right of the main
roof, head up three bolts before placing
some nuts in the crack. If you don't place
gear, you'll definitely deck if you fall. **FA:**
Mike Dahlberg.

103. Gear Fear (5.10a) MIXED ★ Use the
lower three bolts of *Crank-n-Go-Go*, then
move up the left crack. Take gear for the top.
FA: Mike Dahlberg.

104. Crank-n-Go-Go (5.10d) ★★ Blunt
arête with a pretty straight line up through
a rounded nose. **Variations:** Direct start
(5.11b) or try the crack instead of the arête
for a fun bolted crack climb in the 5.10-
range. **FA:** Jeff Engel.

105. Lacuna (5.12b) ★★ No topo. About 25
feet right of *Crank*, scrabble up a dirt ramp
to the base of a chimney-like structure to the
first bolt. Watch for a scary finish. The belay
isn't pleasant. **FA:** Mike Dahlberg.

New Vice Area

The left (east) end of this area starts at a large
eyebolt on a buttress next to the trail. The
buttress forms one wall of a large, right-
facing corner. The trail comes close to the
rock again (near *Two-Tone Zephyr*) about
120 feet west of the eyebolt. This area ends
about 180 feet west of that climb at a dirt-
and-scree pile.

New Vice Area-Left

106. Eye Bolt Approach (5.4) No topo.
Right of the eyebolt is either an easy toprope or an approach route. Not recommended.

The large, right-facing corner just past the eyebolt was previously a route called Jenna's Chimney until major parts collapsed. It *should not* be climbed.

107. Jenna's Face (5.8+ PG13) ★ Follow
up the flake to the right of the corner. The bolts don't start until after the flake, so bring a piece or two to protect the bottom part of the route. It's a slick, tough start before better climbing. The top can be mossy and wet. 3 bolts.

108. New Tomorrow (5.12a) Warm up your
fingers for the opening moves, especially since it's not entirely obvious where the holds are. Depending on recent weather, the top could be choss or straight-up mud for an added "adventure" factor. 4 bolts. **FA:** Nate Postma.

109. Eggs and Darts and Stuff (5.12b) Start
up the ramp/dyke, trying to figure out the

sequence as it slopes upward. At the top, head a touch right before enjoying easier climbing straight up. 5 bolts. **FA:** Nate Postma and Brett Harberts.

110. Stormy (5.11a/b)
★ Find the shallow right-facing dihedral just to the right of *Eggs*. Using the large flake makes this a 10b. Often wet. **FA:** Peter Graupner and Jack Powers.

111. Way Knarly Dudes (5.8 X) TRAD.
Right of *Eggs* is a tall ugly flake that forms two little corners—this is the left one. Stem up into overhanging rock before moving over a bulge to a somewhat nicer (if it's not dirty or muddy) hand and off-width size crack. Follow the crack until it ends at new anchors. Gear is not reliable so be cautious. **FA:** Nate Postma.

112. Syncopation (5.8) TRAD ★ The right-
hand corner crack that starts bigger before closing up a bit. When cleaner, it's a nice route that lets you use a lot of different fun techniques. New anchors at the top. **FA:** Nate Postma.

113. B.F. Bugs (5.9+) ★★ A bolted face
that starts tough on crimps before heading right to the pocketed arête. 5 bolts. **FA:** Nate Postma.

114. Pleasant Summer Absence (5.10a) ★★
Just right of a tiny, right-facing flake-corner. Different types of climbing in a short amount of space. 4 bolts. **FA:** Nate Postma.

115. Spaghetti Before Betty (5.10a/b) ★★ No topo. Left of a seam, head straight up, finding an undercling and crimps. **FA:** Peter Graupner.

The trail passes close to these climbs. A clean crack (*Goofed on Skunkweed*) runs from the ground to the overhangs.

116. Pandemonium (5.10a) ★ A short (possibly dirty) but fun route that isn't (yet) nearly as polished as other 10s at this crag. 4 bolts. **FA:** Nate Postma and Brett Harberts.

117. Vertical Vice (5.9+) ★ A slick, short arête (black on the right, white on the left) that seemingly ends halfway up the wall. Start left of this arête and weave up to chains under a rectangular roof. 5 bolts. **FA:** Nate Postma and Steve Wilgge.

118. Legal Limit (5.10c/d) This linkup starts in *Vertical Vice*'s dihedral, staying to the left of the bolts, then at the third bolt, make a technical traverse over to *Three Chicks* and follow to the top. **FA:** Maggie Moran and Jeff Noel.

119. Three Chicks on a World Tour (5.11b) ★★ Climb up the face, joining *Call* above its corner about 15 feet off the deck. 6 bolts. **FA:** Nate Postma and Dan Meyer.

120. Call of the Mild (5.11b) ★★ Right of *Vertical Vice* is a short dihedral. Go up a short dihedral (you can thread a sling in the drill hole) where you can use either the crack/seam or the crimps before following a slight arête above. 5 bolts. **FA:** Mike Dahlberg.

New Vice Area–Center Left

New Vice Area–Center Right

Maggie Moran on *Frequent Flatulence* (5.10b) PHOTO: TONY MANSOURIAN

121. Goofed on Skunkweed (5.8-) ★★ Look for the crack leading to a ledge before it extends the rest of the way up the cliff. It's fully bolted but also a good trad lead or practice. 5 bolts. **FA:** Nate Postma.

122. Alligator Alimony (5.7+) Up the arête to the anchors. "Loose rock" isn't a strong enough term for this route. 6 bolts. **FA:** Nate Postma.

The following routes are found on the face just west (right) of *Goofed on Skunkweed*. The left side of the face features a crack and the right side is bounded by a right-facing corner. There is a ledge about 5 feet up in the middle and a ledge about 12 feet up to the right.

123. Two-Tone Zephyr (5.9) ★★★ Looks intimidating from the ground, but don't let that stop you from getting on this great route! Climb the face to a small bulge with a crack with good holds. After the bulge, wander to the anchors. 5 bolts. **FA:** Nate Postma and Jeff Engel.

124. Eel Pocket Route (5.10b) ★ Using the *Doctor Limit* anchors, climb 3 feet left of the bolt line looking for pockets on this toprope-only route. **FA:** Nate Postma.

125. Doctor Limit (5.11b/c) ★★ Start at a sloping triangular nose at the left end of the 5-foot ledge. Clean, technical, and fun on delicate moves through a left traverse. This route is intriguing when trying to on-sight. 5 bolts. **FA:** Dan Meyer.

126. Frequent Flatulence (5.10b) ★★★★ In the middle of this face is a thin crack meandering up and right. Start at the left edge of the 5-foot ledge, then head straight up the thin crack, but not necessarily crack climbing. Artful movement. 5 bolts. **FA:** Nate Postma.

127. Doctor Rock (5.10b/c) ★★★ Begin at the right end of the 5-foot ledge and directly below a small overhang. Climb straight up. The top gets thin and crimpy. 4 bolts. **FA:** Nate Postma.

128. Living Postmortems (5.8-) ★ From a dihedral, follow the large left-leaning crack as it cuts up the face. While it has bolts, a bigger hex will give you peace of mind. There's a moveable flake and sand. 4 bolts. **FA:** Nate Postma.

129. No Falling Boys (5.10a) TRAD ★★★ Just right of a black, right-facing dihedral is a finger crack. This is a beautiful little lead with great finger locks. **FA:** Nate Postma.

130. Prairie Fire (5.10c) ★★ Head toward a large hueco for the first bolt, then trend right on crimps to the second bolt. Finally, trend left to the chains of *No Falling Boys*. If you're under 6 feet, it might be in the 5.11 range. 4 bolts. **FA:** Dave Brandt.

131. Dealer's Choice (5.6) ★ Find a gully with chains. For the 5.6, start in the gully and work your way left toward the first bolt, then head straight up, staying out of the corner to the right. **Variation:** A direct start is in the 5.11b range. 3 bolts. **FA:** Jim Blakely (gully); Dave Brandt (direct start).

132. Blue Steel (5.10a) ★ To the right of the dirty corner, follow the bolts. 4 bolts. **FA:** Peter Graupner.

133. Blue Moon (5.10a) ★★ Interesting route with huecos that make the bottom a little tougher before heading up to the anchors. Short yet fun for the grade. **FA:** Jim Craighead.

New Vice Area-Right

Large Roof Area

This area starts 30 feet right of the dirt/scree pile below *Blue Moon* and ends at the large roof 50 yards west. A talus block marks the start of the next three routes, which also share anchors.

In the spring, these routes in particular can be cold, wet, and miserable. In the summer the bugs can rule supreme. The best time to climb is late summer through fall, when the routes are dry and the bugs are gone.

134. In the Pink (5.11c) ★ Shallow and surprisingly tougher holds at the bottom before it eases up near the top. 4 bolts. **FA:** Nate Postma.

135. Quick Draw Moves to Hollywood (5.11a/b) ★★★ The middle line with bolts starting at the top of a pancake flake. This route is all about creativity and finding your

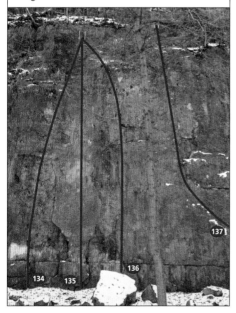

Large Roof Area-Left

sequence. It's crimpy, but not badly so. Watch for ground fall potential on a tough clip. **FA:** Jeff Engel.

136. Space Warp (5.11d) ★★ A tough lieback and bouldery until you reach the shelf. Easier up top. 4 bolts. **FA:** Nate Postma.

137. Tummy Kittens in Space (5.8+) ★★ Scooch right up the ramp. See if you can find the undercling around the third bolt. **Variation:** Direct start from the ground up and over the ramp (5.10a). 3 bolts. **FA:** Peter Graupner.

These next routes lie on the featureless and sometimes dirty wall that stretches left of the large roof. To locate them, walk over to the large roof and find *Needles and Pins*. Work your way back left to locate *Why Doesn't Anybody Climb This?* through *Toll Free*. Beware of poison ivy at the base of a lot of these climbs.

138. Why Doesn't Anybody Climb This? (5.10a) Just right of a line of saplings in a faint corner/seam. Liberally coated with dried scum, and the runout to the second bolt is far more than you may want. 5 bolts. **FA:** Nate Postma.

139. Tub Toys (5.10a) ★ A hueco at the first bolt. 5 bolts. **FA:** Nate Postma.

140. Fish Furniture (5.11a) ★ The next route on the grid. 5 bolts. **FA:** Nate Postma.

141. Multiple Wounds (5.11a) ★★ Great friction and fun movement; stay focused through the crux before that second bolt. 4 bolts. **FA:** Nate Postma.

142. Toll Free (5.9+) Use the anchors from *Needles and Pins* to toprope this route with a loose hueco in the middle. **FA:** Nate Postma.

143. Needles and Pins (5.10a) ★★★ Fifteen feet left of the triangular overhang is a blunt arête on a black wall with a small roof below the first bolt. Climb up to the pocket to get over the bulge at the bottom, pass some small roofs on the right, then some thoughtful, technical climbing. A great low 10. 6 bolts. **FA:** Nate Postma.

144. Dances with Pete (5.11d) ★★ Use a weird slopey pull to get up to a nice jug before happily dancing to the top. 5 bolts. **FA:** Nate Postma and Pete Olson.

145. A Deal with the Devil (5.10c) ★ Start in the dihedral up to the roof before gently traversing left, pull the lip, and gingerly climb up to the anchors. 5 bolts. **FA:** Nate Postma.

146. Talking with God (5.11d) ★★ Start in the dihedral/corner heading up to the big roof on not-great rock, then head slightly right. Pull through the big roof, paying attention to footwork. 5 bolts. **FA:** Nate Postma.

147. Weenies and Nerds (5.10d) ★★ Up the same corner as *Talking*, go right under the roof while avoiding actually pulling the roof, head around the corner to easier terrain, then back left to the *Talking with God* anchors. 5 bolts. **FA:** Nate Postma.

148. Sierra Madre (5.12a/b) ★★★ Follow the *Talking* corner up to the first bolt before heading right up the face to the roof instead of using the dirty corner. Meet back up with *Talking with God* at the roof and finish on that route. **FA:** Jack Powers.

149. Sierra (5.11b/c PG13) ★★★ Follow *Sierra Madre* until you hit the roof, and instead of pulling the lip, head right to follow *Weenies and Nerds* before ending on *Climb or Die*. **FA:** Peter Graupner and Jack Powers.

150. Climb or Die (5.12c) ★★ Moderate and fun moves as you work to the bulge. A tricky crux before easier but exposed climbing through small roofs. 6 bolts. **FA:** Jeremy Mariette.

151. Arachnid Tendencies (5.11d) ★★★ Right of the large roof is a flat face of yellow rock. Start about 2 feet left of the right edge of this face, near a thin crack. Good idea to stick-clip the first bolt. A sporty and tough start as you lieback the face, encounter improbable smearing, and head left to the tooth. Some loose rock may test your helmet. **Variation:** *Arachnophobia*, a direct finish, goes straight up after bolt 5 or 6 (5.12-). 7 bolts. **FA:** Jeff Engel.

152. Dumpster Does Duffels (5.10c) ★★ This is the last route on the bluff, around the corner to the right of *Arachnid Tendencies*. Start on a dirt ramp and climb the black face, generally following a thin seam. A tricky mantle halfway up is one of the technical tests on this route, assuming you get past the vicious sloping start. 7 bolts. **FA:** Nate Postma.

Large Roof Area–Right

Matt Jeffries on *Acid Choir* (5.13a/b) PHOTO: ANDY WICKSTROM

WILLOW RIVER STATE PARK

Walking down the path to the crag, you hear and then spot tumbling waterfalls. As you emerge at a river, your eye is drawn to the giant cave that houses some of the most overhung climbing in the Midwest. Though Willow is one of the smaller crags, it is breathtaking. Be prepared to get so pumped you can hardly get your draws down. While Willow River is technically in Wisconsin (barely!), the Minnesota Climbers Association maintains the crag, hence the inclusion in this book.

You can climb at Willow year-round; in fact, the best time of year to climb with completely dry routes is February. Spring is unpredictable, as the melting winter snow and ice often soaks the routes and causes them to seep (and if the spring snowmelt doesn't soak the rock, the spray from the waterfall will), and there's often dirt in the huecos. Overall, the best climbing is in late summer, fall, and winter.

The best time of day to climb at Willow is in the afternoon (but beware of restrictions, see below), and it's a great idea to check the humidity or dew point for clues as to whether the routes will be wet or not. Anything over 50 percent and the holds are more likely to be wet.

While the steep rock can be intimidating at first and there are only a handful of routes below 5.12, the holds themselves are good—great edges or jugs—and except for a couple of routes like *Dry Lightning* or *Hurtful Pleasure*, it's rare to have a big deviation from the style that makes Willow so unique.

Types of Climbing and Gear

All sport all the time. Most routes use between eight and twelve draws; more are needed for the longer variations or linkups (the longest needs nineteen). A 60-meter rope will work for all of the routes except the long linkups that traverse across the entire wall.

Due to the extreme overhang, use extended draws to reduce rope drag. Bring an emergency sling to help you aid through a route if you can't get up.

Land Acknowledgment

We acknowledge with respect and gratitude that this climbing area is on the traditional lands of the Wahpekute and Očhéthi Šakówiŋ people.

Permits, Local Ethics, and Regulations

You'll need an annual or daily Wisconsin State Parks Pass for your car, which you can get at the office on the way in.

Climbing is permitted only on certain days and at certain times, which are subject to change, so check before you go. At the time of publication, between May 15 and September 15, climbing is not allowed after noon on Friday and Sunday, and not at all on Saturday. This means your draws and ropes must be completely down and off the wall by noon. The rest of the year and Monday through Thursday, climbing is allowed when the park is open.

Climbing is permitted only on the cliff north of the river. The bolted routes on the south side are off-limits.

Avoid climbing on wet rock.

The top of the cliff is inaccessible so all routes must be led.

Dogs must be kept on an 8-foot leash and under control, and please clean up after them.

Getting There and Parking

Located just across the border into Wisconsin. Navigate to the main entrance of Willow River State Park, then turn right past the park office to make your way to the Willow Falls parking lot.

Approach

Follow the wide gravel trail out of the back of the parking lot, staying left when it branches. Head downhill to the river as the trail curves to the right, then over the river bridge. Access to the amphitheater will be on your right.

Camping and Amenities

Willow River State Park has a great campground at the top of the hill. Restrooms are available there, or use the facilities in the park office.

Hazards

Willow is notorious for being chossy. Most of the regular locals have ripped off holds from the wall more than once. Wearing a helmet when belaying and even when just hanging out is a good idea. In addition, tourists often like to walk under the climbs to get to the waterfall, and there's a very real possibility of pulling a rock and accidentally dropping it on someone's head. Some routes, like *Brass Monkey*, *Acid Choir*, or *New Beginnings* might be better left for quiet days when there isn't heavy tourist traffic. Also don't climb on wet rock—it tends to break easily.

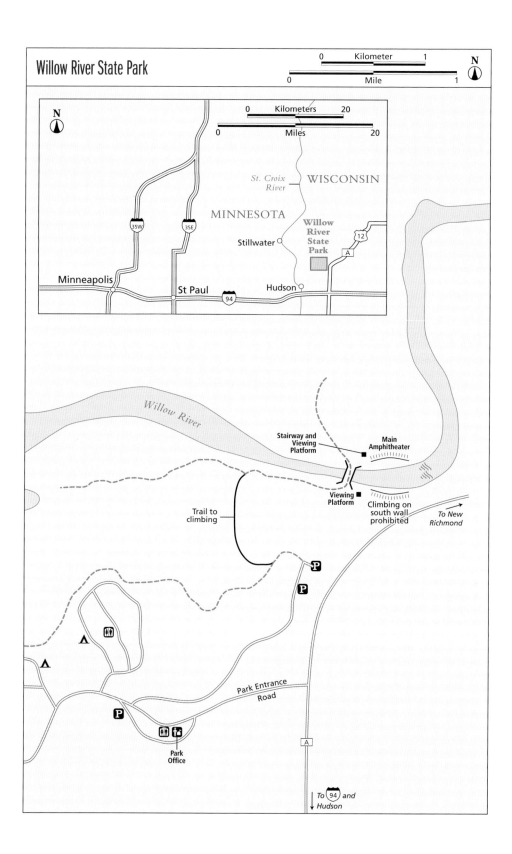

Willow River State Park

N

0   Kilometers   20
0   Miles   20

St. Croix River

WISCONSIN

MINNESOTA

35W   35E

Stillwater

Willow River State Park

12
A

Minneapolis

St Paul   94

Hudson

Willow River

Stairway and Viewing Platform

Main Amphitheater

Trail to climbing

Viewing Platform

Climbing on south wall prohibited

To New Richmond

P

P

Park Entrance Road

P

A

Park Office

To 94 and Hudson

Along those same lines, be cognizant of boinking up a rope when you fall. It's completely possible (and has happened) to rip a piece of rock off the wall with the bolt still attached because of the tension in the system.

The potential for rockfall, and the rushing river and waterfalls right next to the crag, pose serious risks for those not paying attention.

The falls, especially in spring, are so loud that climbing partners often cannot hear each other.

Carry in your own water. The river water has been tested and the nitrate levels alone are off the charts.

Fox snakes are commonly sighted here, both on the ground and on climbs, especially in the spring. While they look similar to rattlesnakes, and even mimic them by shaking their tails, they are not venomous and only want to be left alone.

Routes Not to Miss

Link Up (5.10d), Sudden Shock (5.11d), Natural Selection (5.12c), Couch Time (5.12d), Hurtful Pleasure (5.13a), Dry Lightning (5.13b), High Road to China (5.13b)

The Moderates

1. Quit Your Day Job (5.10a) ★★ Start on the arête of a right-facing dihedral. Head up to a dirty ledge, then move left to find the third bolt through the small roof that leads into the crux. **FA:** Sean Foster.

2. Drop Test (5.10a) ★ Start 8 feet left of *Jar of Flies*, heading straight up through good holds. A nice warm-up for the area. **FA:** Jeff Engel.

3. Jar of Flies (5.9+) Start just right of a small prow a few feet up. Climb a slab to the left of the large horizontal roof to chains located to the left of the crack. Obscure beta and tricky moves make it harder for beginner leaders. Could be called Jar of Wasps on sunny days. **FA:** Josh Helke, Tarek Haddad, and Jeff Engel.

4. White Noise (5.10d) ★★ Start on a small platform just beneath the overhang at the base and climb slightly overhanging rock up. Just before the overhang, head left toward an arête to easier terrain. 9 bolts. **FA:** Todd Peterson.

5. Link Up (5.10d) ★★★ Start up *White Noise*, and once you get to the no-hands rest, traverse right to join *Daily Grind* after two bolts. It's a pumpy route that has a lot of fun options—go straight up, veer around to the right, or get in the big hueco before hitting the roof. 9 bolts.

6. Daily Grind (5.11a) ★★ Start just left of a square inset. Climb slightly overhanging rock that passes just right of the large horizontal roof and clip the right set of anchors. 8 bolts. **FA:** Paul Bjork.

7. Sudden Shock (5.11d) ★★★★ A fantastic climb for the grade that helps you ease into the style at Willow without the commitment of some of the bigger routes—or a good warm-up. Start just right of the square inset (or standing on the boulder if you want), heading toward a hueco about 6 feet off of the ground. Climb up the right side of the large black streak and continue up and left, finding your own sequence through the jugs. 9 bolts. **FA:** Jeff Engel.

8. Sudden Daydreams (5.12b) ★★★ Head up *Sudden Shock* for four bolts before traversing right. You'll heel-hook and traverse on a big jug ledge for two bolts before swinging your feet into a possible kneebar. Reach up for a bad crimp before the crux into a fun finish, ending on *Midsummer Daydream*. **FA:** Jeff Engel.

The Cave

The routes in the cave from this point on begin to turn into wild overhangs and need to be cleaned differently than vertical routes. There is a bit of a learning curve. Don't climb to the top and lower down and try to grab all of the draws; instead, clean from the anchors down to the permadraw (leaving the permadraw clipped), lower down to the ground, then toprope and clean from the ground up to the permadraw. Plan rests at the clips when cleaning, as falling between clips while cleaning from the bottom means having to lower and start again if you can't boink up. It can get tiring after a long day. When finished cleaning, the swing from the permadraw could take you into a tree, and lowering from the top could leave you in the river.

Angie Jacobsen on *Natural Selection* (5.12c) PHOTO: ANDY WICKSTROM

9. Midsummer Daydreams (5.12d) ★★ Look for a big refrigerator-sized boulder where the wall starts to really get steep. Climb up the block, and after the first/main roof, head into a shallow corner before heading left toward a big hueco and up to the top. Kneebars are aplenty on this route, though it was originally done without them. 11 bolts. **FA:** Jeff Engel.

10. Radioactive Man (5.13a) ★★★ No topo. This great route that isn't completely obvious links up some of the tougher parts of two routes. Start on *Midsummer* before heading right just before the second roof for about three or four moves to link up with the top of *Tsunami*.

11. Natural Selection (5.12c) ★★★★ The classic rite-of-passage route at Willow. Start right of a shallow corner to a large pocket where the overhang begins. Follow large pockets up, moving to the left at rails that aren't quite jugs before making a beeline to the top. The last move to finish before clipping the chains could punt you. 12 bolts. **FA:** Jeff Engel.

12. Tsunami (5.13a) ★★ Head up *Natural Selection* to the roof, then go right at the fourth bolt toward and through the hueco. Head right after the hueco into the crux, where you'll find an uncomfortable and weird pinch before finishing on slightly easier terrain. **FA:** Paul Bjork.

13. Middle Cyclone (5.12d) ★★★ Start on *Genesis Effect* until you throw the big move and clip the seventh bolt on your left (not the bolt for *Genesis*, unless you want major rope drag). Shake out, make some tricky moves to the left, and head into the unforgiving upper crux of *Tsunami*, heading toward the bolt in the roof pointing straight down. The clip and the toe hook sequence are fantastic, and then grab the hueco and finish on *Tsunami*. You'll know you're there if you have to get over a bulge before crimping your way up to a big undercling. **FA:** Chris Hirsch.

14. Genesis Effect (5.12c) ★★★★ This is the route that inspired all the others. Three feet left of the black cave at the base, climb the slab to the 45-degree overhang. Pull the roof and head a touch right into a big hueco, which you'll exit with a big move. Keep heading right to another small roof before breathing as you siege to the top. 12 bolts. **FA:** Jeff Engel.

15. Cypher II (5.12d) ★★ Begin on *Genesis Effect*, but after pulling the roof, traverse to the right on jugs before making a big move straight up after clipping the seventh bolt. You'll find one of the best resting jugs at Willow after clipping your eighth bolt. Crimps and pockets make up the crux as you finish on *Genesis Effect*. The tough part could include a tension dead point or a nasty fist jam while saving enough gas in the tank to do the big *Genesis* roof. **FA:** Sid Wright.

16. Couch Time (5.12d) ★★★ Climb *Cypher II* until you get to the seventh bolt, and then head right toward a bolt that will lead up into the crux and finally find the anchors below the roof. **FA:** Jeff Engel.

17. Abel (5.13d) ★★ Twenty feet to the right of *Genesis Effect*, there's (at the time of writing) a brown painted leaver carabiner hanging from the first bolt on the roof. Climb jugs to the roof for the first crux—getting over the lip. Then head straight up to finish on *Couch Time*. **FA:** Chris Hirsch.

18. Cain (5.14b) ★★★ This stellar line is one of the most difficult routes in the Midwest. Start on the opening of *Abel* through the tricky roof section, but instead of heading up after getting through the lip, traverse right (V8 moves) while staying low for two bolts until you're in the black rock. Here, it meets up with *Dry Lightning* for the crux with the little pocket (V11). Your anchors are either those for *Couch Time* or head left climbing 20 more feet to the anchors for *Cain*. **FA:** Andy Raether. **Variation:** *Cabel* (5.14a) A variation that has seen only one ascent was done by Daniel Woods. Instead of heading all the way to *Dry Lightning*, go straight up the left side of the bulging arête toward a bolt (*Cain* climbs the right side) before ending on *Cain*.

19. Business Time (5.13b) ★★★ No topo. Willow's longest route by far, be ready to traverse. Start on *Dry Lightning*, but instead of heading up after the roof lip, keep traversing to the left even farther through pockets for *Cain* and *Couch Time* until you hit the fifth bolt for *Natural Selection*, just where the roof business starts. Finally head up through the roof section to a nice rest before continuing up on *Midsummer Daydreams*. 17 bolts. **FA:** Chris Hirsch.

20. Play Time Is Over (5.13b) ★★ No topo. Go up *Business Time* until you hit the fifth bolt for *Natural*, but instead of heading left, go straight up on *Tsunami*. **FA:** Anthony Vicino.

21. No Crack for Old Men (5.13b) ★★★ No topo. Follows the same start as *Business Time*, but instead of crossing all the way to *Natural*,

The Cave

Note: Colors are only to distinguish route lines. All are bolted sport routes.

move up after your left hand is on a full pocket and your right is heading toward a big horn. Keep going up on *Cypher II* until you clip the anchors for *Genesis*. **FA:** Jeff Engel.

22. Dry Lightning (5.13b) ★★★★
Truly awesome route. Start up *Rejection and Mercy* through the roof crack, but at the lip of the roof, head left on sloping edges without good feet for three bolts until a cruxy few moves. As long as you don't pump off the top, you should be okay. ***Note:*** Don't clip the permadraw on *Couch Time* or your rope drag will be terrible. **FA:** Chris Hirsch.

23. Hurtful Pleasure (5.13a) ★★★★
One of the best and more unique climbs at Willow. This roof crack, with not great jams, starts on *Rejection and Mercy* before heading straight up after you pull the roof. Big holds on steep terrain to another roof make this route beefy and fun and could possibly make your forearms explode. **FFA:** Jeff Engel.

24. Rejection and Mercy (5.13a/b) ★★★
This is the big 12-foot horizontal roof crack in the middle of the amphitheater. You'll climb through the crack, then after the lip, head right before finding a crack up to the anchors. This route feels particularly long. **FA:** Paul Bjork.

25. Mono Mercy (5.13b) ★★★
Start up *Mono Route* before traversing slightly left before the chains and joining up with *Rejection and Mercy*. Full body climbing that could be done multiple ways (see if you can find the no-hands kneebar). **FA:** Chris Hirsch.

26. Mono Route (5.13a) ★★★
Ten feet right of *Rejection and Mercy*, getting to the first clip can be spicy. Head through an intense roof sequence with small edges and a mono finger lock. If you make it through that, it's pretty much over. **FA:** Matt Tschol.

27. High Road to China (5.13b) ★★★★
Start up *Mono*, then two bolts before the chains, follow a bolt line right and up. This is one of the best hard linkups at Willow: The holds are good, but if you don't have the stamina, you won't make it through. **FA:** Chris Hirsch.

28. Low Road (5.12+) ★★★
Possibly one of the longest completely horizontal roofs in Minnesota, it's a shorter route that feels good! Head up three bolts of vertical easier climbing before pulling onto the roof on super jugs. The lip is where the business is. You can clip to the left for the easier way up, or head right if you want more spice. Both variations finish on the face above. **FA:** Rob Pilaczynski.

29. Low Road to China (5.13a) ★★★
Climb *Low Road*, then at the anchors head for the bolts into the top section of *High Road to China*. **FA:** Rob Pilaczynski.

30. Getting Slightly Higher (5.13c) ★★★
Do everything on *Living Slightly Larger*, but traverse over on two bolts and head into the top cruxes for *High Road to China* to finish a route that truly feels like bouldering. **FA:** Nic Oklobzija.

31. Living Slightly Larger (5.13b/c) ★★
A big wingspan will help with the huge reaches on this route. Begin below a two-tiered roof on the tan rock between *Mono* and *Brass Monkey*, heading up to the roof. Huge moves, precision, and some weirdness will get you through. Head to the lip for another couple of bolts. This route technically used to end at the roof. **FA:** Chris Hirsch.

32. Water Music (5.12a) ★★
Starts just right of an 8-foot, shallow black inset. Go straight up to the roof to chains halfway up the main amphitheater, just below a large horizontal

roof. Pulling the roof through crimps is your crux before finishing by traversing left to the anchors. **FA:** Mike Dahlberg.

33. Brass Monkey (5.12d) ★★★ Nails hard. Start on *Water Music* through the anchors, then head up left through the roof. There's a reach, pinches, full body tension, high feet, and a superhero swing at the end. Don't forget about kneebars. If you're not the commitment type, this route might not be for you. **FA:** Chris Hirsch.

34. Acid Choir (5.13 a/b) ★★★ Unique for Willow, this climb requires lots of body and core tension with good foot technique. Start on *Water Music*, and at the chains, traverse to the right for three bolts (the crux) before heading up again, where you'll run into two smaller roof sequences. Expect a lot of rope drag if you don't extend any draws. **FA:** Tyler Hoffart.

35. New Beginnings (5.12a) ★★★ Climb the *Water Music* roof, then head right toward a dihedral. Keep going up and right toward the arête for *Leftovers* and the anchors. This one bakes in the late afternoon, especially on hot summer days. **FA:** Jeff Engel.

36. Leftovers (5.12a PG13) Because of the danger of rockfall, it's advisable to stay off and do the far more fun *New Beginnings* instead. Start on the same first bolt as *Water Music*, but then head up right toward the big dihedral and arête for three bolts to the roof. Follow the arête and the dihedral to the top for exposed climbing. **FA:** Jeff Engel.

The Mezzanine

To get to the Mezzanine, look for three glue-in handlebars (i.e., the "Bolt Ladder") to the right of *Water Music*. It is often wet, and can feel kind of sketchy. To get down, rap from

the chains just above the bolt anchor—downclimbing is not advisable. Bees sometimes like to make their nests in this area, and rock is loose. Stick-clip the first bolt on all of these climbs so no one ends up in the river.

37. Fox Confessor (5.12c) ★★ This starts with a good left-hand pocket and right-hand undercling. Make some big reaches between small holds before pulling through the first roof. Traverse left at the third bolt and be ready for some big moves before finishing on the anchors for *New Beginnings*. **FA:** Tyler Hoffart.

38. Requiem (5.13c) ★★★ A stellar route, start up *Fox Confessor* through the third bolt and then head straight up with two more cruxes in the upper section and a final one at the last roof. **FA:** Ryan Cowell.

Matt Jeffries on *Couch Time* (5.12d) Photo: Andy Wickstrom

The Mezzanine

39. Mermaid (5.12d) ★★★ This shares the first two bolts with *Fox Confessor* before traversing right and up through some crazy dynamic movements that make you feel like a super-hero over the waterfall. Leaver carabiners to assist in lowering. **FA:** Ryan Angelo and Tyler Hoffart.

Just left of *Sunday Sermon* is a set of abandoned anchors from an old project.

40. Sunday Sermon (5.12b) ★★ A deep roof with smaller holds. After two bolts, enjoy some cool campus moves before hitting the last roof with the huge reach. **FA:** Ryan Angelo.

41. Doppler Effect (5.12a) ★★ Nice for the grade, head through some tough and oddly flat underclings to reach the roof. Get through with a big move before a technical middle section and finishing on jugs over a roof, which isn't as easy as you want it to be, especially when covered in mud. **FA:** Josh Helke.

42. Guess and Check (5.10c) ★★ Overall a pumpy route, where getting to the first bolt is the crux. Once you reach the ledge, it's straight up to the anchor.

43. Unknown (5.9) ★ Short with a tough roof pull. It's known to be dirty, but it's hard to argue with climbing directly above the waterfalls. And yes, it really is named *Unknown*.

Sonja Hakanson on *Lost Ego* (5.8-)

TAYLORS FALLS/ INTERSTATE STATE PARK

A wildly popular area, the two Interstate State Parks rise on either side of the St. Croix River, with both Wisconsin and Minnesota making up one of the most visited combo of parks in the Twin Cities area. A warm weekend will find climbers on the cliffs on either side of a river populated with kayakers and fisherfolk. Tourists and hikers share the trails and the clifftops with the climbers, and after a long day, a walk across the road to the city of Taylors Falls will reward outdoorists with ice cream, food, or a cold beverage.

The basalt rocks hold routes from 5.0 scrambles up to 5.13 trad test pieces, and the quality is stellar. Easy access to both sides of the river means you can chase the shade or sun while enjoying both crack and face climbing. The park also has stellar bouldering. No matter what style or side of the river, climbing at Interstate, often referred to as simply "Taylors" by local climbers, is easy, accessible, and good for the soul.

Types of Climbing and Gear

Interstate has traditional climbing and toproping (and boulders). A 60-meter rope and a single rack works well, though a double rack gives more options for parallel cracks. You may want longer webbing or static rope to set anchors on some routes.

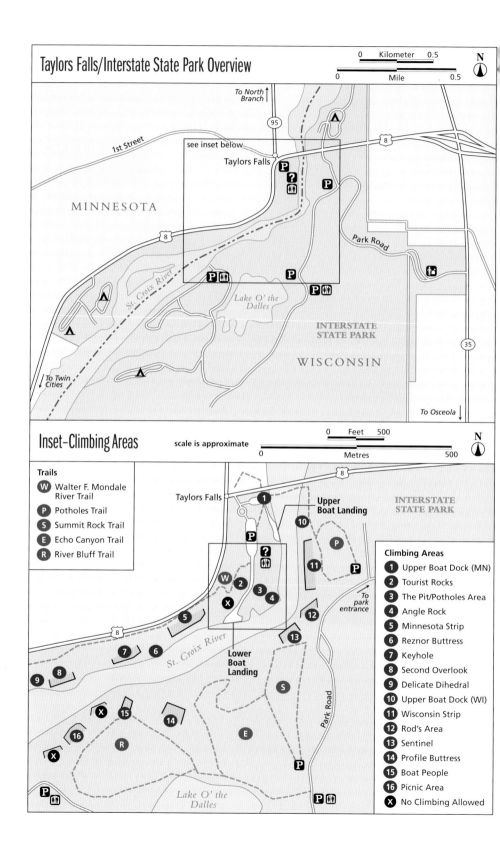

Taylors Falls/Interstate State Park Overview

0 Kilometer 0.5
0 Mile 0.5

N

To North Branch ↑

95

8

1st Street

MINNESOTA

Taylors Falls

see inset below

P
?
P

8

Park Road

St. Croix River

P

P

P

Lake O' the Dalles

INTERSTATE STATE PARK

WISCONSIN

35

To Twin Cities

To Osceola ↓

Inset–Climbing Areas

scale is approximate

0 Feet 500
0 Metres 500

N

Trails

W Walter F. Mondale River Trail
P Potholes Trail
S Summit Rock Trail
E Echo Canyon Trail
R River Bluff Trail

Taylors Falls

8

1 Upper Boat Landing

INTERSTATE STATE PARK

10

P

P

?

11

P

W
2
3
4

X

To park entrance

5

12

8

St. Croix River

7 6

13

Lower Boat Landing

9 8

S

X 15

14

E

Park Road

16

X R

P

P

Lake O' the Dalles

P

Climbing Areas

1 Upper Boat Dock (MN)
2 Tourist Rocks
3 The Pit/Potholes Area
4 Angle Rock
5 Minnesota Strip
6 Reznor Buttress
7 Keyhole
8 Second Overlook
9 Delicate Dihedral
10 Upper Boat Dock (WI)
11 Wisconsin Strip
12 Rod's Area
13 Sentinel
14 Profile Buttress
15 Boat People
16 Picnic Area
X No Climbing Allowed

Land Acknowledgment

We acknowledge with respect and gratitude that this climbing area is on the traditional lands of the Anishinabewaki and Očhéthi Šakówiŋ people.

Camping and Amenities

Interstate State Park has campgrounds inside the park in both Minnesota and Wisconsin, but they can fill up fast. Other campgrounds can be found at Straight Lake State Park and Wild River State Park, plus there are some private campgrounds within a 10-minute drive.

Restrooms are available at the trailheads for most of the climbing areas, as well as picnic areas and water-filling stations. The quaint town of Taylors Falls offers gas, food, beverages, and sometimes live music. There are also watercraft rentals if it's too hot for a

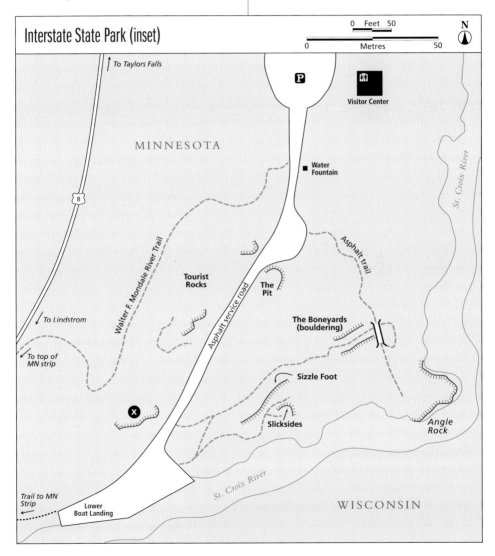

climbing day and you just want to float on the river—check out Taylors Falls Canoe and Kayak Rental just inside the park.

Hazards

The freeze-thaw cycle is particularly harsh on the rock in this area. Gear anchors that were solid one year can be devastating the following year.

Wear your helmet climbing and belaying. Loose rock still falls down regularly, and tourists throw or kick rocks from the tops of cliffs.

Wasps nest in the cracks and can get aggressive on hot, sunny afternoons.

Minnesota Side

Getting There and Parking

For the Minnesota side, park at the "Visitors Center" for "Interstate State Park" just off of US 8. If you go over the bridge into Wisconsin, you've gone too far.

Approach

All routes are accessed from the state park parking lot. Specific access directions are within each area section.

Permits, Local Ethics, and Regulations

Register for a free yearly climbing permit at the kiosk in the parking lot before any climbing. You'll also need a daily or yearly Minnesota state park vehicle permit for your car.

Organized groups need a commercial climbing permit and must contact the park office at least one week prior to set that up.

Some local ethics the state park asks climbers to follow are:

- If you use chalk, use only white chalk, and clean routes when finished.
- Park fixtures such as railings are not to be used when setting up anchors.
- No climbing is allowed in the potholes that are part of the interpretive trail, or those that are filled with water.
- Do not remove vegetation from climbs.
- Keep the park clean and pack in and out everything, including trash.
- Do not leave climbing equipment unattended to reserve climbs. Rangers may move unattended equipment per the park policy.
- Follow established trails to prevent erosion.
- Permanent anchors of any type are prohibited.
- Climbing is **allowed only** in the designated areas, and please respect any closures.
- Dogs must be kept on a leash no longer than 6 feet, and owners must keep them under control and clean up after them.

Routes Not to Miss

Piece of Cake (5.7+), Fallen Knight (5.9), Column Direct (5.9+), The Bulge (5.10a), Fancy Dancer (5.11a)

Upper Boat Dock

These climbs are just north of the upper boat dock and drop into the water.

1. Political Wall (5.9) ★ Find the crack to the climber's right of *Slip Sliding* for adventure climbing over the river.

2. Slip Sliding Away (5.9) ★★★ Look for the slab with a beautiful crack overhanging the river. Dihedral and crack climbing start

Upper Boat Dock

Tourist Rocks-North

things out at the bottom before the crack opens up to a great finish.

3. Drink More Water (5.9) ★★ Head up the corner to the ledge halfway up before taking a corner hand crack to the top.

Tourist Rocks

Top access: Follow the River Trail to access the top of the climbs for setting up anchors and topropes. After the initial uphill climb, you'll see climber access trails heading left toward the cliff edge. Everything from *Noah's Ark* onward is accessible from the top.

Bottom access: All routes are accessed from the service road—you'll see the climbs on your right as you head down the hill.

4. Noah's Ark (5.6-) ★★ The first outcrop on the right side of the road with a gravel patch at the base. From the base of the slab, zig right to good holds, then zag left to an airy step to the top. **Variations:** Work straight up to the final move (5.8) or climb up the face to the right (5.9). **Top access:** Up the slab to the left of the climbs.

5. The Great Flood (5.9) ★★★ Just to the left of *Noah's Ark*, start in the corner before following a gently curving fin. Top out in the same place as *Noah's*.

The *Sonny and Juanita* outcrop is about 100 feet down the road on the right. *Sonny and Juanita* is the dihedral to the right of the large pine growing in the middle of the outcrop.

6. Gorilla Arête (5.10a-c) ★ To the right of *Sonny and Juanita* is an arête capped by an obvious overhang. Climb up the arête, then monkey around looking for a route through the roof—the more direct, the harder the climb.

7. Daphnis and Chloe (5.8) ★ Climb up just right of *Sonny and Juanita* on the face between the dihedral and the arête.

8. Sonny and Juanita (5.5) ★★★ Get atop the ledges in the corner while staying in the dihedral. Full of hand jams great for practicing technique. Pull through overhanging blocks to the top. Beware of a loose yet large block while setting anchors. **Variations:** Lieback a few inches left of the dihedral (5.10) or finish up the steep wall left of the final easier crack (5.11).

9. Bill and Tom (5.7) ★ Start up *Sonny* and cut up and left along the crack to join the arête of *The Cornice.* **Variation:** Climb the face to the left of *Sonny* without using the *Cornice* corner.

10. The Cornice (5.6) ★★ Head up the somewhat broken arête toward the big tree. Move through the crack just to the left of the arête after the tree, then back to the arête to finish at the top.

11. The Other One (5.5) ★★★ A great introduction to Taylors. Climb the face while dancing on horizontal cracks trending toward the tree, then swoop back to the face to finish. It varies depending on where on the face you climb.

12. Push-Me Pull-You (5.4) ★★ This enjoyable corner is a great place to practice placing gear while cruising straight up.

Tourist Rocks-South

The Pit

Access: Near the Potholes Interpretive Trail, across the road from *Noah's Ark*. Head down the gravel trail on the left as it heads toward the Potholes. Spot the triangular overhang with a tree at the top. Please don't use this tree as an anchor.

13. Armpit (5.8+) ★★ Straight up this face without using any of the obvious holds on the right dihedral or the left.

14. Dihedral (5.3) A short and easy corner climb that's good for beginners or practicing gear placements.

15. The Overhang (5.6) ★★ Up the arête and face to the left of the big triangle overhang, using both the arête and the face. Top out on the left of the overhang.

16. The Overhang Face (5.9) ★★ Avoid both corners, head up directly under the point of the overhang on the face. Generally not topped out—the climb ends at the roof.

17. Corner Staircase (Class 4) A great climb for kids up the corner to the right of the overhang.

18. One Thin Fish (5.9+) ★★ Climb the face left of the crack until you get to the very top. Avoid the ledge on your right halfway up for full value.

The Pit

19. The Crack (5.9) ★ A short but fun route to practice crack technique.

20. Boob (5.7) The bulging corner arête to the right of *The Crack*, finishing at the ledge.

Potholes Area

Walk down the service road past *Sonny and Juanita* and turn left on a flat gravel trail. These climbs are across the marsh from *Sonny and Juanita*. There are stellar bouldering problems in this area as well.

The routes are numbered in increasing order as you encounter them while hiking in. This means 21 to 25 are listed right to left.

21. 5.8+ (Likely 5.13) ★ Get up over the block at the bottom before heading through the roof to the right of the thin crack, ending just right of a couple of trees.

22. The Real Thing (5.10a) ★★ A fun chimney/roof in a crack that seems to cut the boulder in half.

23. Genetic Control (5.13a) ★ Climb up into an alcove just left of *The Real Thing*, traverse onto the main face, and forge boldly up the middle of the curved upper section.

24. Sizzlefoot (5.12b) ★★★ About 20 feet left of *The Real Thing*, this stellar route heads straight up from the triangular divot and onto incredible face climbing, where technique and good holds make this climb one of the best at Taylors. **FA:** Mike Dahlberg.

25. Little Sizzler (5.10/5.12) ★ Climb the arête left of *Sizzlefoot* and exit left (5.10) or right to *Sizzlefoot* (5.12).

Potholes Area-*Slicksides*

Potholes Area-*Sizzlefoot*

To reach the next five routes, walk to the boat dock and ascend the trail up the rocks for 50 feet. Descend steps into the semicircular remains of a pothole. Routes are numbered left to right.

These climbs are short, and you should adjust your top anchors as needed to avoid nasty pendulums.

26. The Wheel (5.9) Puzzle out a route to the left of *Lunge or Plunge* up to a little left-facing corner.

27. Lunge or Plunge (5.12b) ★★★★ Climb the arching face left of *Shlocksides*. The lunge at the top has kicked off many climbers.

28. Shlocksides (5.10-) ★★ Head up the right side of the giant divot on the bottom to the sloping crack on big jugs. At the top go straight up. You can set up this climb and *Slicksides* with one rope.

29. Slicksides (5.9+) ★★★ A crack with a high crux and rock so slick your shoes will squeak. The direct start is 5.11ish.

30. Digitalis (5.12-) Around the arête from *Slicksides* on the face, left of a small, left-facing corner.

Angle Rock

Turn left off the service road just before The Pit. Cross a bridge over The Boneyards (good bouldering) and climb up over the high point of Angle Rock to ledges leading down to the edge. These routes may drop into the water depending upon water levels. Routes are described from north to south.

31. Lichens and Spiders and Bears (5.6) This wide crack is in the back of the left-facing corner to the right of *Seat Broken*.

32. Seat Broken (5.6) There are two left-facing corners on the north side of Angle Rock. This is the one closest to the arête of

Dirty Harry. Once you get up the corner, head up the face to the top.

33. Dirty Harry

(5.10b) Climb the face between *Vasectomy* and *Seat Broken*, using the arête occasionally.

34. Vasectomy

(5.11+) ★ Up the very crest of the arête right of *Stretcher*. Watch out for the first move.

35. Stretcher (5.11a-

d) ★★ True in name for those on the shorter side. Head up the crack left of the *Vasectomy* arête. **Setup:** The triangular ledge north of the top of *Iron Ring*.

36. Iron Ring (5.10a)

★★ Climb just right of the iron ring to a ledge two-thirds of the way up. The crux is figuring out the right corner of the overhang.

37. Witch Way (5.10c) ★★★ Start under a

small overhang on a slight outside corner directly under the big overhang. Sequence your way up thin holds to beneath the overhang, then head left to get around it. Harder variations could go directly over the roof.

38. Cosmos (5.10a) ★★ From your anchor,

work your way down and south (Class 2) to the ledge with the eyebolt and belay there. Climb down the chimney, then climb the

Angle Rock

face just right of the easy groove. The crux is the funky basalt at the top.

39. Thin Ice (5.8+) No topo. Drop down to

the water at the eyebolt belay (*Cosmos*), climb a crack, then do the easy groove above.

40. Barnacles and Backsides (5.8+) No

topo. There are some corners downstream of the ledge described on *Cosmos*. This route follows the largest of these corners. There will be vegetation in it.

Minnesota Strip

Easily the busiest area in the park, there's a great number of long, high-quality routes here.

Bottom access: Follow the paved road past Tourist Rock until it dead-ends at the riverboat dock. Turn right onto a hiking trail

Sean Foster rope-soloing *Piece of Pie* (5.8+)

and talus to reach the base of the cliff. A jam crack leads up to a face. This crack is *Piece of Cake*. To the left of a brushy gully is a 25-foot-tall column leaning against the face. This is *The Column*. Climbs will be described north to south relative to those two routes. The routes are very close together in spots.

Top access: From the asphalt path, the easiest is to take the River Trail and keep going past the Tourist Rock trails on your left until you reach the remnants of an old parking lot next to US 8. Veer off the main trail and trend left to the scrambly trail on the river side of the outcropping. There is a scramble on climber's left around the base of *The Bulge*, but it's far more difficult than taking the River Trail.

If you wish to first hike to the bottom of the Minnesota Strip and then head to the top, hike first to the base and then follow a trail as it heads up to the right over the short stone wall, where it will deposit you in the aforementioned old parking lot.

41. Short Crack (5.8) ★
Partway up the eroded access gully, you'll find a short finger crack.

Minnesota Strip Overview

42. Station 62 (5.10c) ★ Hike up and right from *Piece of Cake* until you see a horizontal 2-foot roof with a finger/hand crack running through it. Head straight up to that roof crack, avoiding the ledges to the right. **Variation:** Cut left (5.9+) of the roof to make it easier.

43. Pink Pants Delight (5.9+) ★★★ Climber's right of *Rosebush* is a big open face with lots of choices and possibilities for routes. The easiest way is to head up the face and cut left into the dihedral. For a climb more in the 5.10 range, stay on the face the whole time. Sketchy lead.

44. Rosebush (5.6) ★★★ About 15 feet right of *Piece of Cake* is a short face (crux) that leads to a dihedral capped by a small overhang. *Note:* The rock is a bit loose above the overhang. Setup: In a V-notch with a crack below it.

45. Piece of Pie (5.8+) ★★★ Just right of *Piece of Cake* is an outside corner with a tiny roof. Follow this edge and try to avoid straying left at the crux at two-thirds height. **Variation:** It's possible to force a line that stays left of the *Rosebush* crack and right of *Piece of Pie* (5.8).

46. Piece of Cake (5.7+) ★★★★ The most popular trad climb on the Minnesota Strip, don't let the grade fool you. Start up the crack and follow as it widens, enjoying every inch of easy-to-protect awesomeness. **Variation:** Head left onto easier terrain about halfway up.

47. Good Knight (5.8) ★★ Up the face to the left of *Piece of Cake*, either run out the first 15 feet or get real creative with your gear.

Erik Peterson on *Jammermeister* (5.5)

48. Armor All (5.10a) ★ Go up either side of the arête right of *Fallen Knight*, but pull straight over the roof on fun moves.

49. Fallen Knight (5.9) ★★★ The obvious clean corner left of *Piece of Cake*. Climb up the corner, watching out for pigeon poop. A harder finish is on the arête near the top. **FA:** Nate Beckwith, et al.

50. Organic (5.13a) ★★★ The orange/gold rock 7 feet to the left of *Fallen Knight* holds three boulder problems stacked on top of each other, with the last being the hardest. Start on an overhanging bulge with a thin seam running through it. Surmount this to the horizontal overlap and continue up. Don't use the ledge to the left halfway up. Completely unique compared to the climbs around it. **FA:** Sean Ferrell.

Minnesota Strip-Right

Unknown climber on *Piece of Cake* (5.7+)

Minnesota Strip-Center

53. The Column Direct (5.9+) ★★★

Balance straight up the face of the column, and don't use either edge, including that finger jam on the right. Continue above the column by staying to the right (5.8+) for a direct finish.

54. The Column

(5.6+) ★★ Start in the corner on the left side of the column. From the top of the column, go slightly left as you head toward the block slightly sticking out at the top.

55. Blue Moon (5.6)

★★ Find the big roof 20 feet up to the left of *The Column*. Head up to the right corner under the roof, then move left on huge holds to pull the roof on the left side before easier terrain at the top. **Variations:** Head directly over the roof for a 5.9 or take the right exit for a 5.7, or avoid the overhang completely by following the corner to the left of the overhang.

Between routes 50 and 51 is a broken gully previously called "Death Gully." It is eroded and loose, and only on its best days could be called an access gully.

51. Jammermeister (5.5) ★★ Just to the

right of *Columeister*, start on some blocks and ledges before working your way right to a really fun 15-foot hand crack to the top.

52. Columeister (5.6) ★★ Above and right of

The Column is an outside corner with a short inside corner to its right. Climb up here, finishing in another corner.

56. Nothing Fancy (5.12c) ★ Enjoy the thin seam to the right of *Fancy Dancer* before it joins up with the top easy corner of *Fancy*.

57. Fancy Dancer (5.11a) ★★ Just right of *The Bulge* is a thin seam that leads to a block. Be sure to stretch before this dance for maximum flexibility.

58. The Bulge (aka #6, 5.10a) ★★★★ A Taylors classic. Originally known as #6, it starts on the very left edge of the platform. Avoid the rocks to the left. Climb the thin crack up to and over the bulge, with horizontal and vertical crack goodness that protects beautifully. **FA:** George Bloom.

59. Urology (5.8+) Head up the larger crack on the left part of the wall if you feel like trying something a little dirtier and not as classic.

Minnesota Strip-Left

Route 60: Devil's Chair

Devil's Chair Area

Hike south past the base of *The Bulge* and you'll see the semi-detached tower known as *Devil's Chair* (though the "chair" is gone).

60. Devil's Chair (5.9+) ★★ The first guidebook described it as "a wretched flaring 5-inch crack," with the previous author agreeing. This author believes some might find the Type 2 crack a fun challenge instead.

61. Sweep the Chimney (aka Eagle's Nest, 5.5) ★★ About 50 feet downstream from the Devil's Chair formation, find a slab with a continuous crack that starts next to two trees growing out of the same place. At the ledge, build an anchor to avoid rope drag, and head straight up the face into a dihedral/chimney on the right, then step right to go up through cracks on the headwall.

Devil's Chair Area

62. Mow the Lawn (5.6) ★ Starting 4 feet left of *Sweep the Chimney*'s crack, head up over the bulge to a grassy ledge before finishing up the left face and through the chimney.

Reznor Buttress

This small outcropping rises out of the river downstream of the Minnesota Strip. One steep and narrow chute must be climbed to reach the top. A top-managed system works best here.

63. Into the Void (5.7) ★ Up the diagonal crack or the face to the right to a ledge. Finish on *Me, Not Live*. **Variation:** Work the face to the right (5.10a). **FA:** Gary Nygaard.

64. Me, Not Live (5.7+) ★ The roof right of *The Big Come Down* can be turned either left or right, then follow the left or right side of the detached block. **FA:** Gary Nygaard.

65. The Big Come Down (5.7+) ★ A left-leaning slanting crack cuts through the entire face. **FA:** Gary Nygaard.

66. Ghost IV-32 (5.10b) ★ Stay a couple of feet right of *Just Like You Imagined*, climb the thin crack after the first mini-ledge while avoiding the good holds on either side to make it harder. **FA:** Gary Nygaard.

67. Just Like You Imagined (5.9-) ★ Start in the slice carved out of the bottom of the route before heading straight up through a crack. **FA:** Gary Nygaard.

68. Only (5.8-) ★ Straight up to a roof and exit left to a crack on the sloping face, or climb straight up to the left edge of the roof. **FA:** Gary Nygaard.

Reznor Buttress

Keyhole Area

Take the River Trail from the top of the service road and hike up to US 8. Walk south (next to the highway) to a stone overlook with a plaque and look over the edge—you'll see the ledge at the top of *Keyhole*. A few yards south of this ledge is a detached buttress that is the top of *Double Cracks* (best reached from below). *Reason to Believe* is on the main cliff line south of *Double Cracks*.

Bottom access: Hop over the wall just as you reach the overlook and descend the loose chimney system, which is somewhat hidden in shrubbery.

69. The Horn (5.7) ★★ Trend up and right on this slabtastic route, staying to the right of *Keyhole* in the small seam.

70. Keyhole (5.6) ★★ To unlock the easiest route of ascent, angle up and right past a pin to the keyhole, finishing in the crack as it angles right to the top. A great lead for new trad climbers.

Keyhole Area–Right

Keyhole Area–Center

71. Keyhole Direct (5.9) ★★★ Stay just left of the *Keyhole* crack, left of the arête, and avoid using any holds in the main keyhole crack.

72. Cobra (5.11a) ★★★ Sternly limit yourself to the left side of this face for maximum difficulty.

73. Mongoose (5.8 PG13) ★★ In the gully to the left of *Cobra*, stay in the corner heading toward the roof, eventually traversing under to pull over the roof and following the inside corner to the top. **Variation:** For an all-sorts-of-awkward 5.6, head directly up the corner from the block right above the tree.

74. Double Cracks (aka Hamburger Crack, 5.9–10) ★★ On a slightly detached buttress just south of *Cobra* are two cracks facing the river. Head up both to make it easier, or use just the left crack to make it tougher.

Keyhole Area-Left

75. Hamburger Helper (5.7) ★ Look around the corner just to the left of *Double Cracks*. Climb the face, occasionally using the arête.

76. Short Arête (5.9) ★★ Exactly as described—a short arête.

77. Hamburger Crack (5.9) ★ A short crack in the corner that starts once you get up to the ledge.

78. Reason to Believe (5.11a) ★★ No topo. Some interesting moves make this a worthwhile objective. About 30 feet south of *Double Cracks* is a large cedar tree growing out of a chimney. Climb up right of the tree, traverse right onto a slab, and believe you can get to the top. **FA:** Coleman Miller.

Second Overlook Area

Access: Continue past *Keyhole* along the River Trail to a wooden overlook. Anchor to the rocks, not the overlook itself. Descend to the base to the north (brushier) or south (harder to find at the top).

79. Kornered (5.8) ★★ The arête right of the corner.

80. Minihedral (5.7) ★★ The obvious corner that's a nice lead to the left of the arête.

81. Flopsy (5.10a) ★ Start under the low roof, and prepare for the mantle move over the lower roof. After that, follow the crack up the easier corner to the top.

Second Overlook Area

82. Digit Dance (5.7) ★★ Start in an easy crack left of the roof. Traverse the slab left, then up the final crack above for a great lead and fun climb. **Variation:** Mantle or face-climb up to the left of the easy start (5.10-).

Delicate Dihedral Area

These routes lie on multiple outcrops just past the wooden overlook. The crux may be getting down the descent gully safely.

Bottom access: Descend the gully just north of the *Delicate Dihedral* ridge (5.3+, slippery, consider a rappel and/or belaying inexperienced climbers). Stay to the north, under *Charlie Tuna*. Or descend from the pine ledge above *Dogleg Crack*, swinging down using the trees.

83. Dogleg Crack (5.4) ★★ Head up the short crack splitting an overhang that still has face climbing around it. Walk about 70 feet south of the wooden overlook and you'll

Delicate Dihedral Area

see a large white pine that is rooted on a ledge below. This is near the top of the climb. **Bottom access:** Directly north (across the gully) of *Delicate Dihedral*, you'll find a face that leads to a crack cutting through an overhang, finishing near the pine tree.

84. Charlie Tuna (5.9) ★ Walk a few feet past (south of) the white pine mentioned in *Dogleg Crack* and note a small buttress protruding from the cliff. Climb the clean face past two small roofs to the triangular top. **Bottom access:** *Delicate Dihedral* gully.

Delicate Dihedral and its variations are found at the bottom of a ridge that starts about 150 feet south of the Second Overlook. **Setup:** The "tower" on the ridge. If you down-climb from the top, it's about 5.3.

85. Delicate Dihedral (5.8) ★★ The easiest version takes a crack on the right side of the face up to a ledge. Step across to footholds above the overhang. **Variations:** Lieback the corner, then exit left (5.7) or straight up (5.11ish).

86. Feather Jam (5.7-) ★★ Right of the fin, left of the lieback corner. Start up the slab, then delicately use the thin crack to reach the upper cracks.

87. Fowl Pro (5.8+) ★★★ A great off-width. Head straight up avoiding the fin and the thin crack.

88. Wake Me Up (5.6) ★ To the left of the fin, straight up crack climbing with some lieback moves near the top.

89. Cutting Edge (5.9) No topo. On the south side of the *Delicate Dihedral* formation, walk up the slope for a wall with a little overhang and a dihedral with a finger crack.

90. Thumbs Up (5.7) ★ No topo. Just south of the *Delicate Dihedral* ridge is a gully and a prow of rock. *Thumbs Up* climbs up the face below.

Wisconsin Side

Getting There and Parking

For the Wisconsin side: Skip the final turn into the Minnesota Visitor Center lot, cross the US 8 bridge over the St. Croix, and turn south on SH 35 to the Interstate State Park entrance.

If climbing at the Wisconsin Strip, Rod's Area, Upper Boat Dock, or Sentinel, park at the lot for the Potholes Trail/Ice Age National Scenic Trail (GPS: N45.4001' / W92.6474'), which is nice and shaded throughout the day.

If you're climbing at Boat People or Profile Buttress, continue to follow Park Road to the left past the first parking lot until you see parking on your right, or a touch farther, a huge parking lot on your left at the Meadow Valley Trailhead (GPS: N45.3942' / W92.6498'). For the Picnic Area, park as close as possible to the boat launch.

Permits, Local Ethics, and Regulations

A Wisconsin state park vehicle admission sticker (daily or yearly) is required and can be purchased at the park entrance or online.

For casual day users, a climbing permit is not required by the park; however, guides must contact the park office for a use permit.

Dogs must be on a leash not more than 8 feet long and not left unattended. Pets are prohibited in park buildings, at the swimming beach, and in most picnic areas. Clean up after your dogs.

The areas just south and just north of the Picnic Area are closed to use.

Routes Not to Miss

Air Conditioned (5.7), Lost Ego (5.8-), Sentinel Crack (5.10a), Yosemite Crack (5.10a), Batman (5.10b), Walking on Air (5.10b)

Upper Boat Dock

From the Pothole Trail parking area, take the left fork of the trail and hike until you have passed a wooden overlook. Keep following the trail as it heads right, crossing a small bridge. You'll pass a couple of clearings on your left—look for the upper boat dock, as you'll be climbing directly across from that.

1. Octagenarian (5.10+) ★★ Across from the upper boat dock, directly out of the water. Find a blocky inside corner for your start. Stem through a bright-orange streak before stepping left to a sloping scooped-out area. Get up to the ledge, then do a tiny deviation left before going back right to end.

Route 1: Octagenarian

Upper Boat Dock

Head about 150 feet downstream to find a clearing where out of the river rises a white face with lichen sprinkled on it.

2. Cryptic Crimper (5.11b) ★★★ Start just below the sloping ledge and head straight up through the white rock, avoiding the arête on the right and topping out in a tree. TR only. **FTR:** Logan Dop.

3. Tasty Treats (5.7) ★★ Follow the black face and arête to the left of the big flake.

Wisconsin Strip

This is a fantastic area that is also great for newer climbers learning how to set up anchors or top-manage a system, or for groups with a variety of ability levels. With such a nice collection of great routes on the Wisconsin side, it can get busy with both climbers and hikers.

From the Pothole Trail parking area, take the left fork of the trail, and hike until you have passed a wooden overlook. This should put you at the top of some cliffs with a 2-foot-diameter pothole nearby. You are now above *Outside Corner* and *Rurp City*. To reach *Octogenarian*, turn north and hike toward the bridge.

Bottom access: Walk north past the pothole for a few feet to a blocky gully. Descend the gully to a ledge with a cedar tree (be nice to this old friend), then downclimb (5.4) an 8-foot wall and downclimb the slab. For inexperienced climbers or groups, it's recommended to use anchor material to create a backup belay and/or a handline to help with the short wall and slab downclimb.

The cliff is divided into a series of faces defined by two large, north-facing corners. The northern corner is *Lloyd's Lament*, the southern is *Inside Corner*. South of *Inside Corner* a large block sits at the base, just below *Cathuselum*. Farther south is *The Chimney*. At times of high water, it may be difficult to cross the area beneath *Inside Corner*.

4. Softer than Ice, Harder than Diamonds (5.13+) ★ This route works up the very left edge of the *Deuchler's Corner* face, above the descent tree. **FA:** Chris Ecklund.

5. Deuchler's Corner (5.10c–5.12b) ★★★ This corner is choose-your-own adventure: **5.12b:** Climb the thin crack on the left of the arête **5.11b/c:** Start on the left side of the corner but climb straight up the arête, avoiding the stance out right. **5:10c:** Start at the arête, but figure out how to swing over to the stance on the right. Keep right on the arête and at the roof until finishing left around the corner to the crack.

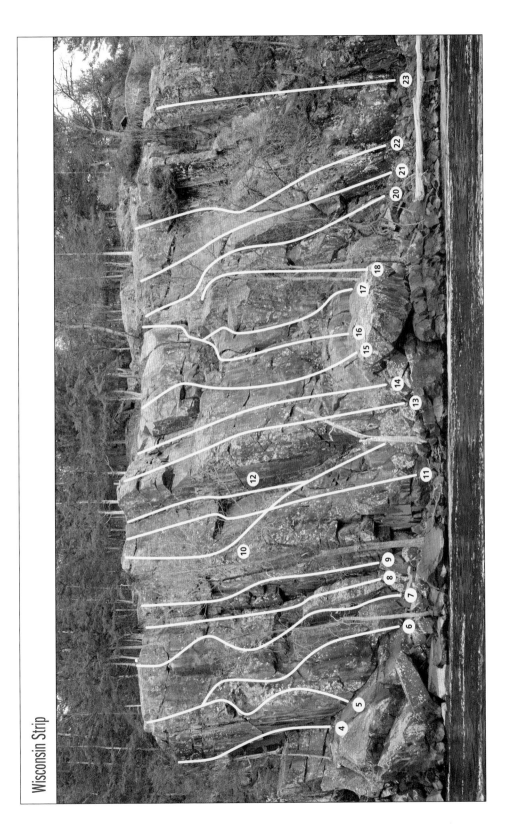

Wisconsin Strip

6. Walking on Air (5.10b) ★★★ At the bottom of the slab ramp, head up the face before moving to the arête just past the mini-roof halfway up. **Variations:** A direct start (5.10b–d) can be found directly below the stance, using holds on the corner to swing up and right to the thin holds. A direct finish is 5.11c. **FA:** Dick Wildberger and Dan Kieffaber.

7. Batman (5.10b) ★★★ A big block at the bottom makes a mini-corner to the left of *Lloyd's Lament*. Gain the top of the large block up that corner. Move left through the overhang on crimps, and zigzag right then left to a small roof at the top of the face, using a wiggly hold.

8. Lloyd's Lament (5.6) ★★ A left-facing corner chimney with a large block forming the bottom. Stem up the corner and finagle through the crux right at the top. A good lead. **Variation:** Climb the face between *Batman* and *Lloyd's Lament* after gaining the top of the block (*Scare Case*, 5.9).

9. Rurp City (5.12b) ★★ Starting from a small talus block on the face to the right of *Lloyd's Lament*, levitate up the center of this north-facing wall to the top of the red streaks, diagonal left, and power up to the second crux.

The next three routes share a face from the arête to the corner crack. The routes are described the original way they were climbed, but any number of combinations of just to the right of the arête, the middle face, and the corner could be used depending on the climber.

10. Outside Corner (5.5) ★★ Start in the inside corner, move all the way across the face left when you get to the roof, then head up the left arête on great holds. Mind your top setup with such a big face to cover.

11. Split the Difference (5.9–5.10c) ★ A bit of an elimination route, head straight up the middle of the face between *Inside Corner* and the arête, avoiding the good holds to the left and right. The truly honed will lieback off some small chips to the right to earn the 10c merit badge.

12. Inside Corner (5.8) ★★★ A truly fun corner with great gear and a bomber hand jam above the roof.

13. The Old Man (5.8-) ★★★ Around the corner for *Inside Corner*, stay on the face to the right of the arête. Expect some big moves. End below the old man's profile in the rock at the top, which you can see from farther down the river.

14. Cathuseleft (5.10b) ★★ Delicate slab climbing while trying to stay in the seam to the right of *The Old Man*. The big roof pull at the top is harder since you're not using the crack or the arête.

15. Cathuselum (5.7) ★★★ Start just left of the crack and weave up the lower-angle, dark face with some good rests. This easier climbing heads straight to the hand crack at the top, which is the crux. **Variation:** The face left of the top crack (5.10).

16. Mother (5.4) ★ A crack just right of *Cathuselum* leads to a ledge system that isn't as easy as one may think moving to the right.

17. Dire Straits (5.7) ★ Thrash up through the vegetation just right of *Mother* and follow a flake to the crux—the transition from overhanging to underhanging. Finishes on *Mother*. **Variation:** Continue straight up the headwall through the curving inside corner (5.11ish).

18. Impossible Crack (5.10b) ★★ About 20 feet right of the large block at the base of

Kristina Suorsa-Johnson on *Impossible Crack* (5.10b) PHOTO: ANTHONY JOHNSON

Cathuselum, you will find a short, overhanging off-width crack. Getting in and out of it is the tricky part. **Variation:** A 5.12 face to the left.

The rock obviously sinks in here, with a big chimney, a roof halfway up the center wall, and a right wall kind of boxing in a handful of fun routes.

19. Chimney Left (5.4) ★ No topo. The crack on the left face of the chimney.

20. The Chimney (5.4) Struggle bus up the chimney.

21. Triple Overhang (5.11a) ★★★ Just right of the chimney is a slabby face. Flow up the face without using either edge for the toughest grade. **FA:** T. Deuchler.

22. Slab Route (5.6) ★ A corner and slab system right of *Triple Overhang* goes up, right onto a crack-filled face, and up on the slab. **Variation:** Start around the arête on the bottom slab and head straight up the slab for a great easy route.

23. Joint Project (5.13a) ★★★ From the base of *Triple Overhang*, look up and south to an attractive north-facing wall. There are several variations. **FA:** Eric Lindquist.

Rod's Area

These routes are located below the stone parapet along the road between the Wisconsin Strip and the Sentinel Area. Park as for the Wisconsin Strip and hike south along the road to a set of steps leading down

through the retaining wall. Locate the top of a south-facing corner with a wide crack (*Thrombus*) or the multiple ledges of *Mickey Mantles*. If you hit flat ground, you've gone too far.

24. Crossover Artist (5.11) ★★ Start near the junction of the wall and the river. Up a slightly overhanging face, then up a finger crack to a very interesting exit over a bulge. Finish up an easier hand crack with a tree growing out the bottom of the crack.

25. Gadget Arms (5.9-) ★★★ To the right of *Crossover Artist*, start in a right-swooping crack that heads straight up after the first ledge before finishing on a heady compression arête.

26. Skin of Rod's Teeth (5.10b) ★★★ Fifty feet climber's right of *Gadget Arms*, find an excellent finger crack that starts from a platform just above the water.

27. Edge Lane (5.10+) ★★★ The arête right of *Skin of Rod's Teeth*, which is angled just oddly enough to make it interesting.

28. Thrombus (5.8) ★★ The obvious flaring crack in the large corner that defines "old-school 5.8."

29. Mickey Mantles (5.9) ★★ Right of *Thrombus*, up several obvious ledges where the mantles look easier than they are.

30. Mental Physics (5.10) ★★ A black, licheny strip leads to a small roof, then up the seam.

31. Hand Jive (5.12) ★ Four feet right of *Mental Physics*, mantle up broken ledges to the horizontal hand jam, then angle up small ledges as they head left.

Sentinel Area

Finding the crag: Park on the right in the Summit Rock Trail parking area, just before you reach the beach. The best approach takes the major trail that proceeds slightly north (right) into the woods.

Take the right fork (Summit Rock Trail), pass along a short cliff on the left, and reach some wooden steps to your left. Ascend the steps, hike past some oaks, and reach the top of *Sentinel* just before another set of wooden steps that descend. The top of *Sentinel* is marked by a double crack that faces the Minnesota Potholes, while *Yosemite Crack* ends on a ledge below and to the right.

Bottom access: To reach the bases of *Sentinel*, *Lost Ego*, and *Yosemite Crack*, continue down the steps to the south end of the railings. Cut north on the rocks back toward *Sentinel*. When the top part of *Sentinel* comes into view, go down left a few feet (near a white pine) and downclimb into a short corner (5.4). It's easy to use anchor material here to set up a rappel or belay to get everyone down safely. Continue down and around a few more feet (usually slippery with pine needles) to a blocky ledge with a large tree. This is the top of *Lost Ego* and the belay ledge for *Sentinel*. Use extreme caution—it can be slippery and dangerous.

Sentinel Area-Overview

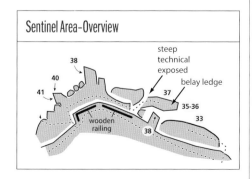

Sentinel Area-Left

Jessica Arnold on *Sentinel Crack* (5.10a)

It is technically easier to approach from Rod's Area, though some groveling up dirt gullies is required. This is the easiest approach if you intend to lead *Lost Ego*.

32. Stay Hungry (5.10b) ★ Start on the bottom slab of *Yosemite Crack* before heading up on the crack and holds 5 feet left of that.

33. Yosemite Crack (5.10a) ★★★ Climb either the face (5.10a) or *Sentinel Crack* at the bottom to reach the ledge where this glorious crack greets you.

34. Sentinel Crack (5.10a) ★★★★ One of the best routes in the area. Swing past a little overhang to double cracks and dream of a full pitch like the top 20 feet.

Sentinel Area-Right

Hillary Waters on *Lost Ego* (5.8-)

35. Lost Ego (5.8-) ★★★★ From the base of *Sentinel*, pick your way down the dirt gully below *Yosemite Crack*. Then climb the crack/face right back up to where you started, with a slightly spicy off-width finish. Good lead with a bit of a crux. Connect with *Sentinel* for a multipitch.

36. Alter Ego (5.8-) ★ This is the face and crack climb to the right of *Lost Ego*.

37. Lost Eagle (5.8) No topo. Climb the crack system around the corner right of *Lost Ego*.

The next four routes are found above and south of the Sentinel Area. **Bottom access:** A short chimney at the south end of the wooden railing.

38. Captain Coconuts (5.10b) ★★ No topo. After leaving the trail to approach *Sentinel*, note a clean prow of rock that extends toward the river. This prow forms the south-facing wall of a large corner. The route goes up this face, about 4 feet left of the corner.

39. Cordless Electric Pus Melon (5.9+) No topo. The face below *Captain Coconuts*—a bunch of blocks.

40. Das Boot (5.10b/c) ★★ No topo. Just south of the base of *Captain Coconuts* around the corner is a short rock with an overhang low and a sharp arête above. The top points at the lower boat dock. This route climbs up the north side of the overhang and prow to a hold on the junction between two faces.

41. The Prow (5.12a) ★★★ No topo. Find this route by ducking under a railing and climbing down a short chimney at the south end. You'll see the obvious triangle face with a prow. Start under the right (north) side and proceed up under the triangular face. Use holds on the right side of the triangle, grab the prow, and continue.

Profile Buttress

This area can be approached in a couple of different ways. The closest approach is to hike past the beach along the north shore of Lake O' the Dalles. Take the first right-hand fork, which is the Echo Canyon Trail. Go past a small pond, pass some cliffs on your left, and reach stone steps that descend to the river. Profile Buttress is the cliff on your left. A human profile can be seen from certain directions. *Mantrap*, etc., are up the talus to the south.

Profile Buttress

Top access: The blocky gully just uphill of Profile Buttress.

42. Little Wing (5.4) ★★ On the uphill side of the buttress is a right-facing corner. Climb the face to the right, with the crux just off the ground, staying to the right of the corner.

43. Profile (5.8) ★ Just right of the prow is a right-facing corner with a jagged crack to the right. Take the easiest finish up and left, heading toward the face profile at the top of the rock.

44. Are You Single? (5.7+) ★ No topo. Around the corner from *Profile* is a nice face covered in horizontal cracks.

The following routes start about 80 feet south of Profile Buttress proper.

45. Air Conditioned (5.7) ★★★★ Your hands will enjoy the cool air as you breeze up the cool crack to a huge ledge, then up somewhat loose blocks to the top.

46. Layback (aka Heat Wave, 5.8) ★★★ Take the deceptive lieback crack just right of *Air Conditioned* and continue up the small dihedral above.

47. Mantrap (5.10c/d) ★★ A small triangle roof is found about 15 feet up, to the right of *Air Conditioned*. Try to get up into the corner, try to surmount the roof (don't cheat right), then head to the top through more powerful moves.

48. Wise Crack (5.8) ★ No topo. Thirty to eighty feet right of *Mantrap* are several corners and cracks of various difficulty, all short. This is the best-looking one and has a tree and a roof.

Profile Buttress-Right

Boat People Rock

About 100 feet downriver from the previous climbs is a tall crag with a mossy slab at its base (very evident from the Minnesota side as you approach the lower boat landing). A prominent prow juts out to the left of the slab. The top is flat and points like an arrow at the lower boat dock. **Bottom access:** It's probably easiest to rappel, though you can scramble down to the north. The nice slab to the south is closed.

Boat People Rock

49. Boat People (5.9+) Takes the black face to the north of the prow.

50. Frequent Flyer (5.11) ★ Right up the triangle point of the prow.

51. Atlas Shrugged (5.10+) ★★ Climb the slightly overhanging face above a higher ledge to the south of the prow.

52. Holiday in Cambodia (5.10+) Up the face to a tree and ledge, then traverse to the left to climb *Atlas Shrugged*.

Picnic Area

These short routes lie just south of the closed area and directly across from Second Overlook.

Finding the cliff: Drive to the picnic grounds by the river and park as close to the boat launch as possible. Hike up and right toward the River Bluff Trail. Stay on the official trail, eventually reaching the edge of the cliffs.

Bottom access: The trail will curve right and climb a few stone steps. A climber's trail leaves the main trail at this point, goes downhill 15 feet to a birch, and proceeds north. You can also descend to the north of the cliff (Class 3).

Top access: Go up the steps to the right and proceed until you see two prows of rock jutting out. The first prow is the top of *Electric Stove Couch* and the second prow is the top of *Picnic Face*. Across the river is a wooden overlook with a short cliff below it. North of these prows are signs marking the closed area.

53. Rock Dove (aka Picnic Crack Left, 5.6) ★ Find the off-width that starts halfway up on the left edge for a fun route.

Picnic Area

55. Picnic Crack Right
(5.8+) ★★ Start on the right-leaning crack, traverse left on the ledge, then up over the little roof to get to the crack and face at the top.

56. Picnic Edge (5.8)
From the top of the cracks on *Picnic Crack Right*, work up the arête above.

57. Trash Patrol (5.6)
No topo. The fist crack right of *Picnic Edge* that starts about 10 feet off the ground, often (unfortunately) filled with trash. Watch for broken glass.

58. Electric Stove Couch (5.8+–5.10d)
★★ No topo. Around to the right of *Picnic Edge* is a right-facing dihedral with a big roof at the top. Do the corner and sneak left for the 5.8+ version, or crimp up over the roof for the harder version.

54. Picnic Face (aka Pine Tree, 5.10a) ★★
Small crimps and face climbing as you delicately pick your way between the cracks and pull the roof.

59. Grishnakh or Gorbag (5.7) No topo. A right-facing corner 90 feet right of *Electric Stove Couch*.

Lan Le on *Compromises* (5.10b) PHOTO: ANTHONY JOHNSON

SANDSTONE/ ROBINSON PARK

Sandstone has everything, sometimes on the same day (weather depending). Boulderers flock near the river for bold freestanding problems. Natural flows and ice farming for the ice and mixed climbers supply fun for the long, cold winters. And covered in this guide, the Hinckley Sandstone rock boasts natural and quarry sport climbing with some of the best hard sport lines in the state with a smattering of adventurous trad. While the climbing is technically located in Robinson Park and Banning State Park, climbers generally lump them together and call the area "Sandstone" after the nearby town. As a midway point between the

Twin Cities and Duluth, it is well placed as a meeting spot for festivals, friends, and fun for the entire state.

Spring and fall are the best times for sport climbing, often right up to the first snowfall. Winter is reserved for the ice climbers. The routes face mostly west and south, and with the walls of the quarry protecting everyone from the wind, it can be one of the warmest places on a chilly weekend, even in the winter. It can, however, turn into a sinkhole for hot and muggy weather in the summer. The mosquitos can get pretty rough, even for Minnesota. Luckily, climbers can bring a swimsuit for a dip in the river after a full day. Awesome multisport climbing day followed by a river dip? Yes, please.

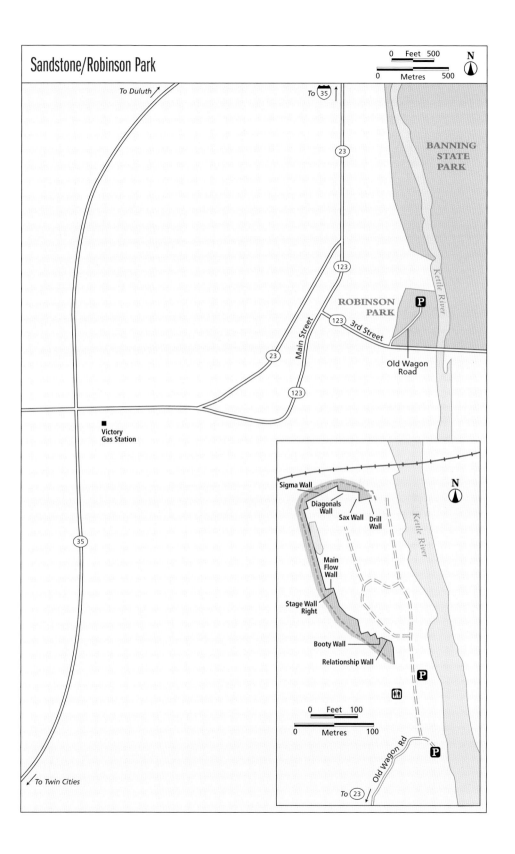

Sandstone/Robinson Park

0 Feet 500
0 Metres 500
N

To Duluth

To 35

23

123

ROBINSON PARK

123

Main Street

123

23

3rd Street

P

Old Wagon Road

BANNING STATE PARK

Kettle River

■ Victory Gas Station

35

N

Sigma Wall

Diagonals Wall

Sax Wall

Drill Wall

Main Flow Wall

Stage Wall Right

Booty Wall

Relationship Wall

Kettle River

P

P

Old Wagon Rd

0 Feet 100
0 Metres 100

To 23

To Twin Cities

Types of Climbing and Gear

Pick your poison depending on what you want to do and what time of year it is. Sport climbing? A 60-meter rope and a set of twelve draws are plenty. Trad climbing? A standard rack works just fine. Bouldering or ice climbing? You aren't using the right book for that (sorry).

Land Acknowledgment

We acknowledge with respect and gratitude that this climbing area is on the traditional lands of the Anishinabewaki and Očhéthi Šakówiŋ people.

Permits, Local Ethics, and Regulations

Parking is free and there's no permit required to climb here. Dogs must be kept on a 6-foot leash and owners must clean up after them. The top of some routes are close to private property, so don't stray far from the edge or trails up top. Stay away from the railroad tracks.

The City of Sandstone has been incredibly open to creating a truly positive relationship with the climbing community, and even has gone so far as to invest money, time, materials, and support toward creating a welcoming atmosphere for climbers. In turn, it's in our best interest to be good stewards by following regulations, keeping areas clean, and (if you can) patronizing local businesses.

Sandstone is very fragile when wet—in the best of conditions (sunny, warm, and windy) please allow *at least* a full 24-hour day after a rain event for the rock to fully dry before climbing.

Getting There and Parking

Boat Landing parking lot GPS: N46.134' / W92.857'

Go to "Robinson Park" in Sandstone. There are a couple of parking lots right at the bottom of the hill next to the river. If you take a left on the gravel road, you'll see a parking lot next to a boat launch. You can also continue to follow the road as it forks to the left (it actually just loops around back to that boat launch parking lot) and you'll first come upon the Relationship Wall. You can also park off that gravel road.

Approach

Straight out of your car and to the cliff of your choice! Start at the Relationship Wall and work your way right.

Camping and Amenities

Robinson Park, where all of the sport climbing resides, is a city-owned park that offers a very small number of tent pads for camping next to the climbs. Just past the parking lot with water access, follow the road to the right to find three city-designated campsites on your right. Outside of festivals, these are the only spots to camp inside the park itself. You'll need to pay for your site at the Victory Gas Station, located right off of the I-35 exit for Sandstone.

You can also check out Banning State Park Campground just a few miles away. They offer both tent pads and electrical hookups and full restrooms.

In the park, there is a permanent building with pit-toilets. It may or may not be stocked with TP.

Hazards

Because this is an old rock quarry, there are a few odd iron bars sticking out in random places that could be devastating to be impaled upon. Some walls have large ledges that could break an ankle if you fall badly. With the freeze-thaw cycle, loose rock is normal and helmets are a good idea.

Check for ticks after a day here, especially in the spring. They love the lush ground cover, which also contains poison ivy.

Routes Not to Miss

Do You Think I'm Saxy? (5.8), Morphine (5.9), Compromises (5.10b), Adoption (5.11d), Sigma (5.12b), Harvest Moon (5.12d), Nexus (5.13a), Derailed (5.13a)

Relationship Wall

From the boat launch parking, follow the road going to the left. You'll see the prominent wall that is the Relationship Wall.

1. KYG (5.7+) ★ An odd warm-up right on the arête, challenging getting off of the ground. The farther left you go, the easier, but stay to the right on the arête for full value. Shares an anchor with *Compromises*. **FA**: Evan Johnson. 4 bolts.

2. Compromises (5.10b) ★★★★ A great climb for the grade. The crux is following the flake at the bottom before just enjoying yourself through pockets and excellent holds to the anchor. **FA:** Jeff Engel. 6 bolts.

3. Adoptomises (5.11a) ★★ Linkup—starts on *Compromises* before traversing to *Adoption* after the fourth bolt. A bolt protects the traverse, and it's a nice way to get in two different cruxes. 7 bolts.

4. Adoption (5.11d) ★★ The lower crux, especially for those a little shorter, is simply reaching the good ledge and then figuring out a way to get your feet up. If you're taller, flexibility will be key. Continue up through horizontal cracks before hitting another crux at the top. **FA:** James Loveridge. 7 bolts.

5. Arbor Day (5.12 a/b) ★ Start on *Adoption* and break off right when the bolts fork instead of going straight up. 7 bolts.

Relationship Wall

6. Stage Fright (5.12d) ★★★ A fantastic but truly difficult climb because of its sustained nature. Start on an undercling before moving into a crimpy traverse and some gastons. **FA:** Kurt Hager. 5 bolts.

Booty Wall

This north-facing wall is around the corner from the Relationship Wall. Under the moss and lichen that has a tendency to build up is a pirate's booty of incredible technical climbs. It does have a tendency to be wet and can take a long time to dry out.

7. Unnamed (Open Project) Arête. 4 bolts.

8. Unnamed (Open Project) Slab to the right of the arête. Anchors only.

9. Harvest Moon (5.12d) ★★ The first bolted line to the right of the arête. Move through the bottom crimps to a really cool crescent-moon-shaped sloper, then delicately pick your way up to big moves to get to the chains. **FA:** Kurt Hager. 6 bolts.

There are three bolted lines with anchors to the right of Harvest Moon that have not seen FAs.

10. Unnamed (Open Project) 6 bolts.

11. Unnamed (Open Project) 6 bolts.

12. Unnamed (Open Project) 5 bolts.

13. Start New (5.10) ★ This corner route goes up the (often mungy) right wall before moving on to the left face and finishing up high. 5 bolts.

Stage Wall Right

These climbs are found at the right edge of steep and smooth Stage Wall. This bolted wall is where a good portion of ice climbing and dry tooling happens, so the rock can be unstable. Most of these routes have runouts at the top that border on PG13 territory, but the climbing usually eases off by then.

Booty Wall

Stage Wall-Right

14. Anchors: Not a Route (5.Moss) There are anchors but no bolts on the face—it's always wet, so feel free to TR if you want a slimefest.

15. Mad Dogs (5.10c/d) ★★ Start off with a sidepull move to get off the ground. Head straight up through lots of sidepull/gaston moves that will work your core a little before hitting the crux just below the last ledge. **FA:** Jeff Engel. 6 bolts.

16. Community Service (5.10d) Getting off the ground to the first bolt is a bit tricky. Once up, stem toward a big right jug before heading back to the left and straight up. The runout at the top can be a little heady, but it's easier climbing. 6 bolts.

17. Dimples (5.10b) ★★ The route is named for the features on the bottom part of the route that you'll have to work your way up with high feet. The seemingly blank middle leads to a good crimp before stepping high up to the flake and another move to the jug. The top is run out but eases off. **FA:** Jeff Engel. 6 bolts.

18. Spray (5.11c/d) ★★ The crux is right off the ground, getting to the second bolt. Get on top of the slopey corner before following the arête to the top. Please *do not* dry-tool. **FA:** Jeff Engel. 6 bolts.

Main Flow Wall

Around the corner from *Spray*.

19. Spray to Play (5.12a) ★★ No topo. Start on *Spray*, traverse at second bolt to walk on the rail for *Derailed* before making a cool balancey slab move to jugs. At the roof of the next break in the wall, directly up is *Derailed*, *or* you can go back to the left to skip that roof and finish on *Spray*. TR only if you do the *Spray* finish, as you go too far right to clip the bolts. **FA:** Gabe Olson.

20. Derailed (5.13a) ★★★★ No topo. Around the corner is this really fun test piece that's currently the only bolted line on the wall. The lower crux is hard but straightforward with a terrible hand rail. Move along it with no feet

Steve Vimola on *Nexus* (5.13a)
PHOTO: RANDALL BAUM

before heading up the face. The top move is a thinker. Clip the anchor shared with *Spray*. It feels like a well-protected comp climb in a gym. **FA:** Gabe Olson. 8 bolts.

Sigma Wall

At the far end of the main quarry wall, you'll find a smooth, yellow wall split by a right-facing corner/flake (*Wild Things*) with a couple of aesthetic cracks on either side. You can set a TR up top, but tie in while doing so as to not slide on the scree.

21. Nexus (5.13a) ★★★★ This superb bolted route is on the far left. It opens with rare dihedral climbing before following up the tiny crack to the heartbreaker crux right at the top. **FA:** Sean Ferrell. 8 bolts.

22. Sigma (5.12b) ★★★★ One of the best sport climbs in Minnesota. Follow the crack up the entire way until it opens out up top (though it's not really a crack climb in the traditional sense). Sustained climbing means everyone will have a different crux. **FA:** Mike Dahlberg. 10 bolts.

23. Wild Things (5.9+ R) TRAD ★ Just to the right of *Sigma*. Follow a right-facing crack/flake to a roof before heading straight up. The top could be called runout, so be solid on the grade if leading.

24. Tool Boy (5.11 R) TRAD ★★ Small cams will protect you on this trad test piece that starts at the same place as *Wild Things*. Head up the flake to the roof, traverse right with big moves to the first niche, then up to the overhang and the off-fingers crack above. **FA:** Mike Dahlberg.

25. Nakoma (5.13b) ★★ This traverses even farther right (use the *Tool Boy* footholds as

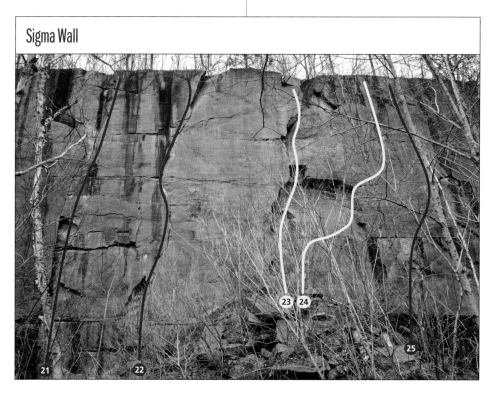

Sigma Wall

Angie Jacobsen on *Sigma* (5.12b)
PHOTO: BRENDA PIEKARSKI

handholds) and follows the thin crack to the right of *Tool Boy*. **FA:** Tyler Hoffart. 6 bolts.

Diagonals Wall

Diagonals Wall and Sax Wall are where you can really tell that this used to be a quarry. All these routes have ledges that could easily break ankles (or worse), so follow the ice leader's mantra and ideally just don't fall. (Or make sure your belayer manages the rope to land you between ledges.) Bolting above the ledges makes some of the bolts feel reachy for shorter climbers.

Do not dry-tool on any of the climbs in this area; it ruins routes.

26. Hot German Babe (5.10) ★ A one-move wonder, most of the route is pretty chill. Follow the arête up the very left edge of Diagonals Wall. Do not start around the corner to the left of the arête as there are big loose blocks there. **FA:** Michael Endrizzi. 5 bolts.

27. Nick the Wonder Dog (5.11b/c) ★★ Up the first set of three drill holes on the very left side of the wall. 6 bolts.

28. Bolts Over Troubled Water (5.10a) ★★ Begin on the 6-foot-tall right-facing flake. With bolt placements, great 10a lead for shorter people. **FA:** Michael Endrizzi. 6 bolts.

29. Ramp of Death (5.9) ★ Follow the obvious left-leaning ramp for interesting moves. 8 bolts.

30. Barron von Mischke (5.11) ★ Same start as *Ramp of Death* but go straight up, finishing on tiny ledges to the right of the anchor. All the business is at the top. 7 bolts.

31. Bolt Bolt Boltin' on Heaven's Door (5.8) ★★ Climb *Barron* to the final ledge and traverse right beneath a little roof under double bolt holes, finishing on the ramp at the top of *FBBME*. . . . **Variation:** (5.10) Go straight up the roof before the ramp. **FA:** Michael Endrizzi.

32. Bolters on the Storm (5.9+) ★★ Start in a notch before heading up and left after the second bolt. Go straight up then left to get over the overhang. **FA:** Michael Endrizzi. 7 bolts.

Diagonals Wall – Left

33. FBBMEAJMFFAMEUFA (5.8X) Start at the very left end of the upper ledge and follow the indistinct ramp up and left. Keep an eye out for the iron rods. **FA:** Michael Endrizzi. 7 bolts.

34. Kletterfreude (5.10a) ★★ The grade is pretty height dependent. Start on *FBBME* . . . then head straight up the bolt line. **FA:** Gaby Brausam. 9 bolts.

35. Dirty Bolts and They're Done Dirt Cheap (5.10) ★★ Seven feet right of *FBBME* . . ., you'll move from an undercling straight up to some small ledges for a unique finish. **FA:** Jeff Engel. 6 bolts.

36. Supercalifragilisticexpi-BOLT-adocious (5.9) ★ A tough start directly beneath the top of the *Cavedago* ramp, then fun face climbing and laybacks up to the anchors. Watch out for iron rods. **FA:** Michael Endrizzi. 6 bolts.

37. Boltway to Heaven (5.10) ★ Nine feet right of *Supercali* . . ., start on some small crimps to get to the first ledge before a unique crack-climbing finish. **FA:** Michael Endrizzi. 5 bolts.

38. Cavedago— Gateway to Spormaggiorre (5.8) ★ Another ramp you'd rather not fall on. **FA:** Michael Endrizzi. 8 bolts.

Diagonals Wall-Center

Diagonals Wall-Right

39. Packen Wir Es An (5.10) ★ Start 2 feet right from the base of the *Cavedago* ramp. Follow some small crimps to hidden underclings before heading straight up. **FA:** Michael Endrizzi. 6 bolts.

40. Unnamed (Open Project) Anchors only.

41. Purple Bolt, Purple Bolt (5.10b) ★★★ The last face climb before rounding the corner to the *Quantum* climbs, this fun route starts with very few options for feet before mixing in interesting moves as you pull past the ledges. **FA:** Michael Endrizzi. 7 bolts.

42. Quantum Chaos (5.9) ★ A variation of *Quantum Order*. Stay just to the left of *Quantum Order* and only use the face—don't use the crack. Clips the same bolts as *Order*. **FA:** Michael Endrizzi.

43. Quantum Order (5.5) ★ This is the obvious huge wide ramp tucked back by the corner. Follow the flake/crack up the very right side of the wall. Use the bolts or trad climb it. **FA:** Michael Endrizzi. 5 bolts.

Sax Wall (aka Muskrat Love Wall)

Sax Wall faces west as a continuation of Diagonals Wall. This is one of the more popular walls at Sandstone due to the easy accessibility of the bolts to set up a toprope. An access trail to the top is around the corner on the right. Watch out: The ledges could still break ankles.

44. Do You Think I'm Saxy? (5.8) ★★★ Despite the choss, sand, dirt, and rocks you'll rain down, this is a good corner climb that has holds for days. **FA:** Michael Endrizzi. 5 bolts.

Sax Wall

45. A Little Spicy (5.10a) ★ A fun climb with sidepulls on drill hole edges as you try to get your feet up. The top gets spicy. **FA:** Michael Endrizzi. 6 bolts.

46. Body and Soul (5.10a/b) ★ An undercling start and a big move to the drill hole before you head up to the chains with a little back-and-forth movement across the bolt line. **FA:** Michael Endrizzi. 7 bolts.

47. Morphine (5.9) ★★ An interesting start trying to get to some small holds right above the first bolt. Climb up and pull through the inverted V-slot before staying on the face after the final ledge. **FA:** Joe Mueller. 7 bolts.

48. Sax-a-holic (5.10a) ★★ You'll like the good feet with the divot at the start, but things get interesting once you pass over *Crack with No Name* and head right after the last bolt to find the chains. Shares an anchor with *Multiple Sax Partners*. **FA:** Joe Mueller. 7 bolts.

49. Multiple Sax Partners (5.11-) ★ Start just under the angling-right crack. Follow the bolts straight up over what will feel like a bunch of right angles. Taller folks will find this route easier. Shares an anchor with *Sax-a-holic*. **FA:** Jeff Engel. 6 bolts.

50. No Such Thang as Too Much Sax (5.10b) ★ This is the bolted line just to the left of the arête. Use small holds or even lay-backing the drill holes to a tough finish. **FA:** Michael Endrizzi. 7 bolts.

51. Crack with No Name (5.9) TRAD ★ This big crack cuts up and left across the face and intersects most of the routes on the wall, ending just left of *Morphine*. Lots of great places for smaller cams, but it can be a little intense for new trad climbers.

Drill Wall

Around the corner from the Sax Wall, there is one toprope route that wanders up the cracks on the right side of this face.

52. Escape (5.11) ★ Up a crack, turn left following the crack after the divot, then back right to the top. If you climb straight up the face from the crack, it can be harder. TR only.

Route 52: Escape

Alex Mlinar on *Dislocation Overhang* (5.6)

ELY'S PEAK

Located just south of Duluth, Ely's Peak boasts a well-maintained and short approach, easy-to-find climbs, and a kid-friendly base hangout. The basalt rock houses routes that are often the first trad climbs for many local Duluth climbers, and the old railroad tunnel boasts some of the hardest dry tooling lines in the entire Midwest. Ely's Peak is a full gambit of fun for outdoorists, shared by hikers and mountain bikers. Other than the busy train tunnel, the climbs are fairly secluded with beautiful panoramic views that are especially stunning during fall colors. You can feel lost while not being very far from Duluth (or the nearest brewery). Ely's Peak is also climbable year-round, with the winter hosting mixed and dry-tool climbing or those practicing for mountaineering.

Types of Climbing and Gear

You'll need a full trad rack to set gear here, as well as a decent amount of extending materials/static line. It's all crack-and-face climbing facing mostly west, with routes from 45 to 60 feet in height.

Land Acknowledgment

We acknowledge with respect and gratitude that this climbing area is on the traditional lands of the Anishinabewaki and Očhéthi Šakówiŋ people.

Permits, Local Ethics, and Regulations

Ely's Peak is owned by the City of Duluth, with no fees or permits required. Please stay on the trails and be respectful of other users. Dogs are welcome, but keep them on a 6-foot leash and clean up after them.

Getting There and Parking

Trailhead GPS: N46.680' / W92.259'

Just south of Duluth off of I-35, go to the "Ely's Peak Parking Area." If you go over the bridge over the railroad tracks, you've gone too far.

Approach

Thanks to the Duluth Climbers Coalition and the Access Fund, there's a boardwalk that heads straight in from the parking lot. Follow this trail up the big stairs and turn right at the top on a wide old train grade. Follow it for 5 minutes until you reach the tunnel access area. From here, you have three options depending on where you want to go. See the individual areas for different approaches, but the tunnel is where the trails all branch off.

Camping and Amenities

Ely's Peak does not have restroom facilities. Either use a WAG bag or take a short drive from the parking lot to a gas station.

Ely's Peak is located within the city of Duluth, which has multiple hotels, motels, Airbnbs, and camping. Jay Cooke State Park in Carlton has beautiful camping only 10 minutes away, with both tent and camper sites available.

Hazards

Ely's Peak is definitely kid-friendly, but with how much loose rock is still around, it's highly advisable that anyone at the bottom of the crag wears a helmet even if not belaying. The City of Duluth has installed nets in the tunnel because of rockfall, so take helmet safety seriously here.

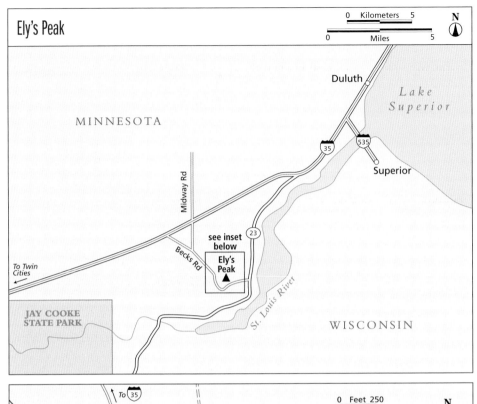

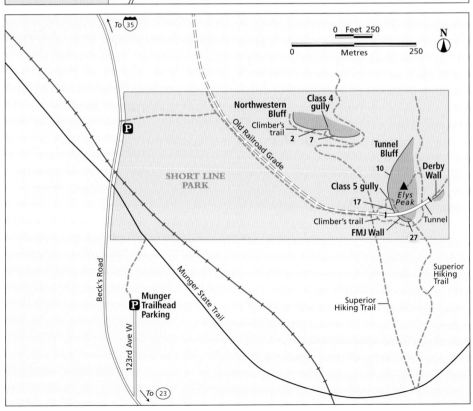

Poison ivy is readily found anywhere off-trail, and wasps, ticks, black flies, and mosquitos hang out when the weather is warm. Wasps like to build nests in some of the flakes and crack climbs. Be cautious about hunters in the fall, and possibly wear bright clothing.

Routes Not to Miss

Corner Geometry (5.6), Dislocation Overhang (5.6), The Flake (5.7), The Bulge (5.8), Bionic Finger Crack (5.12a)

Northwestern Bluff

At the tunnel entrance follow the leftmost trail, staying left at any forks. It starts off level and passes a rock with a bolt after 30 feet. Walk 190 feet from the railroad grade until you are just right of a small streambed (normally dry). Leave the main trail, cross the streambed, and go slightly uphill for about 50 feet. The trail then goes directly up the hill to the base of the Northwestern bluff near *Two Right Feet*. For top access, there's a gully that is on the far right.

1. Carpal Tunnel (5.11) No topo. To the left of *Corner Geometry*, find a thin crack starting off the ground. Reach it, then climb it.

2. Corner Geometry (5.6) ★★ No topo. Another route perfect for first-time trad leaders. Climb a large and obvious right-facing corner on the left side of the Class 3/4 gully.

3. Kindly Step Aside (5.10a) ★★ Look for the triangle roof climber's left of *Take Two*'s smaller roof. Starting with an undercling near the bottom, pull the roof before heading into a small dihedral and then straight up, always staying right of the arête. **FA:** Dave Pagel.

Lucas Kramer on *The Flake* (5.7)

4. Take Two, They're Small (5.10b) ★ Located on the buttress to the left of *Boys of Summer*, start under a block that forms a small roof; there's a thin crack running up the left side of the block. From the block go more or less straight up. **FA:** Dave Pagel and Steve Mankenberg.

5. The Boys of Summer (5.10c) ★★ Just around the corner from *The Bulge*, go up climber's left of the roof, then head right on the face before launching up through the small dihedral. **FA:** Brian Gitar.

6. The Bulge (5.8) ★★★ A crack to climber's left of *The Flake*, this great corner/crack system has a triangle rock at the bottom

pointing your way up. Follow the crack as it goes to the right of the bulge, and then up to a corner. **FA:** Steve Mabley.

7. The Flake (5.7) ★★★★ One of the best cracks at Ely's Peak, follow this beautiful jagged crack as it works up the face and toward the right before finishing in the corner. **FA:** Steve Mabley.

8. Coming Unhinged (5.10d) ★★ The crack in the face climber's right of *The Flake*. Climb toward the roof, bypassing it to the right, and then head up using the left-facing corner. It gets harder than you'd think it should by the end. **FA:** Dave Pagel.

A couple of 5.12ish topropes have been done on the face right of *Coming Unhinged*.

9. Two Right Feet (5.9) ★ No topo. At the right end of the wall to the right of *The Flake*. **FA:** Rick Kollath.

Tunnel Bluff West Face

This is one of the most popular spots for groups, especially with the easy trail access. From the tunnel entrance, of the two trails on your left, follow the right one heading uphill until you reach the obvious face with a nice area to hang out. To access the top, either scramble up the Class 5 gully on

Tunnel Bluff West Face

the left (not recommended) or when at the tunnel, follow the trail to the right past the FMJ wall and up the bluff to the top of Ely's Peak to set up your anchors. You'll have to scramble down a bit, but finding the tops of the climbs and the edges of the cliff is easy. You'll need a fair amount of static line.

10. Royal Robbins F12 Overhang (5.8) ★★
No topo. Follow the cliff face a couple of hundred feet past the *Dislocation Overhang* area and past the gully. This is a fun left-facing corner to smear up before pulling the big overhang and heading up the crack. **FA:** Dave and Jim Mital.

11. Cakewalk (5.5) ★ No topo. Just right of
the gully is a crack that heads up to a big refrigerator block—climb up and around the right side of that big flake, then left at the top of the flake before topping out in the crack. **FA:** Dave and Jim Mital.

The following four routes all start at the same spot down below and can be reached through the same bottom half of the climb.

12. Simple Corner (5.3) ★ An easy right-
facing corner, great for those brand-new to the sport who may be nervous about heights. **FA:** Dave and Jim Mital.

13. Static Is a Four-Letter Word (5.10b) ★
This is the face climb between *Simple Corner* and *Beginner's Crack*, with a height-dependent rating. **FA:** Dave and Jim Mital.

14. Beginner's Crack (5.6) ★ This crack is
just to the left of *New Corner*, and it's a good place for those new to crack climbing. **FA:** Dave and Jim Mital.

15. New Corner (5.5) ★ The prominent left-
facing corner, this is a fantastic first trad lead. **FA:** Dave and Jim Mital.

The next two routes start at the same spot but follow different cracks once midway up.

16. Bionic Finger Crack (5.12a) ★★★ Follow
the same bottom 35 feet as *Dislocation* up to the obvious roof, pull the roof while heading left up the face using the small seam. It's a short but classic route. **FA:** Dave Pagel.

17. Dislocation Overhang (5.6) ★★★★ The
bottom 35 feet follows a pretty obvious crack toward a big roof. Once there, layback up the right-facing corner and pull the roof before heading up the crack in the face. If you don't know the beta, this can be an intimidating first lead. **FA:** Steve Mabley.

18. Jigsaw (5.8) ★ The face climb just right
of *Dislocation Overhang*. If leading, plug gear in *Dislocation*'s crack.

FMJ Bluff

Take the trail to the right of the tunnel going straight up the hill. Routes are described left to right.

19. The Old Path (5.5) To the left of the bulge, find this easy and short scramble.

20. The New Path (5.7) Eight feet right of *Chair Gully*, up and over the bulge on some face climbing that's a touch adventurous. Stay left of the roof.

21. FMJ (5.9) ★★★ This fun climb heads through the large V-cut on the right side of the roof, then navigates slab to reach the flaring dihedral.

22. The Right Path (5.7+) ★ Five feet right of *FMJ*, climb up a broken face to a big ledge.

FMJ Bluff-Left

23. Eminent Domain (5.6) Climb up the "S" ramp on balancey and awkward moves. Be careful of your anchor placement.

24. Chair Direct (5.6) ★ Follow the crack on the climber's left of the "chair," then up the face to the top.

FMJ Bluff-Right

The next three routes can all be belayed from the ground using the bolts above the top-out (a top-managed system on the big, comfortable ledge is even better).

25. Chair Gully (5.5) ★ This is the gully climber's left of the bolted route—follow the ledges that make up the "chair."

26. Waking Up in Duluth (aka The Bolted Route, 5.9) ★★ Make moves dancing around the arête following the bolted line up. **FA:** James Garrett.

27. Dark Side of the Face (5.10) ★★ This face climb around the corner from the bolted line dances up crimpy moves for a surprisingly fun and short route.

Derby Wall

This wall, reached by walking straight through the tunnel, is a fantastic place to bring beginner school groups or someone who is brand-new and nervous about heights. All of the climbs are topropes with natural tree anchors. You can easily reach the top by walking past all of the routes until you see an obvious dirt path on your right that goes up and follows the cliff edge to the trees for setup. Climbs are described from left to right.

1. The Ramp (5.2) An obvious left-leaning dihedral. Follow it all the way up to the rock landing.

2. The Dihedral (5.4) A shallow dihedral that becomes a bit broken in the middle before topping out between two birch trees.

3. Outside the Dihedral (5.4) The prominent dihedral. Start on a small column at the bottom before following the dihedral, then step left onto the face to top out at a big birch tree.

Derby Wall

Karina Krosbakken on *Phantom Crack* (5.9) Photo: Slavomír Tkáč

PALISADE HEAD

Palisade Head is the crown jewel of Minnesota climbing. Rhyolite cliffs tower over Lake Superior, giving the place an air of seriousness, intimidating exposure, and heartbreaking beauty. Traditional climbing leaders will cut their teeth with incredible cliff-length cracks of all widths, fiddly placements to test knowledge, and the possibility of the angry lake tossing weather, waves, and wind while climbers quake above that last piece of suspect pro. You don't need to lead to feel the psych. Many, if not most, toprope and find it heady, isolating, and exposed. Palisade could hit every one of your weaknesses, but it rewards with proud nails-hard sends.

Where the rock is good, it's *really* good. More often, rock will be crumbly or chossy and needs to be evaluated for gear placements. Routes that are not traveled as much have loose rock, the cliffs are battered with wind and weather all winter long, and there is an element of route finding. This only adds to the complete experience that climbers will get the first moment they step to the edge, watch the fog roll in off the lake up the sheer cliff, and get that familiar tingle as they pull their rack out for a full-value day.

Types of Climbing and Gear

Palisade Head is a traditional climbing and toproping paradise. You will need gear (cams, nuts, plus chord or webbing and some sort of padding to protect your rope on the sharp edges) to set anchors and a full rack if you will be leading climbs. Almost all routes can be top-managed (60-meter rope for standard routes, though some require longer ropes as noted). There are a few mixed routes with some bolts as well as a handful of fully bolted sport routes (which still need traditionally set anchors), so having ten to twelve draws (with the majority being alpine draws) isn't a bad idea. These routes are colored on the topos accordingly, and bolt counts have been noted when possible.

Land Acknowledgment

We acknowledge with respect and gratitude that this climbing area is on the traditional lands of the Anishinabewaki people.

Permits, Local Ethics, and Regulations

An annual or daily Minnesota state park vehicle permit is required, which you can pick up in the Tettegouche State Park office, about 2 miles past the turn into Palisade Head. While there also register for a required climbing permit (free).

Don't place any new bolts—there's a process through the DNR route developers have to go through.

There are seasonal route and/or area closures along the cliff for peregrine falcon nesting. Before climbing, either ask in the park office or check the specific state park page on Minnesota's DNR website for route/area closures. Disturbed nests are abandoned by the birds, so please respect the closures.

While Palisade doesn't have areas with cryptobiotic soil roped off, it is all over the tops of the cliffs. Stay on the established trails and on the rock when possible because footprints damage it.

Dogs must be cleaned up after and kept on a 6-foot leash and under control at all times.

If you're leading and decide to rappel in on a fixed line, try to put your line on a non-popular route.

Getting There and Parking

Follow MN 61 to the signed turnoff for Palisade Head, which is just past the Palisade Baptist Church and 2.8 miles east of the stoplight in Silver Bay. This road is gated and locked from 10 p.m. until 8 a.m, as well as during the winter. There's a parking lot before the gate if you wish to come early or stay late, but overnight parking is not allowed. The road snakes to the upper lot, which can often be full but has fast turnover for tourists taking pictures.

Approach

Top access: One of the fastest and easiest approaches in Minnesota, you can see the top of climbs in the amphitheater from your vehicle. All the routes are top-access; getting to the bottom to start is where things get interesting. Ideally the top photos, cliff photos, and descriptions will help you identify landmarks for finding the routes.

A top-managed belay system is the best way to toprope at Palisade. If you've never done that before, it's highly encouraged to take a course, have a mentor, or hire a guide to teach you how to properly execute it.

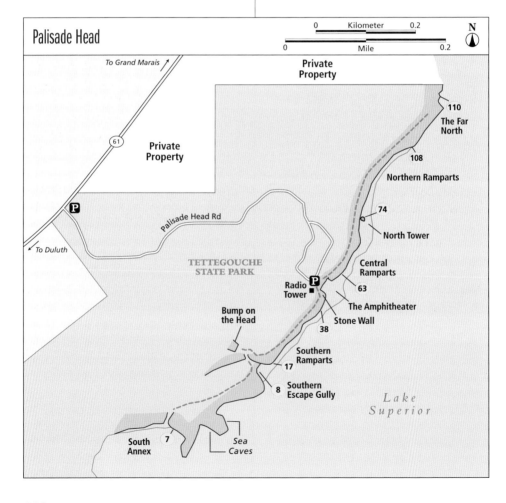

Bottom access: Either rappel or lower down from above. Rappelling reduces the chance of rope damage. Even a longish climb like *Danger High Voltage* can be (barely) toproped from above. To climb *Danger High Voltage* and more southerly routes from the talus, a descent of *The Southern Escape Gully* is the easiest approach. Rappelling into the Amphitheater is the best approach for routes from *Dirty Harry* to North Tower. *Bluebells* is an 80-foot rappel. Reach the talus in the Northern Ramparts by rappelling in the vicinity of *Arms Race*, *V-Max*, or *Water Babies* (80 feet). A 60-meter rope makes life more comfortable.

Traversing the talus below the cliff isn't difficult in good weather except for one stretch below the south edge of the Amphitheater. A boulder cave provides some climbing that is low Class 5, and most climbers will want a belay.

The base of Palisade Head is about the only place in the Midwest that a climber can be seriously marooned. Storms, fog, and heavy surf (and/or ice depending on the time of year) can make the talus impassable, cutting off your escape route. In doubtful weather a strategically placed fixed line (and the gear and skill to use it) can provide peace of mind and is the best upward retreat if one must climb out.

Once you rappel in and pull your rope, know that *The Southern Escape Gully* (5.3 R), *Dirty Harry* (5.7), and *Northern Escape Chimney* (5.8) are the best routes if you need to get out and someone isn't at the top to throw you a line. It could take hours for a boat rescue by local authorities, so it's not a bad idea to identify these lines so you can get out if you need to.

Camping and Amenities

The Tettegouche State Park campground is just a touch north, and there are state forest campgrounds on MN 1 (Eckbeck) and on Lake County Road 6 in Finland.

You'll find restroom facilities at the Tettegouche State Park Visitor Center.

Hazards

Pad the edge of the cliff under your rope. The rock can grind through ropes on just one climb. Be sure your padding is clipped to something so it doesn't drop onto folks below. Rope damage is much less likely if you rappel down rather than having your belayer lower you depending on your setup.

Less-traveled routes often have loose rock, and even well-traveled routes may have loose rock and rockfall after a winter of freeze/thaw. Continuous cracks have adequate protection, though the brittle rock can shatter when stressed. The rock at Palisade Head tends to be more flaky and brittle than at Shovel Point.

There are some bolts and pitons, many of which are old and untrustworthy; inspect on rappel as needed and make your own assessment.

There are seasonal closures for peregrine falcon nests. They are predatory birds that will aggressively defend their nests, even dive-bombing climbers that get too close. The importance of respecting these route closures cannot be overstated.

On warm summer days with little wind, black flies can be particularly bitey and atrocious.

This is a touristy area; a lot of people will be at the top of the cliffs watching, taking pictures, getting closer than they should to the edge, and asking questions.

M*A*S*H* -Top

Laceration Jam and the Southern Escape Gully-Top

Scars and Tripes Forever-Top

Long Distance Commute and Iron Maiden-Top

Swizzlestick Legs to Cul-de-Sac-Top

Driving In Duluth-Top

Urge To Mate and Double-Breasted Anchor-Top

Lord of the Flies-Top

Praise the Many Seraphim-Top

No Sugar, No Baby to The Fall of Ascomycetes-Top

Soli Deo Gloria-Top

Happy Happy, Joy Joy and The Poseidon Adventure-Top

Several species of bats overwinter in the caves and crevices at the base of Palisade Head. The survival of these bats is endangered if they are disturbed while hibernating. It is critical that humans avoid all contact with these caves from mid-fall to mid-spring. Even a quick peek with a flashlight might cause enough disruption to kill the bats weeks later. This is especially notable in the southern areas, near routes like *KGB*.

Routes Not to Miss

The Great Bird Chimney (5.7), Phantom Crack (5.9), Bluebells (5.9), Scars and Tripes Forever (5.10a), Rapprochement (5.10b), Laceration Jam (5.10b), Urge to Mate (5.10c), Hidden Treasure (5.11b), Driving in Duluth (5.11b), Don't Bring a Knife to a Gunfight (5.11b), Mr. Lean (5.11d), The Poseidon Adventure (5.11d), Sunny and Sheer (5.12a), Soli Deo Gloria (5.12b), Oz (5.12b), Palisaid (5.13a), The Gales of November (5.13)

The Bump on the Head

This protuberance is found by walking south to the top of *Laceration Jam* and looking inland. Approach the top from the right. The routes are not very protectable. (See topo p. 156)

1. Phrenology (5.11c) ★ South of *The Noggin* you'll find an undercling flake that leads to a clean face above with a small ledge below an incut at the top. **FA:** Dave Pagel.

2. The Noggin (5.10c) ★ There is a white streak beneath an overhang on the right side of the face. Ascend this and the face above to a bush at the top. **FA:** Dave Pagel.

The South Annex

The South Annex has some adventurous climbs and the potential for more. The rock is traditional Palisade quality, and because of how it's angled, it can be a micro-climate of warmth when the rest of the Head is cold and windy. Recent rockfall (and even a collapsed pillar) has changed and even eliminated some of the routes from past guidebooks.

South Annex

AERIAL PHOTO: BRENDA PIEKARSKI

South Annex

AERIAL PHOTO: BRENDA PIEKARSKI

Continue south, passing the Southern Escape Gully (route 8). You'll pass a trail to your left that takes you over a thin outcropping peninsula, where you can see most of the South Annex. Another access gully between routes 6 and 7 gets you to the beach at the bottom of the South Annex (this is a loose and scary Class 4 scramble with rock that will collapse in your hands; you'll probably wish you roped up or rappelled).

3. A Long Night's Journey Into Day (Open Project) The original chimney route created by a free-standing pillar is gone due to storm activity (taking ⅓ of the original face with it). A big split block at the top marks a sheer face with spots of lichen ready for a new FA. Original route 5.7, likely harder now. **FA:** Rick Kollath.

4. Genetically Correct (5.10b) ★★ A quality crack with a face hold here and there that goes straight up the edge of an obtuse corner shaped a bit like a trapezoid. Finish at the

top right corner. A fun 10 for the head. **FA:** Brian Gitar.

5. M*A*S*H* (5.6) Find the prominent right-facing corner that's easy to protect with a blocky top. **FA:** Rick Kollath.

6. Look Pa and Ma, I'm a Trad Climber (5.8) ★★ The third big notch climber's right from *M*A*S*H**, enjoy a tough start laybacking before transitioning into an obvious crack above. **FA:** Eldon Krosch Jr.

7. Swimsuits and Harnesses (5.10) The beach has disappeared, making this route a free-hanging start above the roof. A discontinuous double crack system at the climber's right of the access gully. **FA:** Dave Pagel.

The Southern Ramparts

This area includes all routes south of the Amphitheater on the main cliff. At the bottom the talus can be easily traversed from *The Southern Escape Gully* to *Danger High Voltage*, but a hike to the Amphitheater ascends a (5.3, slippery) boulder cave. If setting up a top anchor, you may need protection to get to the lip of the following climbs due to a lot of loose rock and scree that could lead to slips or be kicked onto the climber below.

8. The Southern Escape Gully (5.3 R) The easiest top access from the base of the cliff. From the parking lot, follow the trail along the cliff top as it heads down a gully to a flat area until you find a boulder at the top with a bolt for a rappel.

9. KGB (5.7) ★★ The first major corner north of *The Southern Escape Gully* has a ledge near the top. There is a flake, long cracks, and just enough face climbing to allow a 5.7 leader to feel good about gear place-ments. If you use just the crack, it's a grade harder. Loose gravel abounds at the top. **FA:** Dave Pagel.

10. Night Vision (5.11c) ★★ North of *KGB*, this starts on a right-leaning flake heading up a steep thin crack in a left-facing dihedral that gifts you good gear when it gets hard. Look for a big red spot in the middle of the route. **FA:** Steve Mankenberg.

11. Spruce Tips (5.12b) MIXED ★★★ Start up the sharp arête and blank-looking face to the left of a free-standing pillar. Leave the arête and commit to the finger crack on the face. At the top, go a touch left into a diagonal hand crack, finishing on good edges. Beware of loose rock. **FA:** Taylor Krosbakken.

12. Flight School (5.10d) ★ Look for a thin seam in the middle of the face. Near the top, move right onto a big ledge, then ascend a hard overhanging finger crack into a slot/corner. **FA:** Dave Rone.

Southern Ramparts-Left

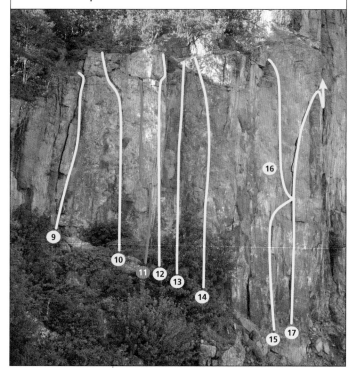

13. Socket Wrench (5.8) ★★ Straight forward mix of crack and face heading up the corner for a fun route at the grade, and a decent lead. **FA:** Dave Pagel.

14. Old Men in Tight Pants (5.10a) ★★ The thin crack into a flake system north of *Socket Wrench*. **FA:** Rick Kollath.

15. Presents (5.11a) ★★ Thin, technical, and aesthetic. Start in the small corner/crack just left of *Laceration Jam* and climb up, then right to a small ledge at the midpoint of pitch 1 of *Laceration Jam*. **FA:** Dave Pagel.

16. Christmas Tree Crack (5.10a) ★★ A lot of loose rock but still a nice climb. Starting where *Presents* ends, slink left and up this dirty crack. This can be toproped as long as everyone understands the belayer may kick massive amounts of dirt and small rocks onto the climber.

17. Laceration Jam (5.10b) ★★★★ A fantastic route that combines sharp crack, hard moves, and a big runout at the end. **P1:** Start in the distinct curving hand crack that widens the higher you go, then move around the corner, traversing a crack wide enough to stick your leg into as you move toward the belay ledge. Bring a #5 for this part. **P2:** Climb through an overhang (5.8) and up a chimney with no real gear (5.6R). **FA:** Jim Kennedy and Dave Mital.

18. Queen of Venus (5.10b) The first shallow corner north of *Laceration Jam* ends just left of the *Laceration Jam* belay. Loose in the upper sections. **FA:** Bob Rossi.

19. Killing Me Softly (5.11b) ★ Ending at the start of the second pitch of *Laceration Jam*, making it interesting. The big flake in the middle is loose. **FA:** Dave Pagel and Rick Kollath.

The next three routes start near a short orange pillar about 50 feet north of *Laceration Jam*.

20. Pussyfoot (5.9+) ★★★ This route has all of the things: crack, face, wide crack, off-width, and a roof. The left side of the flake that hangs down above the pillar ends in a small polygonal roof about 40 feet up. An off-width start (5.9) turns to hands going straight up to the roof. Above the 5.9 roof, follow the hand crack to a belay ledge at its top. Climb left and up the final chimney on *Laceration Jam*.

Paige Orcutt on *Socket Wrench* (5.8) Photo: Taylor Krosbakken

Aerial photo: Brenda Piekarski

It's short enough to do as a single pitch, but if you sew it up, the rope drag will be miserable. **FA:** Rick Kollath and Dave Pagel.

21. Squab (5.7) ★★ A good moderate route that's easily protected. You'll find loose rock.

22. Scars and Tripes Forever (5.10a) ★★★ A long, forbidding, dark corner forms the first major break in the clifftop to the north of *Laceration Jam*. Start about 10 feet north of a right-facing corner and work up to a small bush. Stay in the crack as it gets smaller, and pull through the two roofs. The top is in a corner a few feet lower than the surrounding cliff line. One of the longest routes at Palisade. **FA:** Dave Pagel.

23. Mabley's Traverse (5.8) Look for a decent-sized tree right at the base in an obvious right facing corner—you're heading up the corner. **P1:** Start stepping off a small ledge at the bottom, making some 5.8 moves with bad feet to some broken ledges. Follow crack systems as they head up toward two stubby pillars. **P2:** Traverse on a ledge heading toward a little cave/chimney, climbing through the cave and behind the big rock for your second belay stance inside the dip/cave full of loose rock. **P3:** Climb through the keyhole behind the big rock and enjoy 40 or so feet of off-width until finishing in a chimney. Lots of rockfall and route finding means this route builds a mountaineer's mentality for dangerous terrain. **FA:** Steve Mabley.

24. Lapidarian (5.11b) ★★★ Twenty feet south of *Bridges* is this hidden gem that starts in the middle of the cliff with a bolted anchor and a small ledge for the hanging belay. After some initial crumbly holds, a shallow dihedral leads to big moves that don't let up. **FA:** James Loveridge and Dave Groth.

Southern Ramparts–Right

AERIAL PHOTO: BRENDA PIEKARSKI

Lan Le on *Iron Maiden* (5.10+) PHOTO: ANTHONY JOHNSON

25. Bridges Over Troubled Water (5.10b)
★ Thirty feet climber's right of *Scars*, rappel to the *Mabley's Traverse* ledge about 100 feet down. Make some 5.8 moves up the face to a fist crack and then up your first dihedral to a ledge. Climb the tough second open dihedral, finishing either right or left. **FA:** Rick Kollath.

26. Every Which Way but Up (5.11c) ★★
From the bottom of the cliff, head just north of the cave of the *Mabley's Traverse*. Start is a finger crack that looks easier than it is. Toprope from the big *Mabley's Traverse* ledge. **FA:** John Hoivik and Dave Pagel.

27. Long Distance Commute (5.10a) ★★ In the corner to the left of *Iron Maiden*, follow the left-hand crack in the bottom half until you reach a ledge, and then switch to the right crack. Face climbing switches back to crack before a large block at the top. **FA:** Guy Evans.

28. Iron Maiden (5.10+) ★★★ Off-width—love it or hate it. A hand crack on the north side of the inset opens up to chicken wing awesomeness. You get a ledge before the squeeze chimney at the top. Excellent torture the whole way up. **FA:** Dave Pagel.

29. Swizzlestick Legs (5.11c) MIXED ★★
The face left of *Smearjob*. Rappel to a ledge less than halfway down and follow the bolts before running it out at the top. Bring a couple of small cams to lead it. **FA:** Peter L. Scott and Scott Brockmeier.

30. Smearjob (5.10c) ★ Fifteen feet climber's right of *Swizzlestick*, this finger/thin hands crack could be so good if it didn't bleed so much dirt, despite years of climbers attempting to clean it out. Most climbers start from the big ledge but climb from the talus to add some dirty 5.9. **FA:** Steve Mabley.

31. Jim's Crack (5.10a) ★★ An off-width starting on broken ledges. See if you can find the "hug" part of the route in between the jamming and the odd face holds. **FA:** Jim Ronnigen, Steve Mabley, and Rick Kollath.

32. Smuggler's Cove (5.13-) MIXED ★★★ Ten feet climber's right of *Jim's Crack*, start from the lowest ledge about 50 feet above the water just above Class 4 climbing (a 70-meter will just reach the ledge). Open with 5.11 face climbing heading into a shallow corner to gain the headwall. Then sustained climbing along the arête for 60 feet on tiny tricky moves before toasting with a tiki drink at the top. 8 bolts, supplement with some small cams and runners. **FA:** Randall Baum.

33. Cul-de-sac (5.10c) The next larger crack north of *Jim's Crack* and *Smuggler's*. **FA:** Rick Kollath.

34. Yellow Feather (5.11c) ★★★ Short but high quality, this climbs only the top half of the wall. Begin on a fixed belay on the ledge, heading up well-protected thin stemming and finish working left. Bring small cams and micro-nuts and a couple medium-sized cams for the top section, which can get run out. **Variation:** Do the first pitch of *Oz*, then

break off left to finish on *Yellow Feather*. **FA:** Jeremy Schlick.

35. Oz (5.12b) MIXED ★★★★ Possibly the best trad route of its grade in the Midwest, this route requires the full arsenal of technique in order to send the whole line with big moves at the bottom and crack technique at the top. About 30 feet climber's left of *Danger*, there is a small bush about 10 feet from the top. Rappel down, stopping on a sloping belay ledge about 30 feet above the water. Start here. Climb right to a chunky buttress and up through a bulge and some bolts to the stunning crack for 70 feet. **FA:** James Loveridge.

Kurt Hager on *The Gales of November* (5.13)
PHOTO: CRAIG HUANG

36. The Gales of November (5.13) MIXED
★★★★ This incredible climb gently follows a
seam to the left of *Danger* and the lightning
cable. You'll need a 70-meter rope if lowering
from the top, or if you decide to do it in one
long push. **P1:** Enjoy pumpy, sustained, and
technical climbing before graduating through
crimps while traversing left to the belay
ledge. **P2:** Follow the seam through three
powerful bouldery moves. **FA:** Kurt Hager.

37. Mind Forever Free (5.13) This second
pitch variation follows *Gales* until the traverse to the belay ledge; instead of doing the
traverse, continue straight up for a 200-foot
endurance-fest that's a true test piece for the
grade. You can't just toprope it without a
directional because if you fall, you won't be
able to get back in to the wall. **FA:**
Eric Enquist.

38. Danger High Voltage (5.8) ★★★ This
chimney-ish off-width crack route follows
the lightning cable climber's right into the
corner, and the second pitch is a great quick
toprope. If leading, best done in two pitches.
A 60-meter rope will reach the bottom. If
toproping, flip the rope behind the lower
flake or arrange a directional to avoid swinging if you fall down low. **P1:** Start right of
the cables and improvise your way up into
the off-width crack. Belay at the obvious
ledge. **P2:** Work up and right of the flake to
the top. A 5.9+ variation requires climbing
the off-width to the left of the final flake.
FA: Steve Mabley and Rick Kollath.

39. Pamplemoose (5.12b) MIXED ★★ Start
on a small ledge below and right of the large
DHV ledges halfway down the cliff. Head
slightly left, then up the face, finding the rest
ledge out left. The meat of the climb ends

with a flake system on the left, then trends
right to a ledge and easy climbing. **FA:**
Taylor Krosbakken.

40. A Feathery Tong (5.10c) MIXED ★★★
A few yards north of the top of *Danger High
Voltage* is a pointed orange rock right on the
edge. Rappel down to a semi-hanging bolted
belay ledge to start, or rappel all the way to
the bottom to add about 20 to 30 feet of
climbing and three bolts. Great stemming
in a dihedral, but the crux is on steep edges.
This is mostly bolted, but bring three or four
small cams and some shoulder-length runners. Rappelling on a 70-meter will not get
you all the way down, but there's a bolted
anchor midway down. **FA:** Scott Brockmeier
and Peter L. Scott.

The Amphitheater

Just a hop and a skip from the parking lot is
a rock wall that marks the Amphitheater, a
popular tourist picture spot as well as some
of the most traveled climbs at Palisade.
Bluebells and *Quetico Crack* can be toproped
from below on a 60-meter rope; other routes
must be belayed from a top-managed system
or led. Avoid leaving a fixed line on the
popular climbs in the Amphitheater.

41. Dirty Harry (5.7) ★ This is the best escape
route from the Amphitheater area. From the
southern corner of the Amphitheater, a line
of ledges ascends up and left. Access to these
ledges is barred by a corner topped by an
overhang. Ascend the corner (5.7), belay, and
scramble up the Class 3 ledges to the top.
Pulling the overhang can be intense for new
trad leaders, but it's a straightforward lead for
the grade.

42. Sudden Impact (5.11d) ★★ If the contrived crux moves at the top are avoided, the route is somewhat easier (5.11b). From the belay ledge at the top of the *Dirty Harry* dihedral, paw your way up the shallow corner above. The crux moves are a few feet below the top, just left of the *Ex Nihilo* finish. **FA:** Dave Pagel.

43. Ex Nihilo (5.10b R) ★★★ Climb the large dihedral (5.6) immediately north of the *Dirty Harry* start and belay. The right-facing corner and cracks above form the crux pitch where the runout is as you try to stem. The top is

a 2-by-2-foot ledge below the edge of the cliff, a few feet right of the wall. **FA:** Dean Einerson.

44. The Fool's Progress (5.12b) MIXED ★★ Follow the bolts up the corner between *Rapprochement* and *Ex Nihilo* before moving to the right arête to a ledge. Finish on a slightly overhanging face on tiny steep edges. **FA:** Scott Brockmeier and Peter L. Scott.

45. Rapprochement (5.10b) ★★★★ A reach near the bottom leads to fun corner-climbing above. Start on the face between *Ex Nihilo* and *Sunny and Sheer*. Climb up through

Amphitheater-Left

AERIAL PHOTO: BRENDA PIEKARSKI

Joe Lee on *Hidden Treasure* (5.11b) Photo: Anthony Johnson

double cracklets (crux at pin) and enter the 5.9 corner above. A popular lead. Top: centerish of the tourist wall.

46. Sunny and Sheer (5.12a R) ★★★★ This arête between *Rapprochement* and *Hidden Treasure* is continuous and strenuous, climbing on knife edges with precise and technical sequences through quartz pockets. **FA:** Kris Gorny.

47. Palisaid (5.13a) MIXED ★★★★ Incredible face climbing on sound rock. Up seams to the left of *Hidden Treasure*. **FA:** Dave Groth.

48. Hidden Treasure (5.11b R) ★★★★ The major corner right of *Sunny and Sheer* runs the full height of the cliff and is overhanging most of the way up. This beautiful corner has

shallow and shattered rock that spits out gear and has broken bones. **FA:** Jim Kennedy.

49. Phantom Crack (5.9) ★★★ Start on the slabs at the bottom (5.6, limited protection) or begin at the ledge for 30 feet of a left-leaning hand crack that widens out at the top. A classic for the Head.

50. Phantom Corner (5.11+) ★★ Up the tough corner to the right of *Phantom Crack*, where you'll need small gear and no fear. **FA:** Eli Curry.

The back wall of the Amphitheater is defined by *Bluebells* on the south and *Superior Crack* on the north.

51. Bluebells (5.9) ★★★★ Easily the most popular and most traveled 5.9 at Palisade. Jam

Amphitheater-Right

AERIAL PHOTO: BRENDA PIEKARSKI

your way up the marvelous (and slippery) finger crack in the right-facing dihedral closest to the parking lot. **FA:** Dick Wildberger and Dan Kieffaber.

52. Warrior's Last Dance on Earth (5.12a) Fifteen feet to the climber's right of *Bluebells*, hard moves up the face lead to an overhang and finish right. **FA:** Steve Mankenberg.

53. False Prophet (5.11) Start in a short wide dihedral. At the top of the dihedral, make a big reach left before following the face straight up to the top. **FA:** Peter L. Scott and Scott Brockmeier.

54. Gift of the Magi (5.11d) ★ Begin in a corner and trend up and right, finishing closer to *Quetico Crack*. **FA:** Roger Harkess.

55. Quetico Crack (5.8-) ★★ The big chimney and flake system just left of *Superior Crack*. It's a great first outdoor climb at the head.

56. Superior Crack (5.8+) ★★★ A wide crack/corner on the north edge of the Amphitheater, you can either practice stemming inside the corner or head straight into the off-width (or a fun mixture of both). You'll swing if you fall, as it's slightly overhung.

57. Superior Arête (5.12c R) ★★★ This beautiful arête is hard to miss and an incredible climb because of the pure physical movement and exposure. Start up *Superior Crack* for 15 feet or so until you can traverse right onto the arête via edges. The route weaves up the arête, switching sides now and then. Excellent stone and movement, but scary runouts on gear. **FA:** Rob Pilaczynski.

58. Wise Guy (5.12a R) ★★★ Excellent, varied, and unique climbing that could feel like the gym if it weren't for the lake breeze and some crumbles. Start to the left of the rotten, rightward-trending, overhanging crack. Keep your cool placing dicey gear in a crumbly crack before the prominent 5-foot-wide "tombstone" jutting from the wall about 15 feet below the top. Head up the left side for an easier variation. **FA:** Mike Dahlberg.

59. Driving in Duluth (5.11b R) ★★★★ Begin in a shallow dihedral below a notch as you balance and dance around on this meandering route. **FA:** Kris Gorny.

The Central Ramparts

The rock from here north can be unstable and might flake easily. There are still some incredibly stellar routes, so don't let that hamper your excitement.

60. Queen of the Damned (5.12a) ★ Start in a corner at the bottom before ascending up thin face when the crack peters out. Watch out for loose rock in the middle of this one. Top is to the climber's left of a diagonal. **FA:** James Loveridge and Dave Groth (TR).

61. Attention Wanders (5.9) Climb the hand crack to the first belay of *A Hard Rain*.

62. A Hard Rain (5.12b) **P1:** Climb shallow corners/dihedrals to a belay (old bolts) beneath a left-facing corner capped by a roof (40 feet). **P2:** Up the corner and through the roof, eventually trending right to the belay ledge on *Urge to Mate* (150 feet). **P3:** Up a thin crack just south of *Urge to Mate* (40 feet). **FA:** James Loveridge and Dave Groth (TR).

63. Urge to Mate (5.10c) ★★★★ A glorious hand crack that starts at a ledge and goes straight up with some good rests. **FA:** Peter L. Scott and Chris Holbeck.

Central Ramparts-Left

AERIAL PHOTO: BRENDA PIEKARSKI

64. Double-Breasted Anchor (5.8) ★★ A hanging hand/fist crack that finishes just a few feet north of *Urge to Mate*, it's a great lead with exposure. On toprope, start from the higher, northern ledge. You'll wish it were longer. **FA:** Chris Holbeck and Peter L. Scott.

65. The Great Bird Chimney (5.7) ★★★★ For a fantastic chimney experience from wide to squeeze, this is well protected (by occasional bats).

66. Haulbags Are People Too (5.10d) Up to the base of *The Great Bird Chimney*, then cut right up a seam and the corner to the right of *The Great. . . .* **FA:** Rick Kollath and Bill Gitar.

67. Lord of the Flies (5.12b) ★★★ MIXED
Amazing 80-foot dihedral with some difficult stemming (crux at mid-height) reminiscent of *Poseidon Adventure*. Bring small cams to 1.5 inches and a set of stoppers to supplement the two bolts. Start on the ledge where there's a fixed belay, not at the water. **FA:** Dave Groth.

68. Mr. Lean (5.11d) ★★★★ Often accused of being sandbagged, this incredible route is long, exposed, and climbs clean with fantastic gear. Start on hand cracks before balancing on a tiny ledge. Crank through the finger crack and slight overhang to a ledge with a tree on the left before the last 20 feet ending in a rounded buttress. **FA:** Dave Rone.

69. Bugaboo (5.13+) MIXED ★★★ To the right of Mr. Lean, starts with Class 5 scrambling with no pro before a bolt. From there, a 5.11 intro to a laser-cut seam leads to a chimney that's open-ended at the bottom and threatens to spit you out as it gets steeper toward a notch at the end. **FA:** Randall Baum.

70. Mack the Knife (5.10b) ★★★ A classic 5.10 crack. At the top an acute inside corner has a birch tree with a block at its base. Forge up the corner to start, topping out either in the crack or by scootching around right for easier terrain. **FA:** Rick Kollath.

71. Northern Escape Chimney (5.8)
Technically the easiest escape if you are north of the Amphitheater. A short 5.8 section ends with a tricky mantle protected by small gear, which then leads to Class 3 scrambling (loose) to the notch behind the North Tower. From here, it's a straightforward chimney. It's a good one to identify for "just in case" situations. When setting an anchor, keep in mind that the route starts climber's right from where it tops out. A variation starts to the right of the "notch" going straight up toward the chimney.

Jump across to the North Tower (carefully).

72. North Tower, South Face (5.10c PG13) ★★ The south face starts as scramble up some 5.5 to a pedestal. There are small flakes before a finger crack up at the top. If you stay in the corner, it's closer to 5.9, but for safety's sake stay on the headwall.

Sarah Vanderheiden rope-soloing *Mr. Lean* (5.11d)

Central Ramparts–Right and North Tower

AERIAL PHOTO: BRENDA PIEKARSKI

73. Faith (5.12b) ★★ **P1:** Begin near a cedar tree in a pit on the left side of the north face. Head up a crumbly corner with poor gear that ends on a big belay ledge. **P2:** A tough boulder problem and an upper head wall crux after a bolt. The top makes the crumbly bottom worth it. **FA:** Taylor Krosbakken.

74. Don't Bring a Knife to a Gunfight

(5.11b) MIXED ★★★★ Excellent route with consistent moves throughout. Start from the pedestal and move up and left on edges (passing two bolts) to gain the start of a crack. Follow the crack up to a ledge you could eat a sandwich on, then up a crack to a dirty alcove, and traverse left to follow another crack to the top. If toproping, you'll want to place some directionals as you lower. **FA:** James Loveridge.

75. Withering Heights (5.10)

This off-width is on the north side of the North Tower right below a rock-filled gully area, sharing the same opening as *Gunfight*. Be careful of loose rocks. **FA:** Rick Kollath.

The Northern Ramparts

As you move north of the North Tower, the cliff drops down and the trail moves away from the cliff edge. For climbs in the vicinity of *Arms Race*, spot a grove of tall birches while you are on North Tower. Keep an eye out for loose rock due to lower traffic on this end of the Head.

The routes from *Whodunit* to *Hidden Agenda* sit higher up in the talus, surrounded by a grove of trees.

76. Whodunit (5.9+) Up a left-leaning ramp to the crack, climb to the right of several bushes, and beware of loose rock at the top.

77. Father's Day (aka Sunday Excursion, 5.11d) MIXED ★ Up the corner the tough crack is now protected by six bolts. At a triangular overhang go left. **FA:** Josh Columb.

78. Keystone (5.12b/c) MIXED ★ North of *Father's Day*. Ascend the chimney to the corner heading into keyhole alcove. **FA:** James Loveridge (TR).

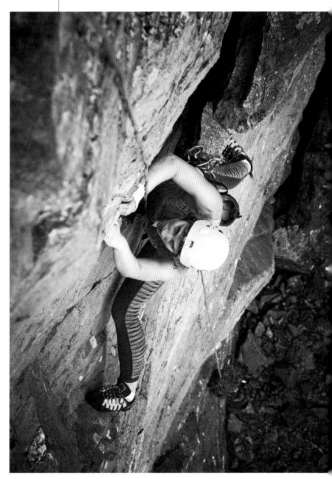

Ellen Wiederhoft rope-soloing *Don't Bring a Knife to a Gunfight* (5.11b)

79. Feces Mortibus (5.10a) Right of *Keystone*, you'll find a pillar near the bottom. Go right of that little pillar to a crack, up to a ledge and a hand crack. Loose. **FA:** Rick Kollath and Bob Bickford.

80. Bearded Cabbage (5.11a) Just north of *Feces Mortibus*. Up left of the wide crack to thin seams. **FA:** Brian Gitar.

81. Arms Race (5.11c) At the top look for an eroded area that looks like a water-draining ditch leading to a dihedral. On the bottom, start on a small ledge a few feet up, following a smooth but flared crack about 10 feet south of *Grunge Off*. Watch for chossy rock before a ledge. **FA:** Dave Pagel.

82. Grey Expectations (5.11a) Often loose and dirty, this crack is just south of *Grunge Off*.

83. Grunge Off (aka Goliath's Finger Crack, 5.9+) ★ Gravelly top; find a major wide crack in a corner. Enjoy the off-width, but choss and flakes make for a spicy lead. **FA:** Bob Bickford.

84. A Twister With Teeth (5.9 PG13) ★★ On the arête 20 feet north of *Grunge Off*, follow the detached pillar up into a finger crack and a ledge. Continue up the dihedral through some sloping face and a tiny overhang. **FA:** Zachary Strong and Charlie Hazelroth.

85. A Moveable Piece (5.9) From the bottom north of *Grunge Off* is an arête that is broken at the top. Just north of this arête is a flake. Climb the thin crack up the left side of this flake and cut right under a bush near the top. Dirty, crumbly, and loose. **Variation:** Up the right side (5.11). **FA:** Brian Gitar.

86. In the Wash (5.9) Up the next flake north of *A Moveable Piece*, minding the bush in the middle and at the top of the route. **FA:** Brian Gitar.

87. V-Max (5.11c) This route begins 30 feet south of *Water Babies* as an acute dihedral with a small cedar about 20 feet up. Dirty and loose. **FA:** Rick Kollath.

88. Water Babies (5.8) ★★ Just left of *Contender* is a smaller corner with a shrubby tree halfway up and a ledge caked with bird poop. Face climbing with a little crack, it feels isolated with the water behind you as you climb. Tops onto vegetation. **FA:** Brian Gitar and Bill Gitar.

89. I Could've Been a Contender (5.8) ★★ Start in a finger crack. At the ledge decide if you're doing hand/finger crack (left) or off-width (right) or just do all the things. The ledges at the top usually have loose stuff. **FA:** Dave Pagel.

90. Mohammed Ali (5.12) ★ Up the blank-looking face of the buttress. Start on the pedestal, then move left onto the face. **FA:** Mike Dahlberg.

91. Hidden Agenda (5.9) ★ This is the corner to the right of *Mohammed*'s blank face. Up the hand crack to a ledge. Very loose at the top and not a good toprope. There are old bolts at the top. **FA:** Rick Kollath.

92. The Sound of One Hand Jamming (5.10d) ★ Your body size will decide how many hands you can get in the jam when in the tight and awkward dihedral. From the right edge of the ledge, climb up the flake and corner. Crux is near the top. **FA:** Rick Kollath and Roger Harkess.

The next three routes climb to a large ledge before finishing together up top.

93. Praise the Many Seraphim (5.8) MIXED ★★★ Look for a line of bolts 20 feet left of *Ecclesiastes*. This full-value climb starts at the water heading up a right-facing corner until a ledge. Traverse right just a touch on

Northern Ramparts–Left

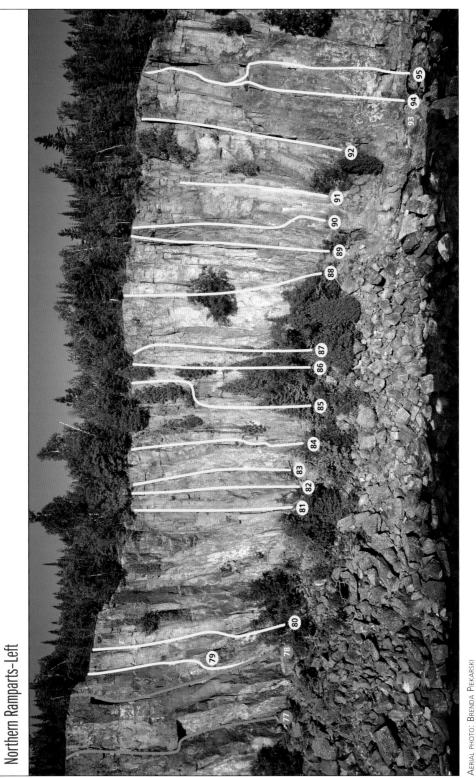

AERIAL PHOTO: BRENDA PIEKARSKI

the face following four bolts before dealer's choice between two wide cracks and a giant ledge before topping out. Good beginner lead. **FA:** Rick Kollath.

94. Ecclesiastes 1 (5.12a PG13) ★★ This finger crack immediately right of *Praise* used to be easier before Lake Superior storms blew whole boulders off the start. You can start up *Praise* and traverse left (with unknown protection). Alternatively, start on a boulder problem going straight up for a harder (5.12c), more dangerous climb. **FA:** Paul Bjork.

95. A Sinner's Last Gift (5.11d) ★★ Another route cleaned but this time downgraded by Superior's storms, you start on flat ground below a small overhang. Follow a thin seam up as it widens. **FA:** Jeremy Schlick.

96. The Metamorphosis (5.10b) ★ Of the two corners making up *Metamorphosis* and *Mann Act*, head up the one on the climber's left. Follow the corner and crack, encountering large loose rocks to a dirt top. **FA:** Scott Brockmeier and Peter L. Scott.

97. The Mann Act (5.11 R) ★ Jam and stem the right corner crack with good gear placements before runout face climbing. **FA:** Kris Gorny.

98. Soli Deo Gloria (5.12a) MIXED ★★★★ A fantastic lead that protects well. Start at a flake left of *The Choice* and reach the thin crack. Pass through two tiny roofs and zigzag on crimps and sidepulls to the top. Big moves don't let up until you pull over the edge. 2 bolts. **FA:** Dave Groth.

99. The Choice of a New Generation (5.11d) ★★ About 10 feet north of *Soli*, look for a white inset/roof marking the start. Climb a very thin crack that mutates into a small right-facing corner. The bottom half

has excellent rock, but the top is loose. **FA:** Dave Groth.

100. No Sugar, No Baby (5.9) ★★ At the last trees along the talus on the bottom, this is a clean dihedral with a hand crack. Start on the ledge just above the tree if you don't want to get in a fight with vegetation. To set anchors, set the face on the climber's right of a huge corner. **FA:** Rick Kollath.

101. Hiawatha's Journey to Gitche Gumee (5.9) Climb straight up the right side of the arête east of *No Sugar*. **FA:** Suzanne Johnson and Peter L. Scott.

102. Mital's Roof (A3) ★★ **Pitch 1:** Head toward the obvious roof, praying your gear doesn't pull. Pull the roof to a bolt station. **Pitch 2:** Finger crack. **FA:** Dave Mital.

103. The Fall of Ascomycetes (5.11b) ★★★ Starts right of the first pitch of *Mital's Roof*, heading through a series of roofs and a dihedral before joining with *Mital's* finger crack after the roof and above the old bolted belay. This is a free version of pitch 2 of *Mital's Roof*. **FA:** Alex Ristow.

104. Rejuvenation (aka The Sound and the Fury, 5.12+) SPORT with no bolted anchor ★★★ A stunning line tackles the roof on the north end of Palisade Head. Hardest climbing at the start, bizarre corner sequences, and a thin traverse around the roof. Great holds before sustained movement up the beautifully colored headwall. **FA:** Kurt Hager.

105. Aching Alms (5.12a/b) ★ Fifteen feet to the south of *Happy*, follow a dihedral with a crack through a roof, clawing through off-width to reach a rappel station partway up. **FA:** Seth Dyer.

Northern Ramparts–Right

AERIAL PHOTO: BRENDA PIEKARSKI

Krzysztof (Kris) Gorny on the FA of *The Mann Act* (5.11R) Photo: Kris Gorny's camera on a tripod

106. Hyper Light Drifter (5.13-) SPORT
with no bolted anchor ★★★ Climb *Aching
Alms* to the anchor, then pull a series of roofs
trending right before finishing in the little
notch, allowing you to link up the entire
cliff for one wildly big climb. 8 bolts. **FA:**
Randall Baum.

107. Happy Happy, Joy Joy (aka Echoes
and Echoes Extension, 5.13b) SPORT with
no bolted anchor ★★★ **P1:** The dihedral just
south of *The Poseidon Adventure* start (5.11b).
Gain the ledge used for *Poseidon*. **P2:** Traverse
left off the ledge to climb the bolted face for
an utterly fantastic technical line with incredible exposure over Lake Superior (5.13b).
FA: Travis Melin.

108. The Poseidon Adventure (5.11d) ★★★★
One of the best continuous finger crack
dihedrals on the north shore. At the very
north end of the talus, climb up the lower
shallow corner (5.9), step right, then continue up the sustained dihedral above. Most
start from the ledge since the bottom crack is
loose. **FA:** Dave Pagel and Rick Kollath.

The Far North

To find this area, head past *Poseidon* along
the cliff line for another 400 feet or so, staying on the high side. Look for a baby pine
tree on the top of a dihedral corner to locate
the next two climbs.

109. Blowing in the Wind (5.13c) SPORT
with no bolted anchor ★★★ A chill slab that
slowly gets harder as it becomes a gentle
overhang. Sustained climbing leads to a short
slab finish. 8 bolts, bolted hanging belay at
the bottom. **FA:** Coulter Holden.

The Far North

AERIAL PHOTO: BRENDA PIEKARSKI

110. Johnny Tsunami (5.12a PG13) ★★★
Getting to the start of the route, whether
on lead or TR, is half of the battle. **P1:** The
first belay ledge is barely above Superior, so
belayers may get wet if there are any waves
at all—consider boating to the bottom if
leading. Toproping means directionals and
intense rope management. Start through a
chimney into an overhanging hand and fist
crack heading to the right. Use a finger crack
through a horizontal roof to a ledge. **P2:**
Ascend the dihedral. **FA:** Taylor Krosbakken.

Sophie Kedrowski on Dance of the *Sugar-Plump Faeries* (5.7–5.10d)

SHOVEL POINT

Shovel Point is an exceptional base camp for weekend climbing adventures along Lake Superior. There are fewer routes, but don't underestimate it just because it's smaller. The views are breathtaking, the approach and amenities are excellent, and if you want a relaxing day with a top-managed system, this is a fantastic choice. If the weather is bad at Palisade, don't rule out Shovel—the southwest-facing wall means that it often avoids the cold winds that can come in off the lake. There are days when those climbing at Palisade are in puffy jackets and those at Shovel are overwarm in their T-shirts.

This crag is for everyone. Despite the rumors that Shovel is mostly an "easy" or "moderate" crag, there are a few tough classics for those looking for a challenge and a wide range of grades for all ability levels. Truly fantastic 5.6 climbs for the beginner alongside stellar 5.10s, 5.11s, and a 5.12 means a party with a wide range of abilities will have a fantastic full-value day at Shovel Point.

Types of Climbing and Gear

There's more slab climbing here than a lot of places in Minnesota, along with plenty of face climbing, cracks, and dihedrals.

You'll want long anchor material (webbing or static rope) for most of the routes, and a 60-meter rope is more than enough. If you want to lead, a single rack works just fine. Lower in and build a bottom anchor to belay from, often perched precariously above the water or in a hanging belay.

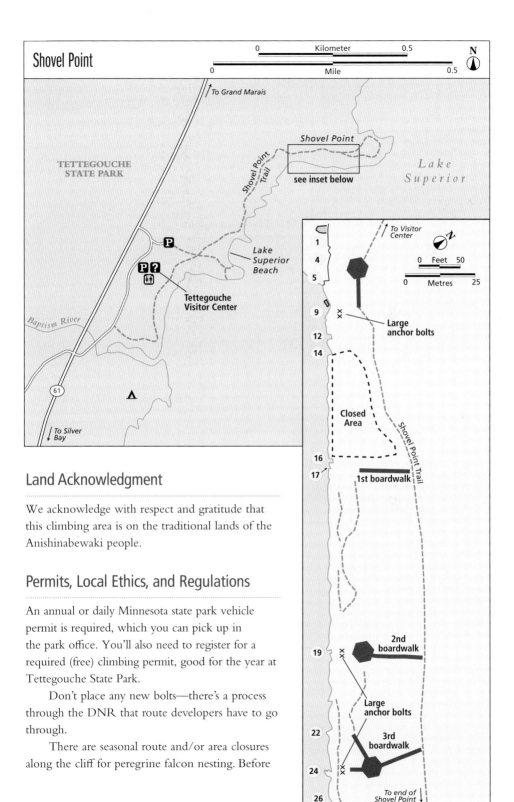

Shovel Point

TETTEGOUCHE
STATE PARK

To Grand Marais

Shovel Point

see inset below

Lake
Superior

Lake
Superior
Beach

Tettegouche
Visitor Center

Baptism River

61

To Silver
Bay

To Visitor
Center

Large
anchor bolts

Closed
Area

Shovel Point Trail

1st boardwalk

2nd
boardwalk

Large
anchor bolts

3rd
boardwalk

To end of
Shovel Point

Land Acknowledgment

We acknowledge with respect and gratitude that
this climbing area is on the traditional lands of the
Anishinabewaki people.

Permits, Local Ethics, and Regulations

An annual or daily Minnesota state park vehicle
permit is required, which you can pick up in
the park office. You'll also need to register for a
required (free) climbing permit, good for the year at
Tettegouche State Park.

Don't place any new bolts—there's a process
through the DNR that route developers have to go
through.

There are seasonal route and/or area closures
along the cliff for peregrine falcon nesting. Before

climbing, either ask in the park office or check the specific state park page on Minnesota's DNR website for route/area closures. Respect the closures. There are also many areas of cryptobiotic soil restoration that are roped off, so please stay out of those areas.

Dogs are allowed but must be kept on a 6-foot leash and under control at all times, and owners must clean up after them.

Getting There and Parking

Tettegouche Parking Lot GPS: N47.338' / W91.196'

While heading north on MN 61 just past mile marker 58, watch for the signs for the Tettegouche State Park Visitor Center on the right.

Approach

The trail to the climbs is popular with hikers, and it's well maintained. If you take one of the viewpoint spur trails along the main trail on the hike in, you can see the cliff and the climbs. After ascending a long set of wooden steps a half mile in, you emerge onto an observation platform, which serves as a starting point for locating the climbs.

A number of routes can start from the talus that can be seen below the observation platform area, though depending on the year, the talus could be underwater. All access descriptions refer to the top of each climb. Usually, a 40- to 80-foot rappel will deposit you on a small ledge or tree that marks the bottom of the pitch.

Camping and Amenities

Tettegouche State Park, hosting both Shovel Point and Palisade Head, has its own campground and cabin lodging. You can also camp at the state forest campground on MN 1 called Eckbeck or up Lake County Road 6 in Finland.

For restrooms, simply hike back to the Tettegouche State Park Visitor Center.

Hazards

The rhyolite rock can be quite loose, with flakes or blocks that could pull off when on-route, especially on routes that don't see much traffic.

Pad the edge to protect your rope. Don't trust the old bolts and pitons.

The park service installed some truly magnanimous bolts at the top of some popular routes to help with erosion. When setting natural anchors, you'll want to carefully evaluate some of the shallow-rooted trees at the top before using them. Longer webbing will enable you to use bigger trees or cracks—or the huge bolts.

Be careful not to toss the ends of your rope into the lake.

Basic knowledge of hauling is nice if your climber can't get back up the route.

On non-windy days in the summer, black flies can be abundant and bitey.

Routes Not to Miss

The Great Yawn (5.6), Dance of the Sugar-Plump Faeries (5.7–5.10d), Ross's Crack (5.10b), Gold Plated (5.10b), Sacred Biscuit (5.11a), Narcoleptic Epic (5.11d)

To set up the first two routes, walk west from the observation platform for about 100 feet. Descend a few feet to a clean platform that juts toward the lake. *The Tree Route* ends in the east-facing corner; *Straight, No Chaser* ends about 5 feet east at a slightly higher ledge with a tree.

1. The Tree Route (5.10a) ★★ A nice long route that's good for the grade. From the talus, a brushy start leads to a nice thin crack that leads to another nice thin crack that leads to a dying cedar about 50 feet up. From the cedar, scamper up easier slabs to a flake and the corner at the top. Use gear, not the tree, as a directional.

2. Straight, No Chaser (5.10b) ★ A few feet east of *The Tree Route* is a climb with a few neat moves that are a bit technical and require some balance. Zip up to the shrub to the right of the tree on *The Tree Route*. Join that route, but then near the top, move into the short, thin crack above the flake. Clean and fun. **FA:** Brian Gitar.

3. Ego-itis (5.12a R) ★★ Don't set up the right side of the roof if you're TR. Be wary

of using the bolts. **P1:** (5.9) Look for the old piton to mark the start, and enjoy stellar climbing that protects well. Your belay stance is just below the roof. **P2:** (5.12a) A fantastic and intimidating overhang that requires some tricky moves to pull the roof on the left side. The crux is not easily protected, earning the route the R. **FA:** Rick Kollath.

4. The Great Barrier Roof (C3/5.11+) ★★★ Head up the right side of the same roof of *Ego-itis* for this climb. The free version can be done in three pitches, but feel free to link it for one glorious pitch. If you're aiding, bring small RPs and a hook or two. **P1:** Often wet (80 feet, 5.10+); several bolts under the roof. **P2:** (5.11+/12-) Head up into an odd tight corner/wide chimney feature traversing up the right side of the

Shovel Point-Left

AERIAL PHOTO: BRENDA PIEKARSKI

roof to pull it. Set up your belay after you turn the roof. (5.11+). **P3:** Follow the right-trending crack until it disappears, then go left to the top. **FA:** Mike Dahlberg.

5. Ross's Crack (5.10b) ★★★ The first dihedral just east of the lookout platform. Most people start from the tree about 60 feet down, but feel free to do the 5.8 approach pitch from the talus below. The pins in the crack are very old. This is a great corner climb that doesn't have a ton of crack climbing but makes up for it with fun, flexible, and twisty moves. **FA:** Paul Ross.

6. Balance of Power (5.11c) ★★ Do the first few feet of *Ross's Crack*, then cut up and right past two small roofs. Head up the tiny corner above the second roof for the crux, using tiny edges for balancing on this strenuous route. **FA:** Dave Pagel.

The next set of routes are found along the clean cliff edge just east of the observation platform. There are a pair of huge bolts for your belay anchors that could legitimately hold one of Superior's giant ore boats in place. Many groups can share these anchors at the same time. Treat the trees kindly and stay off their roots.

7. Did Plato Love Trees? (5.9 PG13) You'll need your route-finding skills for this meandering route. The thin pro with rock that could easily pull off along with the possibility of taking huge swings earn it the PG13 rating. **P1:** Set up at the end of the talus, heading up toward the base of the *Ross's Crack* with the tree. **P2:** Cruise up and right following a thin crack to reach a dihedral. Climb through some bushes before traversing across some jugs and then down into the tree belay just below *Faeries*. **P3:** Head up the corner to the left of the *Faeries* slab. **FA:** Rick Kollath, Dave Mital, and Jim Mital.

8. Gravity Assist (5.10c) ★★ Look for the short, shallow corner climber's left of the overhang for this fun route. Climb 5.8 crack and face, then go left just below the small overhang toward a thin crack, where you'll meet the crux as you maneuver the crack and the face. Avoid the hand crack through the overhang. **FA:** Dave Rone and Dan Wilkinson.

9. Dance of the Sugar-Plump Faeries (5.7–5.10d) ★★★★ The shining star of Shovel Point. About 15 yards past the wooden lookout is a clean low-angled slab. From the tree below, you can swing into and up the inside corner (5.7); maneuver up the thin crack a few feet right of the corner (5.8); dance up the face between the crack and the arête (5.10b/c); or wander up the right edge (5.10d). Use the ginormous bolts to set up your top-managed belay. While most climbers begin at the tree, you can lower all the way to the water and climb the bottom 30 feet.

10. Sacred Biscuit (5.11a) ★★★ Just east of the *Faeries* slab is this fantastic and technical crack and slab climb. Start at a cedar beneath an overhang. Go left of the first roof, then right of the second to the crux crack. **FA:** Brian Gitar.

11. A Study in Scarlet (5.10b) ★★★ Start at the same place as *Sacred Biscuit* and go right around the roof and up the middle of the clean face above for similar but easier movement than *Biscuit*. **FA:** Dave Pagel.

12. A Dream of White Sheep (5.9) ★★ Look for a rotten indentation 10 feet west of the trees at the top of *Narcoleptic Epic*. This is a fantastic climb for those wanting some good stemming. Follow the diagonal fault that lies to your left as you lower down from above. Following the natural fall line of the rope on the right is a little easier. Belayers: Be careful

Andy Tollefson on *Ross's Crack* (5.10b)

not to kick loose rock on your climber.

13. Straw House

(5.11a) ★★★ Often overlooked, this is a gem of a climb with just enough features to make it work. Just west of the *Narcoleptic Epic* dihedral is an outside corner. Cruise up this, cut left to a tree beneath a roof, then pull the roof and truly enjoy the top. **FA:** Roger Harkess.

14. Narcoleptic Epic

(5.11d) ★★★★ Sixty feet east of *Faeries* and directly below a tree at the edge of the cliff is a very clean dihedral. The crux is maintaining your cool on the entire route through very technical and thin stemming. **FA:** Dave Pagel.

15. Wake Up and Smell the Coffee (5.9)

This is a big fin to the right of the *Narcoleptic*

Shovel Point-Center

AERIAL PHOTO: BRENDA PIEKARSKI

corner. It's passable if you peter out while trying *Narcoleptic* and need an escape route. **FA:** Rick Kollath.

From the observation platform, walk east on the main trail to skirt an eroded slope closed for revegetation. Take the first wooden boardwalk back toward the cliff edge. You will be almost directly over *A Touch of Leather and Lace*. Set up the next two routes slightly to the right (west) of their crack/corners to minimize any swings.

16. Rise Over Run (5.7-) ★★ At the bottom of the gravel slope, just left of the closure when facing the lake, is a notch with some smallish blocks at the top. There's a horn on the right side of the notch that can be used as a directional anchor. Start at the ledge and head up the corner.

Shovel Point-Right

Giant anchor bolts XX

Giant anchor bolts XX

19

20

21

22

23

24

25

26

AERIAL PHOTO: BRENDA PIEKARSKI

17. Cornered (5.9) ★★ A few feet east of *Rise Over Run*. **FA:** Dave Mital.

18. A Touch of Leather and Lace (5.7) ★ Immediately in front of the boardwalk. **FA:** Raven Corbett.

Keep walking east on the main trail to skirt an eroded slope closed for revegetation. Take the second boardwalk leading toward the cliff edge. There is a wooden platform and a second set of giant bolts. *Out on a Limb* is directly below the bolts.

19. Out on a Limb (5.6) ★★ This is a fantastic beginner climb. Immediately below the bolts, start on a ledge with a curved branch. Almost always occupied, and with good reason. Avoid the bolt halfway down if you decide to lead this route.

20. Only the Lonely (5.7) ★★ Twenty feet east of *Out on a Limb* is an obvious notch that marks this route. You'll enjoy some crack and big moves to jugs that work a newer climber's technique. Near the top, traverse right. **FA:** Rick Kollath.

21. Only the Looney (5.9) A few feet east of *Only the Lonely*. A finger crack leads to a thin traverse right at the top. **FA:** Rick Kollath.

While walking east on the main trail, take the third boardwalk leading toward the cliff edge. There is another wooden platform and a third set of giant bolts. *The Great Yawn* is the west-facing corner in line with the bolts.

22. Soldier of God (5.5) ★★ A fun little climb that's great for first-timers. This is 65 feet up from *The Great Yawn*. Locate an unusually clean section of cliff top that faces a little peninsula (where an arch collapsed). Descend 30 feet to the start of the climb. **Variation:** If you decide to lower all the way to the water, you can enjoy a low-angle slab up really small holds for some fun 5.9 climbing. **FA:** Rick Kollath.

23. I Laughed, I Cried, It Became a Part of Me (5.10a) Head west of *The Great Yawn* to find a chossy crack. **FA:** Dave Pagel.

24. The Great Yawn (5.6) ★★★★ This is a fantastic beginner climb, especially if you want to practice jamming. The top is in the obvious notch straight down from the giant bolts. When lowering, you can start at a small ledge 25 feet off the water, or lower all the way to the water to climb up the dihedral with the big crack.

25. Undercover (5.10c) Just east of *The Great Yawn*, hidden in a forest. **FA:** Dave Pagel and Jim Kennedy.

Walk east along the cliff edge for 80 feet from *The Great Yawn* bolts. The trail goes through a slight depression and then climbs for 2 vertical feet. Turn right before the little rise to see the notch that is the top of *Gold Plated*. Drop your rope a couple of feet right of this notch.

26. Gold Plated (5.10b) ★★★★ One of the best 5.10s on the North Shore, this starts about 40 feet or so past *The Great Yawn* after the broken tree and by three trees in a row. Rappel down to an obvious ledge with lichen that gives the route its name, and enjoy incredible crack and dihedral climbing with a couple of roofs thrown in for good measure.

Sam Taggart on *Gold Plated* (5.10b)

Sarah Lofald on *Sisyphus* (5.7)

WOLF RIDGE AREA

Wolf Ridge Environmental Learning Center is reminiscent of isolated adventure climbing while keeping things accessible with fun routes, solid rock, and some of the most beautiful views on the North Shore. While at the top of the Mystical Mountain crag, climbers can enjoy a 360-degree panorama that rivals the overlook at Palisade. The big lake and cliffs stretch out to one side, Wolf and Raven Lakes on another, and the forest wraps around the peak with the Baptism River and Sawmill Creek snaking through the green.

The cliffs are the same rock-hard quality anorthosite that is typical of the inland north shore climbing areas. The Environmental Learning Center has been in existence since 1971 with the Wolf Ridge campus opening in 1988, hosting programs for all ages.

Folks come from all over the Midwest to get outside, connect to the outdoors, and learn about natural sciences and adventure. For some Minnesota climbers (like this guidebook writer!), this was their first rock-climbing experience.

Types of Climbing and Gear

This is also a trad/toprope climbing area only. The climbs are long, with some up to 130 feet high, so you'll want at minimum a 60-meter rope, with a 70 being better. For setting up topropes, bring a lot of anchor material and a fair amount of padding, as the rocks are *sharp*.

A single rack works fine, but a double rack will give you far more options on the longer climbs. Some routes, such as *Gollum's Staircase*, require big pro.

Land Acknowledgment

We acknowledge with respect and gratitude that this climbing area is on the traditional lands of the Anishinabewaki people.

Permits, Local Ethics, and Regulations

This area is private land, owned by Wolf Ridge ELC. The private-property owners request this of climbers:

- When you arrive, you must sign in with the main office, as well as sign a liability waiver. Their updated office hours can always be found on their website, as well as via a phone number where you can check ahead of time the hours of the day you plan on climbing. In spring and fall, call ahead for weekend hours.
- Wolf Ridge staff will not come looking for you if you fail to check out, but please do so as a courtesy.
- Upon check-in, Wolf Ridge will provide updates on access, trails, nesting site closures, or route/area closures due to concurrent Wolf Ridge programming.
- This is the only place on the North Shore that has a strict written rule against using chalk.
- Wolf Ridge retains the right to reserve climbing areas/routes for Wolf Ridge programming needs. Please cooperate with, respect, and yield to Wolf Ridge students and staff.
- Wolf Ridge also requests that climbers head straight to the office from the parking lot, and then straight to the crag without wandering the grounds. Same on the way back. If you wish to hike the trails at Wolf Ridge, please get permission from staff at the office prior to hiking.

- Please respect the natural environment. Stay on established trails, minimize erosion, and do not litter. Practice Leave No Trace ethics.
- Dogs must be leashed at all times, and dog waste must be picked up and disposed of properly.
- All commercial and guiding groups must contact Wolf Ridge to coordinate any climbing programs that are planned on Wolf Ridge property prior to arrival. Such groups must provide Wolf Ridge with a certificate of insurance naming Wolf Ridge as an additionally insured party prior to arrival. Upon arrival, groups must check in at the Wolf Ridge office before heading out to the climbing area.

Wolf Ridge has been and continues to be friendly to climbers; please abide by these rules so we can keep it that way. Wolf Ridge assumes no liability or responsibility for climbers on their property or in the area in general. You are climbing at your own risk. By climbing here, you agree that Wolf Ridge is not liable or responsible for anything that happens to you in this area.

Historically, there have been other cliffs in this area that have been climbed and named. These cliffs are currently on private property, and the current landowners have not granted climbers permission to access their land to climb them.

Getting There and Parking

From SH 61, turn inland on Lake County 6, following signs for Wolf Ridge. Turn on Cranberry Road, follow to the end of the drive, and park in one of the three lots on the left. Please drive slowly on the driveway

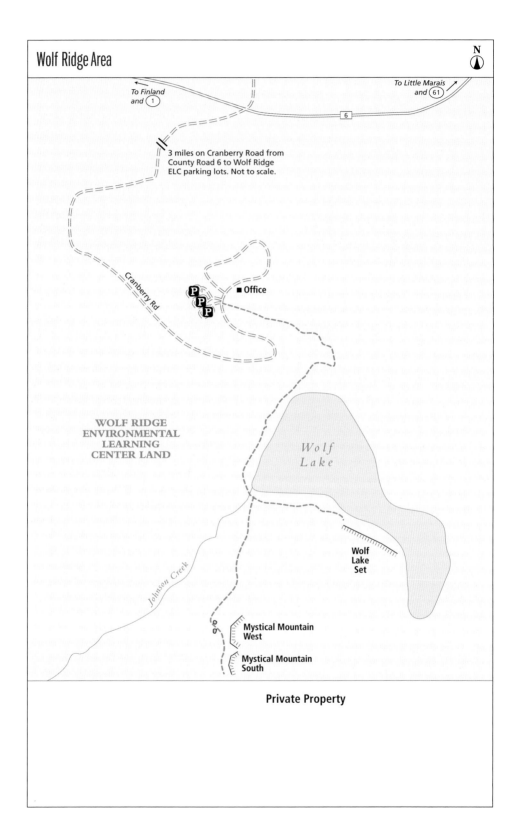

Wolf Ridge Area

N

To Finland and ①

To Little Marais and ⑥①

6

3 miles on Cranberry Road from County Road 6 to Wolf Ridge ELC parking lots. Not to scale.

Cranberry Rd

P P P

■ Office

WOLF RIDGE
ENVIRONMENTAL
LEARNING
CENTER LAND

Wolf Lake

Wolf Lake Set

Johnson Creek

Mystical Mountain West

Mystical Mountain South

Private Property

as there are often a *lot* of young kids on the grounds.

The folks at Wolf Ridge ask that climbers *only* park in the lots and not on the road.

The main office is across the road from the parking lots. Head over there to sign in before hiking to the crag.

Approach

From the main office and the information board, follow signs to the Lake Study Area (take every right-hand turn on gravel trails; avoid grassy ski trails). In a couple of minutes, you'll descend some wooden steps. Pass by the canoe dock and ignore the side trail to your right, continuing to hug the path next to the lake instead. Pass the swimming area and reach the Lake Study Area. Cross the bridge over Johnson Creek.

After you cross over Johnson Creek, you'll either follow the less-maintained trail to the right as it heads toward Mystical Mountain, or go left if you're looking for Wolf Lake. Specific approach instructions for each of those places are told more in depth below.

While you'll see other offshoots of trails throughout the property, Wolf Ridge requests that climbers stick only to the main trail down, the approach trails to the climbs, and the climbing areas, and not wander the property.

Camping and Amenities

Restrooms are located in the Wolf Ridge Main Office.

Camping is prohibited on Wolf Ridge property, including in your car.

The closest campground is the Finland Campground followed by Eckbeck, both on state forest land, or Tettegouche State Park.

Hazards

There's a fair amount of loose rock. Keep an eye out for poison ivy, and know the rock is very abrasive—padding the edges for your rope is a must. Bears are common around here.

Routes Not to Miss

Over the Rainbow (5.7+), Swords of Zanzibar (5.9), Black Gate (5.10a), Jack Be Nimble (5.10a), Cirith Ungol (5.11c)

Wolf Lake Set

As you hike down the trail toward the lake, these are the obvious beautiful cliffs calling out to be climbed right across the water. Head left after crossing over the bridge, then follow the path as it stays near the lakeshore before the lake narrows off. Head up to the cliffs, scrambling over some serious talus through the trees, which may require a little bit of bushwhacking.

The approach gully passes to the right of the main crag (just right of Sixty-Second Crack) and is steep but passable. If you find yourself doing desperate lunges up collapsing dirt gullies, you're in the wrong place. Another approach would be to climb up and left of Mystical Mountain, go over the ridgetop, and find a faint trail above the cliffs.

There is a falcon-nesting box on the cliff. Wolf Ridge staff will inform you if it's occupied and the cliff is closed.

1. Crow Crack (5.9+) An off-width that heads straight up and could quite possibly be sandbagged. **FA:** Steve Mabley and Jim Ronnigen.

2. Crow's Nest Traverse (5.5) Named so because there are usually ravens that actually nest here. Please keep away until mid-June. This traverse is the wide farthest-left escape

Wolf Lake Set

from the crux of *Crow Crack*. **FA:** Steve Mabley and Jim Ronnigen.

3. Caw Caw (5.10b) Ditto on avoiding the ravens. Climb *Crow Crack* until the traverse, but instead of going far left, go a little left and head up the crack that's more on the face. **FA:** Steve Mabley and Jim Ronnigen.

4. Blue-Eyed Delight (5.8) Go up the left side of an overhang to a fist crack and follow that straight up. **FA:** Steve Mabley and Jim Ronnigen.

5. Two Cent's Worth (5.7) Head up the bottom half of *Blue-Eyed Delight*, but instead of taking the hand crack up, duck out to the left instead. **FA:** Steve Mabley and Rick Kollath.

6. Shriek Foot (5.9) ★ Head up the bottom third of *Blue-Eyed Delight*, and before the route moves to the left, head up a crack to the right instead.

7. Slippery Razor Spittoon (5.8) The off-width to the right of the bottom of the *Blue-Eyed* crack. **FA:** Steve Mabley and Jim Ronnigen.

8. Physical Negotiation (5.10c) ★ Head directly up the prow (though you can come in from the right) and through the overhang. **FA:** Jim Blakley.

9. Greasy Gulch (5.7) On the right side of the gully find a crack leading to a left-facing corner. This is the bottom of a handful of routes. **FA:** Steve Mabley and Jim Ronnigen.

10. Puddle Paddler (5.9+) Start below and right of *Greasy Gulch* in a corner leading to vegetation. Not really the best way to access the upper climbs. **FA:** Steve Mabley.

11. Bushwhack Crack (5.7) Climb a crack near some vegetation, to the left of the top of *Greasy Gulch*. **FA:** Steve Mabley and Jim Ronnigen.

12. Up Your Crack (5.9-) ★★ From the broken ledges halfway up the cliff, climb a black corner/face until you reach the overhang. Work up and right, then up the crack to the top. This is the most straight line up from *Greasy Gulch*, and a great climb for this wall. **FA:** Steve Mabley and Jim Ronnigen.

13. Pratt Fraternity (5.6) This is the easiest way to escape the ledge above *Greasy Gulch*; traverse to the right until you find a chimney in the corner to go up. **FA:** Rick Kollath.

14. Loose as a Goose (5.9) ★★ On the southeast face of the West Column, you can see this crack around the corner to the left of the nest box. **FA:** Steve Mabley and Rick Kollath.

The peregrine nest box sits on the face of the column. Birds have nested there more than once; please do not disturb the box.

15. West Column Ramp (5.5) On the right side of the West Column, this feels more like a ramp than the rest of the straight up climbs in the area. **FA:** Jim Ronnigen.

16. Sixty-Second Crack (5.8) ★★ The left wall of the approach gully has a set of disjointed cracks; look up to see them and then climb them. **FA:** Steve Mabley and Rick Kollath.

Mystical Mountain

This is (perhaps surprisingly) one of the tallest crags in the entire state, with some routes reaching 130 feet. You'll want to either lead or do a top-managed system if you have a 60-meter rope here, and rappels with a rope of that length would need to be to an intermediate ledge where you could set up a slingshot toprope or a second rappel station.

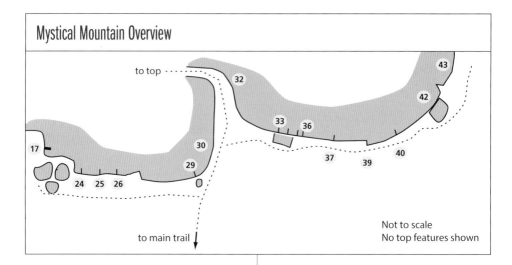

Mystical Mountain Overview

to top ···· ·

32

43

42

33 36

30

17

29

37 39

40

24 25 26

Not to scale
No top features shown

to main trail

Finding the crag: After going over the bridge, take a right on the climber's trail to hike next to a stream. After 100 feet climb a bit to reach a level, dry area. The trail zigs up and left, soon reaching a large, white boulder. Skirt the boulder to the left and head directly uphill on an eroded trail. You will end up at the right end of Mystical Mountain West, beneath *Black Gate* and *Horner's Corner.*

Top access: The cliff is naturally divided into two sections: Mystical Mountain West (the first section encountered on the approach from below) and Mystical Mountain South (up and right of Mystical Mountain West). Access to the top is via a gully between the two sections. This gully is eroding badly, so please tread lightly. Cut left up this root-laced gully that usually has a fixed rope (Class 2–3). This puts you above *Black Gate.* To reach the south section, climb up a few more feet and reach an obvious trail to the right. The south section may also be reached from the far right end of that cliff.

Mystical Mountain West

Setup: The cliff is about 130 feet tall on its left side. Slingshot topropes can be set up on *Jack Be Nimble* and many other routes from midway ledges.

Route 17: Gollum's Stairwell

17

Mystical Mountain West-Left

Walk to the left side of the cliff and stand beneath some blocks. The slanting white corner of *Over the Rainbow* is obvious above.

17. Gollum's Stairwell (5.9) ★★★ Just left around the corner from *Jack Be Nimble* is an impressive off-width, truly unique for the area. **FA:** Steve Mabley and Rick Kollath.

18. Jack Be Nimble (5.10a) ★★★★ The white corner with a roof left of *Over the Rainbow*. Pull the roof (crux) to a ledge and hand cracks above for a climb that requires technique and a dash of endurance. **FA:** Steve Mabley and Rick Kollath.

19. Fractured Fairy Tail (5.6) ★★ Climb the jaggedy crack/chimney past a small cedar. Finish on the hand crack of *Jack Be Nimble*, with a possibility for a 5.7 variation if you head straight up. The straight-up option is better if on a top belay. **FA:** Dan Koch.

20. Over the Rainbow (5.7+) ★★★ The white, left-facing corner. Lieback the corner, then climb up and right in a thin crack. Continue up into an A-shaped alcove in the roof. Be nice to the cedars growing in the crack. **FA:** Rick Kollath.

21. Claw Marks of the Cave Bear (5.10d) ★ Climb on the white face to the right of

Mystical Mountain West-Center

Rainbow, up and over the roof, move to the right then pull the last little roof onto the face between the cracks. **FA:** Rick Kollath.

22. Hobbit's Demise

(5.10b) ★★ Start up the large, vegetated, left-facing corner. Cut left up a steep ramp/ corner with black rock. Traverse right to the crack right of the *Over the Rainbow* finish. **FA:** Rick Kollath.

23. Walking Toto (5.7) Start on the ledge, you'll head up the crack to the right of the *Hobbit's Demise* finish, ending on face at the top. **FA:** Brian Gitar.

The next five routes are found on the black wall to the left of the low roof.

24. Danse Macabre (5.11d) ★ Fifteen feet right of the left edge of the black face is a small, right-facing corner that morphs into a crack. It ends on the midway ledge. **FA:** Jim Blakley.

25. Mephisto Waltz (5.11c) ★★ Twenty feet right of *Danse Macabre* is a thin seam with a pocket about 8 feet above the sloping ledge with a triangle at the base. Head up the left side of the triangle. Good luck finding tiny jams for your fingers. **FA:** Jim Blakley and Steve Mabley.

26. Nymphiad (5.11a) ★ Fourteen feet right of *Mephisto Waltz* is a right-facing corner with a thin seam and a large talus block at its base. Climb up past a bush to the ledge, then continue up the face for the last 30 feet with no pro. **FA:** Rick Kollath.

Paige Orcutt on *Black Gate* (5.10a)

27. Humpty Dumpty (5.7) No topo. The right side of the black wall degenerates into an ugly, broken corner system. This route starts at the left end of the overhang that is 7 feet above the ground. Often wet and covered in lichen. **FA:** Steve Mabley and Jim Ronnigen.

28. Trickster (5.8) At the right end of the overhang is a short and sweet 25-foot crack, great for learning trad. **FA:** Steve Mabley and Jim Ronnigen.

29. Black Gate (5.10a) ★★★ Twelve feet right of the overhang is a thin crack, just left of a large talus block. Up the crack, traverse slightly left to a finger crack, then enjoy the crux at the top. See if you can find some no-hands rests. **FA:** Steve Mabley.

30. Horner's Corner (5.5) ★ On the right edge of the main face is a low-angle crack with a ledgey area and a cedar tree at its base. Up this crack to a hanging dihedral. **FA:** Steve Mabley and Rick Kollath.

31. Noah's Arc (5.5) ★ Use the same start as *Horner's Corner*. At the first cedar ledge,

veer left and away to follow an arcing and enjoyable alternative to *Horner's Corner*. The two routes meet to become one again as the climb gets abruptly vertical before easing at the top. **FA:** Peter Smerud.

Mystical Mountain South

From the bottom of the access gully, walk right past a block forming a ledge (*Cirith Ungol*, etc.). The trail descends along the base of the rock, around a corner, and bends right (near *Mother Goose*) into a pretty grove of cedars forming a nice base area, especially for those with kids.

Setup: From the top of the access gully, work up and right to a defined trail and follow it to the South section. In the vicinity of *Oz Before the Wizard*, the cliff is about 130 feet tall, making slingshot topropes problematic. The difficult cracks starting from the vegetated ledge can be set up from a lower ledge, reached by rappel.

32. Surrender Dorothy (5.11c) ★ No topo. Just about where you turn left to climb up the root-laced approach gully, look right. A small right-facing corner leads to a seam. **FA:** Rick Kollath.

The next two routes begin from a large, vegetated, but pleasant ledge about 15 feet above the ground.

Mystical Mountain West-Right

Mystical Mountain South-Left

Mystical Mountain South-Center

33. The Lair of Shelob (5.12a) ★ The left crack hits a horizontal crack 20 feet up, where you'll traverse right to join the top of *Cirith Ungol*. **FA:** Steve Mabley and Jim Blakley.

34. Cirith Ungol (5.11c) ★★★ The continuous crack in the middle of the face that rises from the ledge. **FA:** Steve Mabley and Jim Blakley.

35. Swords of Zanzibar (5.9) ★★ Walk down and right around the block forming the ledge mentioned in *Cirith Ungol*. Just right of this block you'll find two cracks—this is the left crack with a hollow rock at shoulder height. You can also start this route from the ledge. **FA:** Steve Mabley and Rick Kollath.

36. Arrows and Slings (5.11b) ★★ The right-hand crack; the crux is near the top where the rock slopes. You'll need extremely long anchor-setup material.

37. Three Hacks at a Crack (5.11c) ★★ About 30 feet right of *Swords of Zanzibar* is a white area of rock. A thin crack starts 10 feet right of a small, right-facing corner. After intersecting a horizontal crack about 12 feet up, it curves to the right and widens occasionally (crux). Cut left up another crack (5.9) or right (5.7-) to reach the top. **FA:** Dave Pagel.

38. Oz Before the Wizard (5.7) ★★ No topo. Walk past *Three Hacks* and around a corner. Start across from a large birch, at cracks directly below a tall pine 30 feet up. Jam the cracks (5.7) to the pine, ascend a recess to a small ledge, then follow a neat, low-angle finger crack

(5.7-) to the top. A bit more of an adventure climb. **FA:** Rick Kollath.

39. Mother Goose (5.5) ⋆
Twenty feet right of *Oz Before the Wizard*, a left-facing corner/chimney leads to the right end of the pine ledge. Continue up slabs and corners to the top. The run-out on the top is huge and not for the faint of heart.

Continue right past *Mother Goose* for about 30 feet to a flat area with a large boulder leaning against the wall.

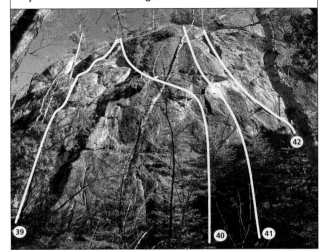

Mystical Mountain South-Right

40. Sisyphus (5.7) ⋆⋆ About 30 feet right of *Mother Goose*, climb up a thin crack, eventually traversing really far left to a tree and flake. Do not climb the loose flakes directly below the ledge; climb up, then traverse left, where you'll meet the top of *Mother Goose*. **FA:** Steve Mabley and Jim Blakley.

41. Ode to a Newt (5.8) The face left of *Old Number Nine*.

42. Old Number Nine (5.7) ⋆⋆⋆⋆ A great route for a new trad leader, this one is super-fun and well protected. A large boulder leans against the wall. Climb the clean corner to the dead pine, then zip to the top. **FA:** Rick Kollath and Dan Koch.

43. The Desolation of Smaug (5.11) No topo. Right of the boulder is a short, right-facing corner. Turn the roof to the right and head up the face, finishing right of the crack. **FA:** Dave Pagel.

44. Advice from a Caterpillar (5.9) No topo. Stay right of *The Desolation of Smaug*, finishing on the 5.9 finger crack. **FA:** Dave Pagel.

Liz Johnson on *Mother Goose* (5.5)

Haley Rasmussen on *Banana Stand* (5.8)

SAWMILL CREEK DOME AND SECTION 13

Tucked back from the lake, these two areas have stellar climbs that tower on domes over well-known bouldering with biting anorthosite rock. Routes are 60 feet long, encompassing the full gambit of slab, crack, and corner climbing on cliffs that test your head game. The gear is good, the low amount of traffic makes it better, and the climbs are incredible. If you want to pack in a full weekend of hard roped climbing and bouldering when the popular crags are stuffed with people, come here.

Types of Climbing and Gear

Trad and TR. The anorthosite rock protects well with a single rack of gear, though bring more to sew things up or to have extra pieces to build anchors. A 60-meter rope works fine. Padding the edge will save rope wear and tear. Some anchors, especially at Sawmill Creek Dome, require fairly long anchor material.

Land Acknowledgment

We acknowledge with respect and gratitude that this climbing area is on the traditional lands of the Anishinabewaki people.

Permits, Local Ethics, and Regulations

Both areas are on county land and require no permits or parking passes.

While there are no leash regulations, keep dogs under control and clean up after them.

Getting There and Parking

Parking lot GPS coordinates: N47.411' / W91.154'

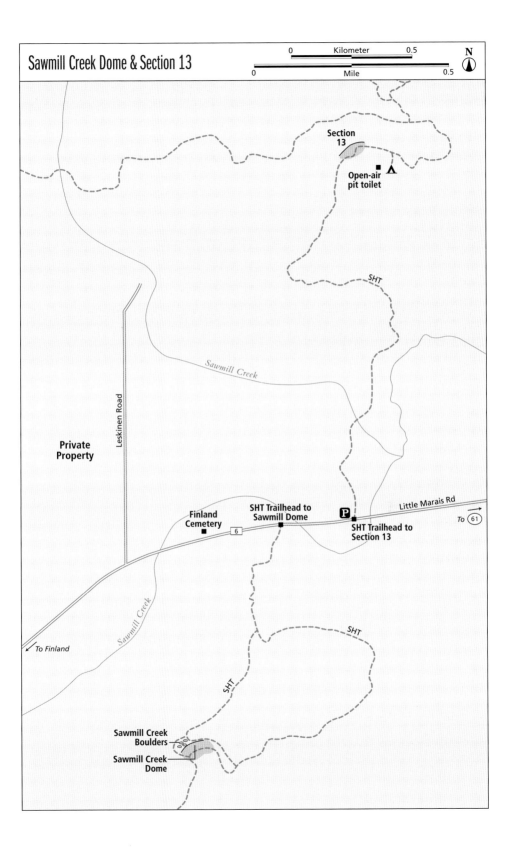

Sawmill Creek Dome & Section 13

0   Kilometer   0.5
0   Mile   0.5

N

Section 13

Open-air pit toilet

SHT

Sawmill Creek

Leskinen Road

Private Property

Finland Cemetery

SHT Trailhead to Sawmill Dome

6

SHT Trailhead to Section 13

Little Marais Rd

To 61

Sawmill Creek

To Finland

SHT

SHT

Sawmill Creek Boulders

Sawmill Creek Dome

Park at the same lot for both crags. Turn inland from MN 61 up Lake County Road 6 for 1.1 miles to the big new Superior Hiking Trail parking lot. The trail heading north out of the parking lot brings you to Section 13; 0.3 mile west on the road, you'll find the Superior Hiking Trail (SHT) that heads south into the woods toward Sawmill Dome.

Camping and Amenities

There currently aren't any restrooms at the trailhead. Stop in the town of Finland before you head this way, or follow LNT principles if you have to go while climbing.

For easy camping, check out Tettegouche State Park or the state forest campgrounds on MN 1 (Eckbeck) and on Lake County Road 6 in Finland.

If you want to camp near Section 13, there's a designated Superior Hiking Trail campsite less than 100 feet past the crag along the trail. You'll have to hike all of your camping gear in, but there's a backcountry toilet, tent pads, and a campfire ring for a great multiday setup.

Hazards

There is the potential for loose rock around this area.

You're farther into the woods up here—don't be surprised if you see a bear or a moose. Give them their space.

These areas are on county land where deer and grouse hunting is popular, so wearing orange during hunting season is a great idea.

Sawmill Creek Dome

Incredible views of the forest will take your breath away as much as the biting rock as you crack climb here. This is a great place to start

your day or weekend, as the moderates are varied and truly enjoyable. Don't forget to wave "hello" to the boulderers below you.

Approach

Trail start GPS coordinates: N47.40773' / W91.15972'

From the parking lot, hike west along the road for 0.3 mile (near the top of a small rise) and turn left (south) onto the trail. Gain about 250 vertical feet, descend steeply, then climb to a ridgeline with beautiful views and a small cliff below. The trail then bends around to the base of the summit dome, where the Picnic Rock spur trail branches right.

Trail split GPS coordinates: N47.40288' / W91.10608'

Top access: Continue on the SHT as it climbs steeply to the top, then hike to a terraced rock overlook with a few large and sparse pines. You are now above *Birch Flakes*.

Base access: Turn right and follow the Picnic Rock spur trail. The trail has a level start and is well maintained. After passing an overhanging boulder, the trail becomes less obvious, goes uphill, and then descends through an eroded section to flatter ground at the base of the dome. You'll see a lot of the bouldering at the bottom of the crag, as well as some wild boulderers that may have emerged from their winter crash-pad stashing caves. You can recognize them by the beanies on their heads, no matter the air temperature. Don't disturb them. Weave through boulders and continue around the dome before turning left and bushwhacking toward the dome to find the obvious beautiful crack of *Birch Flakes*, which is a great landmark to find the rest of the climbs.

The top or bottom *can* also be reached via the gully next to *Birch Flakes* (it's pretty

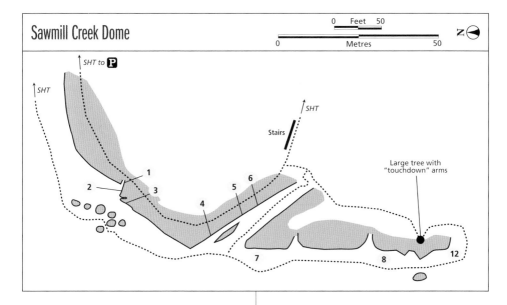

Sawmill Creek Dome

scrambly and steep Class 4) or by hiking up around the far end past *Bubble Up*.

Routes Not to Miss

Banana Stand (5.8), Birch Flakes (5.9), A Farewell to Arms (5.11b)

Northeast Section

A few routes are rumored to exist left of those documented. Because of the minimal information for route finding them, they have been omitted here. The following routes start to the left of *Birch Flakes*.

1. No Rest for the Wicked (5.11c) The corner immediately left of *Blueberry Jam*. Follow the corner all the way to the top (if it's not wet). **FA:** Steve Mabley and Jim Blakley.

2. Blueberry Jam (5.8) A beautiful fist crack in a streaked face on the right side of a north-facing wall. The upper half gently trends left. **FA:** Steve Mabley and Jim Blakley.

Sawmill Creek Dome-Northeast

Sawmill-Central Top

AERIAL PHOTO: BRENDA PIEKARSKI

3. Hummock, Tussock, Stomach (5.8) No topo. Around the corner right of *Blueberry Jam*, go farther right past a Class 4 gully to find a crack that gets thinner the higher you go before a runout face to the top.

Central Section

4. Birch Flakes (5.9) ★★★★ A sustained and beautiful climb to the right of an obvious two-step roof with a birch tree halfway up the route. A great lead, start at the base of a small ridge of rock at the bottom of the descent gully. The crux is at the bottom with small fingers, then easy cruising past the tree to the top.

Sawmill Creek Dome-Central

AERIAL PHOTO: BRENDA PIEKARSKI

Bring mostly finger-sized cams. **FA:** Steve Mabley and Jim Blakley.

5. The Wonderful World of Huecos

(5.9+) ★★★ To the right of *Birch Flakes*, look for the ledge beginning *Julie Gets Flowers*, traverse left and up, then head right and up. Great movement, but wanders a lot and the easiest way up isn't immediately obvious (plus the rock bites). **FA:** Rick Kollath.

6. Julie Gets Flowers (5.9-) ★★ Start

from a ledge 30 feet above the bottom of the gully, follow the crack on the right as it heads up. **FA:** Rick Kollath.

7. Banana Stand (5.8) ★★ To the right

of the access gully, locate a huge roof for this really fun and varied route. Start by climbing up the inside left corner to the roof, then turn the roof in that corner for the crux. Enjoy easier face climbing up the slab to the top, complete with incredible views and not much protection. **FA:** Steve Mabley and Jim Blakley.

West Section

If this is your first visit to these climbs, it may be easier to approach from below (described at the beginning of the Sawmill Creek Dome section). You can scope out the climbs and then reach the top via the gully by *Birch Flakes* or by traversing right and up the SHT to the top.

To approach these climbs from above, hike to the top of *Birch Flakes*. Climb up a few feet on the trail and turn right at a birch with a trail marker, just before some steps. Instead of descending in the gully by *Birch Flakes*, stay left, paralleling the cliff edge, then drop down a few feet and note an overlook on your right. There are no routes there. Continue until you find yourself standing on a ledge with a pine tree that appears to have its arms raised to signal a

Paige Orcutt on *Birch Flakes* (5.9)

touchdown. Below is another ledge, which forms the top of the following climbs. The large V-cleft is the top of *Micropedimorph*. Reach the base by continuing in the same direction and down, or by rappelling.

8. A Farewell to Arms (5.11b) ★★★★ Want

to feel like Thor? Lead this beast. To the left of an 8-foot-high block are two shallow corners. Climb the right one to the saplings and head for the crack/flake in the roof left of *Micropedimorph*. At the roof take three deep breaths, say a prayer to the climbing gods, and go for it. **FA:** Steve Mabley and Jim Blakley.

Sawmill-West Top

AERIAL PHOTO: BRENDA PIEKARSKI

Sawmill Creek Dome-West

AERIAL PHOTO: BRENDA PIEKARSKI

9. Micropedimorph (5.8) ★ If toproping, go straight up the black streak to a big notch in the roof. To lead this (not recommended), start as for *A Farewell to Arms* and traverse a long way right to the notch instead of heading up into the *Farewell* roof. **FA:** Steve Mabley.

10. Once in a While (5.11d) ★★ Right of *Micropedimorph*, locate the last larger roof crack before the roof tapers off. Start in a lichen-covered seam a few feet right of the roof crack for a boulder problem–type crux, then find easier terrain as you head up. At the roof, follow the crack to the left. **FA:** Jim Blakley.

11. That Hideous Strength (5.11c) ★ The lower overhang is interrupted by a prow of sorts 8 feet right of *Once in a While*. Get the juglet on top of this, then fire up and slightly right to the steep, dark face (just left of the final crack on *Bubble Up*) for technical face climbing that doesn't let up. This route and *Bubble Up* can be toproped from the same setup.

12. Bubble Up (5.9) ★★ At the right end of the lower overhangs, slightly around the corner, you'll find a block the size of a twelve-pack about 6 feet up. Grunt up onto this, then forge straight up (or slightly right) to a serrated crack near the top. **Setup:** In a notch just right of a large birch at the left end of the ledge. **FA:** Pete Holler and Roy McDonald.

Section 13

Section 13 offers some incredible inland views, so don't forget to look behind you (if you can!) midroute. The routes are shorter and some are often damp or wet, but this is possibly one of the best places on the shore to lead easier crack climbs without the commitment of Palisade Head. The singularly unique *We Don't Need No Steenkin' Ledges* is great sustained slab training for *Snake Dike* on Yosemite's Half Dome.

Approach

Locate the trail as it exits the SHT parking lot going north. This 1.3-mile hike is uphill with a few places to stop and appreciate the view. At the top there are two blue blazes painted on the rock and a sign on a tree showing a right turn on the trail. Climbers should turn left toward the open and expansive overlook. Allow 30 to 45 minutes for the approach, depending on your cardio fitness. If you do any significant downhill, or see a campsite, you've gone too far.

Many of the routes start from a narrow ledge about 60 feet below the top of the cliff, reached by rappel. Starting from the very bottom is possible, but it's dirty and scrambly and not recommended. To belay from the ledge, take a couple of 2- to 3-inch cams for anchors as the trees are not reliable, or fix a line down. Belaying from above is recommended for toproping.

Section 13 Top

AERIAL PHOTO: BRENDA PIEKARSKI

Claire Miller on *The Path of Fierce Black Wolves* (5.10a)

Routes Not to Miss

We Don't Need No Steenkin' Ledges (5.8–5.10), Arrowhead Direct (5.9), Rubble Trouble Direct (5.9), Digit Damage (5.11a)

1. Junk Culture (5.8) ★★ Start at a clear ledge that follows the crack as it starts hand-sized then gets smaller (going to the bottom means being lowered way climber's left, and a fall will have a pendulum swing). Once past the tree halfway up, it gets easier with multiple ledges and good feet. The crux will probably be cleaning the moss out of the crack and getting around the tree. **FA:** Charles Bernick and Rick Kollath.

2. Reading Braille (5.11b) ★★★ Sustained fun face climbing—a great route that is often overlooked. Follow a thin crack until it trends right. Stay on the face at the top for crimps and good feet. Avoid the gully on the right.

3. The Path of Fierce Black Wolves (5.10a) ★★ Follow the obvious dike showing a water line. The little knobs sprinkled on the route are fun. The bottom ledge isn't great, and if it has recently rained, this climb is probably wet. **FA:** Rick Kollath.

4. In Limbo (5.10d) ★★★ To the right of the water dike, follow up the left side of a flake, then head on to some cool face-climbing shenanigans, staying right of *Fierce Black Wolves*.

5. In the Valley (5.10d) ★★★ Climb the right side of the flake, then traverse right to a thin crack. **FA:** Steve Mankenberg.

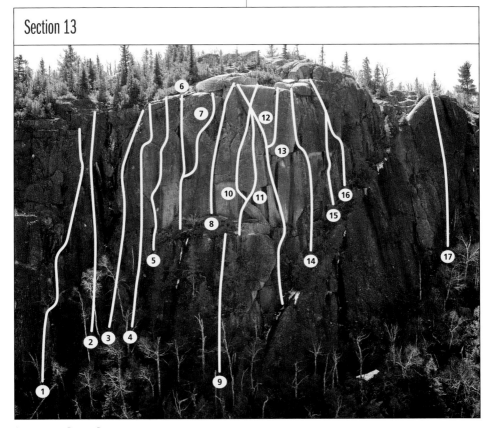

Section 13

AERIAL PHOTO: BRENDA PIEKARSKI

Hillary Waters on *Rubble Trouble Direct* (5.9)

There are also nice pockets and features outside of the crack. Set an anchor at the top of the *Rubble Trouble* ramp to climb *Equinox* and *Arrowhead Left* (but not *Rubble Trouble*). **FA:** Jim Blakley.

9. Lower Slab (5.8) ★ If you decide to build an anchor at the ledge just below the start of the *Arrowhead* routes and then lower again, you'll find this slab. There's no really good ledge to start this climb, once lowered, and it's really only been done on TR.

10. Arrowhead Left (5.8-) ★ Gain the top of the leaning block under the arrowhead-shaped flake and following a left-facing corner. A nice clean crack with good gear. At the top follow the ramp left (the top of *Rubble Trouble*) or the thin crack straight up. **FA:** Jim Blakley.

6. Macho Pitchu (5.9+) ★★ A shallow, yellowish corner is the start of this route and the next. After the corner head up the dihedral before following the easiest path at the top. **FA:** Steve Mabley.

7. Brenda's Last Fling (5.10c) ★★ Begin in the same yellow shallow corner as *Macho Pitchu* before heading right at the dihedral and through some technical bits as the route trends right toward the top. **FA:** Dave Pagel.

8. Equinox (5.10a) ★★★★ This is full-value amazing 5.10 crack climbing. About 20 feet left of *Arrowhead Left* is an obvious sloping finger/hand crack starting on the ledge. The crux is getting off the ledge before enjoying glorious hand jams until it squeezes down to fingers and tips right up at the top.

11. Arrowhead Direct (5.9) ★★★ Head up to the point on the arrowhead, then make the tough moves to get from the ramp onto the main face. The friction is delightful—head straight up on pockets and small knobs that you just have to trust for the final 30 feet. **FA:** Rick Kollath.

12. Rubble Trouble (5.7) ★★ Right of the leaning block is a tall, sharp pillar. Gain the top via the left for a dihedral and hand crack (5.6) or right for some off-width fun (5.8), then follow the left-trending corner to a short, thin crack (the top of *Arrowhead Left*), or up the ramp. Use a full 70-meter rope to get to the base, where you'll do some Class 5 scrambling to get to the bottom of the pillar to lead. **FA:** Rick Kollath.

13. Rubble Trouble Direct

(5.9) ★★★★ A stellar crack that is fantastic for the grade and especially glorious for new crack climbers. The exposure is excellent and the gear is good. Head up the dihedral corner for the bottom of *Rubble Trouble*, then up right through a slightly overhanging crux into the finger crack before it eases into hand-size at the top on lower-angled terrain. **FA:** Steve Mabley.

14. Digit Damage (5.11a)

★★★★ Incredible technical climbing. Start on the massive ledge in the middle of the wall and work up the face through an overhang. Keep to the left as you head up a second crack to the top. Enjoy the sequences and weight shifts that make this climb a gem. If you lead, it's a blind gear placement at the crux. **FA:** Dave Pagel.

15. Minas Tirith (5.11b) ★★ Start about 6 feet left of *Seam's Hard* on some fun features before joining with it about 50 feet up. Finish directly up the large block. **FA:** Sean Ferrell.

16. Seam's Hard (5.11b) ★★ Head climber's right of *Digit Damage* to find a small dihedral to yet another thin crack, which is the top for this climb and *Minas Tirith*. **FA:** Dave Pagel.

Christine Waters on *We Don't Need No Steenkin' Ledges* (5.8–5.10)

17. We Don't Need No Steenkin' Ledges

(5.8–5.10) ★★★★ This incredible slab is one of the best in Minnesota, and the sharp rock is reassuring. Just like *Sugar Plump Faeries* at Shovel Point, the difficulty changes depending on where you climb. At the bottom, start under a mini roof about 10 feet off the ground. Follow a series of cracks and faults with lots of holds before the slab opens up in all of its glory with indents, divots, and dishy ledges. Pure delight.

Jessica Arnold on *Group Project* (5.7)

CARLTON PEAK

At 900 feet above the lake, Carlton Peak is the highest point on the North Shore, and the anorthosite dome offers incredible views of Lake Superior and the surrounding forests. While it doesn't have quite the reputation of the cliffs right along Lake Superior, it's not to be overlooked. The climbing here is just a little more adventurous, and it's a great place for newer climbers to practice setting anchors. Located not far inland from the lake, Carlton Peak is also a great backup to climb when Palisade Head or Shovel Point have bad weather, as the lake effect means Carlton often has its own microclimate and can be sunny when the shore itself is rainy or foggy.

Originally owned by the 3M Corporation and bought by the Nature Conservancy, Carlton has been climbed for well over fifty years, with rumors that locals watched the moon landing in 1969 before driving out to climb at Carlton. It's now part of the Temperance River State Park and still boasts the old foundations from the fire tower at the summit. A nearby quarry offers potential for future climbing, and ambitious locals are currently exploring that potential with the appropriate landowners.

Types of Climbing and Gear

The routes here are anywhere from 60 to 80 feet tall and are face, crack, and corners in the rough anorthosite facing mostly west and southwest. A standard single rack works great.

The ratings showcase that this area was established a while before others in Minnesota. A 5.6 might feel just a little bit harder than expected.

Bring a lot of long anchor line and padding for toproping. You'll be able to use trees as natural anchors, but they are sometimes sparse and quite a way back from the tops of the climbs.

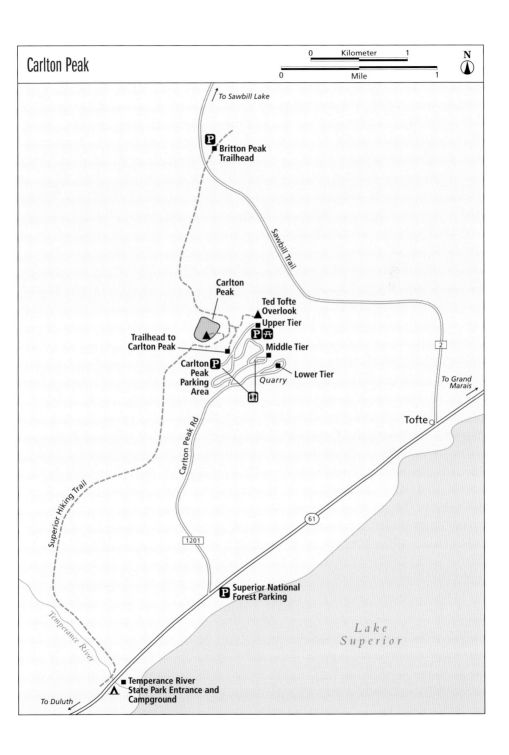

Carlton Peak

0 Kilometer 1
0 Mile 1

N

To Sawbill Lake

Britton Peak
Trailhead

Sawbill Trail

Carlton
Peak

Ted Tofte
Overlook
Upper Tier

Trailhead to
Carlton Peak

Middle Tier

Carlton
Peak
Parking
Area

Lower Tier

Quarry

Carlton Peak Rd

2

To Grand
Marais

Tofte

Superior Hiking Trail

61

1201

Superior National
Forest Parking

Lake
Superior

Temperance River

Temperance River
State Park Entrance and
Campground

To Duluth

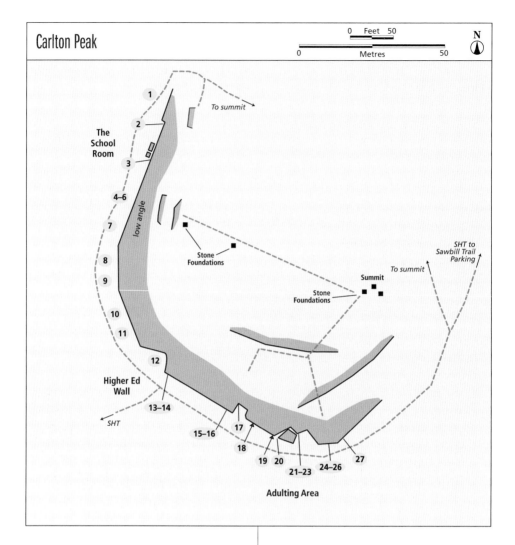

Carlton Peak

0 Feet 50
0 Metres 50
N

1
2
The School Room
3
To summit
4–6
7
low angle
Stone Foundations
8
9
10
11
12
Higher Ed Wall
13–14
SHT
15–16
17
18
19 20
21–23
24–26
27
Adulting Area
Stone Foundations
Summit
To summit
SHT to Sawbill Trail Parking

Land Acknowledgment

We acknowledge with respect and gratitude that this climbing area is on the traditional lands of the Anishinabewaki people.

Permits, Local Ethics, and Regulations

A Minnesota state park vehicle permit is required at the trailhead, as is a (free) state park climbing permit. There's a self-service kiosk for a climbing permit at the Carlton Peak parking area, where you can obtain

your yearly pass. Otherwise you can visit the Temperance River State Park Visitor Center (just south of Tofte, directly off 61) to get it.

Dogs must be kept under control and on a leash no longer than 6 feet, and you must clean up after them.

Getting There and Parking

There are two different parking lots available depending on how long you want the approach hike to be and the ground clearance of your vehicle.

GPS for Britton Peak Trailhead parking: N47 35.923' / W90 51.734'

If you do not have a high-clearance vehicle, this is the safer, but longer, option. Drive up to Tofte and turn north on Cook County Road 2 up the Sawbill Trail, following signs for Britton Peak parking lot, about 2.6 miles up the road. Use the lot—don't park on the road. Once parked, follow the Superior Hiking Trail across the road as it starts on boardwalks and follow signs toward Carlton Peak. This approach takes about 30 to 40 minutes and trends uphill.

GPS for Carlton Peak parking area: N47.5822' / W90.8579'

The second approach is a tad more precarious, though it's gotten better in recent years. The road can and has been done in low-clearance vehicles, but it's not recommended, especially after a big rain. Heading north on MN 61, cross over the Temperance River bridge, continue for 0.8 mile, and turn left onto FR 1201 (gravel), which is opposite the Superior National Forest sign. Head inland toward Carlton Peak for 2.7 miles, passing some turns and trails and some schwoops in the road before reaching the small Carlton Peak parking area. There will be a trailhead for the Superior Hiking Trail and a self-registering climbing permit kiosk.

Approach

From the Britton Peak Trailhead parking lot, take the Superior Hiking Trail (SHT) across the road, along boardwalks, and follow the signs for Carlton Peak. You'll pass the Ted Tofte spur trail on your left near the end of the hike. Continue along the base past the intersection with the summit trail and to the base of the route *Older than Dirt*. Follow the climber's trail to the left to find the rest of the climbs.

If approaching from the Carlton Peak parking area, hike up the well-marked Superior Hiking Trail to the base of Carlton Peak near routes 25 to 27.

To get to the summit for setting up topropes, hike to the register box at the high point of the SHT, and take the summit trail uphill, instead of following the main SHT. Anything other than easy hiking means you've lost the trail. You're on top when you reach the stone foundation of the former fire tower.

Approach and setup suggestions are given for many routes, but they are not always obvious because the top is rounded and has many repetitive features.

Camping and Amenities

The Carlton Peak parking area has a restroom.

The Temperance River Campground is nearby and does not require reservations. Do not park overnight or camp in the quarry next to Carlton. The nearby towns of Tofte and Shroeder are only a mile or two away and offer food, coffee, amenities, and even a small grocery store.

Hazards

Be wary of the sharp rock, as it likes to chew on your ropes and your hands.

This is one of the places in the state where bear encounters are more common. Hunters are also in these woods in the fall, so wear bright clothing during hunting season.

Routes Not to Miss

Schoolhouse Rock (5.6), Citation Needed (5.8), Protractor (5.10d), Setting the Curve (5.10d)

Note: In all previous printed guidebooks for this area, there are no FAs listed because Carlton has been climbed for a long time with no real documentation—the history is simply word of mouth. Previous guidebook authors for the area simply numbered the routes, and those numbers became the route names. In the years since, new routes have been added and other routes have disappeared due to rockfall or have been combined, making the numbering confusing. To help alleviate the confusion, new route names are being introduced along with the old route numbers for reference.

The School Room (aka West Face)

The School Room is a great place for beginners and young climbers, both in types of climbs and the open space below for parties to camp out for the day. While some of the most obvious lines are described below, a lot of these routes could have multiple variations depending on where you begin the route. Have fun thinking up new variations of these climbs!

Top access from the summit: Take the right-hand approach and walk about 160 feet to the second fire tower foundation pier (covered in orange lichen). Below and to your right is a ledge with a large dead pine and a large living pine, along with some smaller pines. *Schoolhouse Rock* is directly below the living pine. You can also reach this ledge by continuing up from the setup ledge for *Teacher's Pet* and *Conjunction Junction*.

Teacher's Pet through *Schoolhouse Rock* are found on the slab, split by cracks. This can be a good place to learn to lead if the anchors are preset. A big open black slab that has three distinct black streaks at the top is between *Protractor* and *Recess*.

The School Room-Left

Top access from the bottom: Walk left of *Teacher's Pet* to a 20-foot-wide, completely vegetated gully. Hike up the gully, then cut back right on slabs and dirt (Class 2++) to a bit of a ledge with a tree for your setup.

1. Teacher's Pet (aka #1, 5.6) ★★ No topo. Thirty feet left of *Conjunction Junction* is a thin crack that starts about 4 feet off the ground, just left of a sloping ledge. A well-protected, fun lead.

2. Conjunction Junction (aka #2, 5.5) ★★ Look for the big white patch of rock under a roof. The corner leading up the left side of that roof is the top of this route, with the start being 30 feet left of *Protractor*. Climb this to the right end of a ledge.

3. Protractor (aka #3, 5.10d) ★★★ The right side of the roof shared with *Conjunction Junction*. To start, find a thin crack up to the roof. Great face climbing tests your footwork on knobs with poor pro for the first 20 feet or so. Take your pick of which crack to follow and pull the roof around the big flake for a bouldery finish.

4. Recess (aka #4, 5.7) The bottom of this mushy crack follows it straight up. The jams aren't there, so you'll use more slab technique for the tougher bottom of the route before entering a great crack at the roof.

5. Late Assignment (aka #5, 5.6) The crack to the right of *Recess* heads up the face with the option for crack holds. Head for the right side of the overhang. Pull through the overhang, or exit left on the roof for *Recess* instead. Usually mossy and dirty.

6. Schoolhouse Rock (aka #6, 5.6) ★★★ Just right of *Late Assignment*. This is a great route

for new trad leaders. Start up the pleasant crack and zigzag at the tree, going right to the crack in the middle of the face. Work up to the right-facing corner. The last 10 feet is a little heady and exposed, but with a big hand crack and jugs before finishing at the cedar tree.

7. Tricams Are the Way (5.3) No topo. About 30 feet right of *Schoolhouse Rock*, look for where the rock dips into a V. It starts on the little foot slope that moves down to the right and heads straight up toward a crack before topping out on the right side of the little overhang. This is a great route for newer climbers and truly has a lot of variations depending on where the climber climbs in that V.

8. Cheating (aka #7, 5.3) Head up and follow a gently curving flake.

9. Detention (aka #8, 5.6) ★ Find a dark recess with a 5-by-2-foot block 8 feet up. Climb the block and continue up in the hand crack, aiming toward a tree at the top. Often wet.

The School Room–Right and Higher Ed Wall Left

Higher Ed Wall (aka South Buttress)

The climbs on the Higher Ed Wall are just around the corner from *Detention*'s dark recess. To the right of *Group Project*, the climber's trail meets up with the Superior Hiking Trail as it ascends to follow the base of the cliff.

Top access: If you are okay with a little Class 5 scrambling, head up the ledges for *Midterm* to the right of *Citation Needed*. If you take the summit trail at the top of the SHT and are looking for these routes to the left, the routes *All-Nighter* to *Publish or Perish* may require a rappel to a lower ledge (take some gear as the trees aren't trustworthy).

10. All-Nighter (aka #9, 5.10c) ★ This crack starts under a small roof, heads up, then follows the left side of the roof before heading straight to the top.

11. Setting the Curve (aka #10, 5.10d) ★★ Six feet right of *All-Nighter* is a thin seam. Climb 5 feet, then move left and up at your first chance to end in an easier crack heading to the top.

The wall to the left around the arête from *Citation Needed* is home to routes 12 through 15.

12. Group Project (aka #11, 5.7) Find a dirt alcove with several downed trees. There's been some recent rockfall in here, so be wary. Follow the crack that heads straight toward a tree. Get around the tree, either going right to navigate the overhang (harder with the recent rockfall; alpine draws recommended) or stay in the alcove and head straight up for the safest path.

Higher Ed Wall-Left

13. Publish or Perish (aka #12, 5.10a) ★★★ Start up the left-leaning crack and pull left through a pocketed face, following the crack as it bulges to the right before heading into the hand crack through the roof. Setup: At the right end of a line of junipers about 30 feet right of *Citation Needed*.

14. Plagiarism (aka #13, 5.10d) ★★★ A nifty little route. Forage to get to a small left-facing corner, then go up a left- and then right-leaning crack toward a V-groove that lacks all the right holds and is covered in lichen. Setup: Over the edge at the left end of a line of junipers about 30 feet right of *Citation Needed*.

15. Office Hours (aka #14, 5.10d) Start left of *Cram* on the main wall instead of on the flake, then move right to join that route once you reach the last corner section.

16. Cram (aka #15, 5.11c) ★★ Find a pointed flake on the main wall. Take the thin crack on the face and then get into the left-facing corner above. **Variation:** For the bottom of the route, climb an incredible hand crack around the right side of the pointed flake until you're standing on top of the flake and take the thin crack from there (5.7).

The large, right-facing corner crack of *Citation Needed* starts from a ledge about 12 feet off the ground.

Katie Berg on the variation start of *Cram* (5.7)

17. Citation Needed (aka #16, 5.8) ★★★ A gem at Carlton. The major right-facing corner heads up over a little bulge before excellent finger locks to an overhang (watch for loose stuff). **Variation** (5.9) Go up the thin crack on the left wall about two-thirds of the way up, exiting left at the top. For a TR setup, look for a small corner with trees, just left of a large, downsloping slab with a tree ledge just below and to the right of the slab.

Higher Ed Wall-Center

Higher Ed Wall-Right

18. Midterm (aka #17, 5.6) Fifteen feet right of *Citation Needed* is a crack rising from the ledge. Get up on that ledge, and then follow the crack before it turns into a ramp heading up to the right.

19. Final (aka #18, 5.10c) ★ Just left of the chimney formed by the large block is a pointed talus block. Climb up, staying right of the lower trees, to a stance just left of a tree. Move up and left to a small seam.

Adulting Area (aka South Face)

This is the face with the most non-climber traffic due to the Superior Hiking Trail heading right alongside it.

Top access: Follow the left approach from the summit and drop over a small wall after about 100 feet. Go left and drop over another small wall to reach the area of *Mortgage* to *Early Retirement*. Descend right, parallel to the wall for about 30 feet before turning left for 20 feet. Hopefully you'll be able to find *Citation Needed*, etc. from here.

Experienced climbers can reach the same area by hiking up and right on the Superior Hiking Trail. From the base of *Early Retirement*, either go 15 feet right to head up the 5.3 access gully of *Older Than Dirt*, or head about 100 feet right to find a set of ledges that stair-steps on your left for a Class 2+ ascent up the ledges (the bottom is where the SHT levels out). Once up, cut left to a worn area at the top of *Rugrats* to *Early Retirement*.

Base access: From the junction of the Superior Hiking Trail and the summit spur trail, continue past some low-angle slabs for a few hundred feet. You'll come to a 25-foot-tall block resting against the cliff and an A-shaped overhang just to its right. *Aches & Pains* to *Older Than Dirt* are found here.

20. Overeducated (aka #19, 5.10+ PG13) Follow the SHT around the outside of the big rock outcropping to find an A-shaped cave that's a nice hideout if it starts raining. Inside the little cave is a fantastic crack on the right wall. Falling wouldn't be fun.

Adulting Area

21. Mortgage (aka #20 and #21, 5.5) This chimney route splits into two different finishes. Start on a big block and head up the chimney (on the outside or squeezing in). When you get to the top, you can go straight up for a 5.5 finish. **Variation:** Go far right around the overhang (formerly #22, about 5.7).

22. Aches & Pains (aka #23, 5.12a) ★★ While looking up at the big roof, start up the left side of the A-shaped overhang following a crack into the corner. Pull through the roof, staying to the left of the big horn, while finding an odd foothold or two that you'll feel later on.

23. Climbing the Ladder (aka #24, 5.12b) Look up at the big roof—that's your end-game. Start up the right side of the A-shaped overhang and traverse left to join *Aches & Pains* just before you head into the main overhang of the roof. Stay to the left of the horn at the top.

24. Rugrats (aka #25, 5.9) ★★ Fifteen feet right of the big stepped roof, look for the small left-facing corner with an obvious finger crack that heads all the way to the top. A tricky start over a bulge just left of the crack leads to easier climbing past the right side of a tree.

25. Landline (aka #26, 5.8) ★ On the broken face, start about 6 feet right of *Rugrats* on a flake to a shallow dihedral before making a big move left to a big jug. Follow the rest of the broken dihedral as it aims up and then right, heading toward the tree.

26. Early Retirement (aka #27, 5.8) ★ About 12 feet right of *Rugrats* is a left-leaning finger crack and dihedral. The right side follows a continuous fault with the crux right off the ground, and it stays sustained at finger crack size all the way up.

27. Older Than Dirt (aka #28, 5.3) ★ No topo. This is an access gully that is located about 15 feet right of *Early Retirement* and is the farthest-right rock area on the South Face before it turns into bushes. It can feel a little scrappy with loose rocks and dirt everywhere.

Jane Roskowski on *Mortgage* (5.5)

Kendra Stritch on *Papaya?Banana!* (5.12-) PHOTO: SEAN FOSTER

CRANE LAKE

Poised on the edge of the BWCA, Crane Lake is a place where generations of families come to boat, fish, and slow their lives down a little. A trip that is only an hour longer from the cities compared to the North Shore crags or Blue Mounds, Crane Lake feels like backcountry climbing, but the approaches are short, you can grab a post-climb dinner at the nearby resort or catch your dinner instead, and you can choose between a campsite and cabins. Crane Lake is perfect if you want both the ambience of the Northern Minnesota BWCA and the convenience of amenities nearby.

While there are remnants of old pitons and button head bolts from past youth groups, the bolting and development of the area and the connections to the local community were spearheaded more recently by Sean Foster during the summer of 2015. Through community-supported efforts to buy bolts, he strived to create a crag that was as accessible as it is unique. It's almost overwhelming how many walls and possibilities for more climbing development there are in the area. The two main areas, M&M Hill and Government Bay, are included in this book, but there are other places you could climb a wall straight from a boat, rappel over a cliff into a gorge, or throw down on some stellar boulder problems. With routes ranging in difficulty from 5.7 to 5.12, Crane Lake is a recently added gem to the stellar lineup of crags in the state.

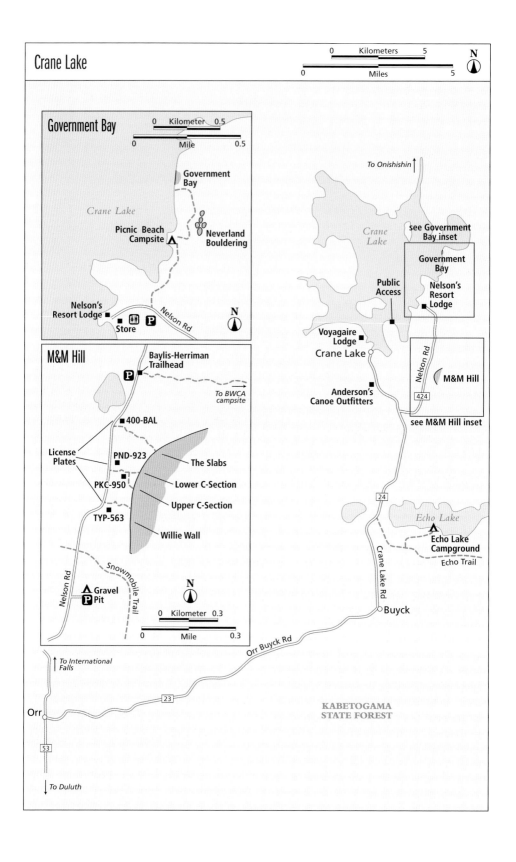

Crane Lake

0   Kilometers   5

0   Miles   5

N

Government Bay

0   Kilometer   0.5

0   Mile   0.5

Crane Lake

Government Bay

Picnic Beach Campsite

Neverland Bouldering

Nelson's Resort Lodge

Store

Nelson Rd

N

To Onishishin

Crane Lake

see Government Bay inset

Government Bay

Nelson's Resort Lodge

Public Access

Voyagaire Lodge

Crane Lake

Anderson's Canoe Outfitters

Nelson Rd

M&M Hill

424

see M&M Hill inset

M&M Hill

Baylis-Herriman Trailhead

To BWCA campsite

400-BAL

License Plates

PND-923

The Slabs

PKC-950

Lower C-Section

Upper C-Section

TYP-563

Willie Wall

Nelson Rd

Snowmobile Trail

Gravel Pit

N

0   Kilometer   0.3

0   Mile   0.3

24

Echo Lake

Echo Lake Campground

Echo Trail

Crane Lake Rd

Buyck

Orr Buyck Rd

To International Falls

23

Orr

53

To Duluth

KABETOGAMA STATE FOREST

Types of Climbing and Gear

The majority of the climbs are sport routes, and ten draws and a 60-meter rope will have you covered. There are also a handful of trad routes, so bringing a single rack gives you options.

The majority of the trees near the cliff edges (especially at M&M Hill) are old and/or rotted, so they're not advisable to use as anchors. There are better trees farther away from the cliff, and there are limited cracks and boulders at the top if you're trying to access the anchors to set up topropes.

Land Acknowledgment

We acknowledge with respect and gratitude that this climbing area is on the traditional lands of the Anishinabewaki and Očhéthi Šakówin people.

Permits, Local Ethics, and Regulations

No permits needed. Use your own gear for toproping; the last climber should lower through the fixed hardware.

Getting There and Parking

Drive to the town of Orr then turn east onto CR 23 toward Crane Lake. After 28 miles and before the town of Crane Lake, you'll turn right onto Nelson Road for 0.8 mile until the gravel pit near M&M Hill or, if you are staying at Nelson's or Picnic Beach, continue 3 miles on gravel road to Nelson's Resort.

Parking is easy at the gravel pit (for free). Nelson's Resort is also a great place to stay if you'd like a bed. You can also park there for Picnic Beach or easy access to Government Bay. It's $5 per night per vehicle, or $10 per night for a vehicle and trailer. Pay at the store across the gravel road from the lodge.

Camping and Amenities

If you need gas, liquor, or anything other than basic groceries, stop in Virginia on your drive up for the best options. Orr is the closest town, about 29 miles/40 minutes from the crags, and they have gas and a small grocery store.

Nelson's Resort is close to the climbing and provides a parking area and restaurant/bar for relaxing after climbing, and a basic camping shop with minimal supplies and groceries. They also have water—there's a big sink outside of the restroom building facing the docks, perfect for filling water bottles or jugs. They're open from the fishing opener in May through the first weekend in October.

Showers are available for $3 per person, or treat yourself to a sauna *and* shower for $5. Pay at the store, where you can borrow a clean loaner towel if you need one.

There are three places you can camp if you don't stay at Nelson's Resort:

- **Picnic Beach** GPS: N48.2778' / W92.4565'
  - This is a fantastic place to camp, but there's only one site and fisherfolk also camp there. It's secluded and on the lake and has room for a couple of tents, a short cliff you can jump off of into the lake, and a pit toilet a short walk away. There are a few bolted climbs and some trad lines a short walk past the toilet.

- The site is on Government Bay, so you can hike 25 minutes or paddle to get to the crag from the campsite (the trail is often overgrown, so canoeing/kayaking is best).
- Park at Nelson's for the hike.
- Everything is pack it in, pack it out and Leave No Trace.
- **The gravel pit** GPS: N48.1421' / W 92.2746'
  - This is the easiest place to camp. Down Nelson Road 0.8 mile from CR-23, look for a gravel pit on your right. It's state forest land that is still occasionally used to mine gravel, but it's flat, graded, free, and wide open yet surrounded by trees and hidden from the road.
  - You can park and camp for free here. There's plenty of room for many tents and cars. There is no designated fire ring.
- **Baylis Herriman Trailhead**
  - This trail is about a mile and a half down Nelson Road, leading to a backcountry campsite roughly 2 miles in on Knute Lake within the BWCA. Park in the horseshoe-shaped pullout on the opposite side of the road. Pack everything in and out, and be sure to sign up for a permit at the trailhead.

Hazards

Watch out for the usual suspects in northern Minnesota: bears, ticks, moose, poison ivy.

While Minnesota is known for bad bugs, it cannot be overstated how overwhelming the bugs can be in the opening months of summer. Think of plague-level infestations and you might be getting close to the horrifying reality of late-spring and early-summer

conditions. Early spring and late summer to fall are better seasons to avoid the mosquitos.

M&M Hill

Called M&M Hill far before modern-day climbers got there, this area was originally frequented by groups of camping kids wearing colored helmets that the locals thought from a distance looked like candy. With plenty of moderates and a relatively flat base, it still provides great climbing for kids if any tag along.

Approach: There are three trail entry points right on Nelson Road that you take to hike into M&M Hill. Look for license plates nailed to trees for your trail markers. From north to south, the license plate 400-BAL will bring you to The Slabs, PND-923

Michelle Schull on *Slabbatical* (5.7)
PHOTO: SEAN FOSTER

brings you to Upper and Lower C-Section, and TYP-563 brings you to the Willie Wall. Routes are listed left to right, or in this case, north to south. To get from area to area, it's recommended to go back to the road or trail split instead of bushwhacking along the wall.

For top access, go climber's right past *Mammas* at Willie Wall and you'll find a scrambly path to the top. Many of the edges are slopey and difficult for setting up topropes.

Routes Not to Miss

Clouds (5.9), Time Slips Away (5.9), Crazy (5.10), Cascade (5.11-), The Crunge (5.12-)

Lower C-Section

PHOTO: BOBBY OMANN

The Slabs

Currently there's only one route established here, but there's plenty of room for more to be added in the future. The trail drops you about 40 feet right of *Slabbatical*.

1. Slabbatical (5.7) ★★★ No topo. Enjoy a slightly arching route with a crux around the third bolt. 5 bolts. **FA:** Sunnie Ainsley.

Lower C-Section

The trail meets the cliff at Clouds.

2. The Crunge (5.12-) ★★★★ No topo. Twenty-five feet left of *Hanging Chad*, you can start either in the dihedral to the right before moving left at the crimp shelf, or a direct start with a V 6/7 boulder problem. Be as efficient as possible as you climb through pumpy but super-fun moves, with a dash of finger strength required at the top in a crack. 3 bolts. **FA:** Sean Foster.

3. Hanging Chad (5.8) ★★There are good ledges and holds in this straightforward route. 4 bolts. **FA:** Sean Foster.

4. Crab Legs (5.9) ★★★ This stellar 5.9 begins with great feet and holds before turning into a cryptic gym climb with little holds and lots of thought halfway up. 4 bolts. **FA:** Sean Foster.

5. Clouds (5.9) ★★★★ Start on the left side of a small roof lower to the ground, and finish on a large pillar at the top. One of the longer routes for the hill, this climb combines fun and balancey movements with a few heady clips for a full experience. 8 bolts. **FA:** Brent Barghahn.

6. C Saw (5.8) ★★ A great climb for someone newer to sport climbing, it has ledges for rests and good holds. 8 bolts. **FA:** Chad Anderson.

7. Assassin's Creed (5.10) ★★★ The route farthest right in the area boasts a wide variety of holds with the option to climb it as two pitches. 3 bolts to chain anchors, above that are 2 more bolts (one with a permadraw) and a second set of anchors. **FA:** Dustin Schull.

Upper C-Section

The trail takes you to the base of Cascade.

8. Cascade (5.11-) ★★★★ No topo. Begin on a big jug toward a lieback to a corner before heading toward a dihedral as it kicks into overhang mode near the top. 5 bolts. **FA:** Jeff Engel.

9. Calypso (5.10+) ★★★ This route is all about figuring out the sequence and crimping hard. **FA:** Sean Foster. 3 bolts.

10. Coal Mine (5.11) ★★★ Head up the vertical face on small holds while trying to figure out the sequence. **FA:** Angie Jacobsen. 4 bolts.

11. Coalnary (5.11+) ★★★★ Start up *Coal Mine* for the first two bolts before moving right into the third bolt of *Canary*. **FA:** Sean Foster.

12. Canary Into Coal Mine (5.9) ★★★ Start up *Canary* for two bolts, then head left, skipping the third bolt for both climbs, clip the fourth bolt of *Coal Mine*, and head up to finish. **FA:** Sean Foster.

13. Canary (5.10+) ★★★ Enjoy a straight-up fun vertical face. **FA:** Ben Scheele. 3 bolts.

14. Crimson (5.10) ★★ Find the flaring detached flakes and the main wall—go straight up before heading up the arête. 4 bolts. **FA:** Brent Barghahn.

Upper C-Section

15. Pillar of the Community (5.10) ★★★ No topo. Named after the local climbing community that helped fund all of the bolts for Crane Lake, this route starts at the spray-painted "C" before heading up the arête on the right side of a pillar. **FA:** Sean Foster. 3 bolts.

Willie Wall

The trail will lead you to *Remember Me.*

16. Bloody Mary Morning (5.9) ★★ No topo. The farthest left route bolted on the wall. Climb over two ledges before hitting anchors just past a tree. **FA:** Julie Ahlbrecht. 4 bolts.

17. Roll Me Up (and Smoke Me When I Die) (5.8) ★★★ Look for the black streak, where you'll climb fun moves on a particularly well-bolted climb. **FA:** Sean Foster. 5 bolts.

18. Band of Gypsies (5.8) ★★ Start up the first two bolts of *On the Road Again* before heading left through a linkup bolt and joining up with *Roll Me Up*'s fifth bolt to the top. **FA:** Sean Foster.

19. On the Road Again (Track 5) (5.10) ★★ Find the spray-painted "5" and enjoy the melodies of amazing holds before the crux at the top. 4 bolts. **FA:** Ben Scheele.

20. Time Slips Away (5.9) ★★★★ A glory of a route that properly earns "one of the best 5.9s at this area" credit. 4 bolts. **FA:** Elysia Gerber.

21. Teatro (5.10) ★★ Head up this arête as it bulges using thoughtful hand movements. Three words: Find the underclings. **FA:** Jacob Gerber. 4 bolts.

Angie Jacobsen on *Calypso* (5.10+) PHOTO: SEAN FOSTER

Willie Wall-Left

22. Chocolate Box
(5.8) TRAD ★★ Head up the face into a right-facing arête on the black face. This leads into a left-facing corner and up between two black streaks. The gear is a little inventive, but that's part of the fun. **FA:** Brent Barghahn.

23. Crazy (5.10) ★★★★ The "don't miss" route of the area, enjoy every type of move climbing could come up with thrown at you as you smile the entire way to the top. 4 bolts. **FA:** Sean Foster.

Willie Wall-Center

24. Remember Me (Track 4) (5.10) ★★ Above the spray-painted "4" are some blocks to navigate before heading over a mini roof as it chills out to the top. 4 bolts. **FA:** Sean Foster.

25. Whiskey River (5.12) ★★★ Look for the arête to the right of *Remember Me* and start on the ledge on the left face. You'll move to the arête after the first bolt. 3 bolts. **FA:** Scott Hogenson.

26. Lefty (5.10) ★★★ Start around the corner to the right of *Whiskey* and go straight up the bolts to the lip before traversing right to the anchors shared with Pancho. 5 bolts. **FA:** Sean Foster.

27. Pancho and Lefty (5.10) ★★ Clip the first bolt of *Pancho* before heading left using a linkup bolt and joining with *Lefty* for the rest of the route. 5 bolts. **FA:** Sean Foster.

28. Pancho (5.9) ★★ On the right side of the dihedral, find this crimpy and sequency route that's a great lead. 4 bolts. **FA:** Sean Foster.

29. Blue Skies (5.9+) TRAD ★★ Love the laybacks on this route just to the left of *Stardust*. The crack eats small gear. Use the anchors for *Stardust*. **FA:** Sean Foster.

30. Stardust (5.12-) TRAD ★★★ Pick and choose between three seams for both gear and what moves you want to do before hitting the tough bouldery moves above. Has

not yet been led. **FTR:** Brent Barghahn.

31. Mammas, Don't Let Your Babies Grow Up to Be Aid Climbers (5.8 A0 PG13) TRAD ★★ No topo. Eight feet to the right of *Stardust*, head up into a right-facing upper dihedral with a few old rusty pins pounded into the crack (it's up to you if you clip and trust them). **FA:** Andrew Knoflicek.

Government Bay

If you're looking for a leisurely day of climbing next to a big open lake with great sunsets, this is the place for you. If you're a 5.9 climber, this is a great place to challenge yourself. Either way, Government Bay is worth the approach, with one of the best 5.11s in the state.

Approach (Crag GPS: N48.2812' / W92.4559'): Boating is the easiest way to get to this crag, as two routes, *Papaya? Banana!* and *Blueberry Fortress*, are only accessible by boat, but with dry land you can belay from. Just park your boat in the small channel between the giant rock and the shore and hop out. The big rock is a great place for spectators to cheer on climbers. There are lots of good spots to park a boat to access the routes on the right side of the cliff.

Willie Wall-Right

If you decide to hike, you'll only have access to the five routes on the right side of the cliff. Hike to the Picnic Beach campsite, then keep following the trail up and left, past the Neverland bouldering area, until you reach the cliff where you'll scramble down a gully to the base. It's about 15 minutes to Picnic Beach, and a farther 25 minutes to reach Government Bay.

Routes Not to Miss

Pineapple Jazz (5.7), Blueberry Fortress (5.11+)

1. Papaya?Banana! (Open Project) TRAD ★★★ If you feel strong, follow the single crack to the left of *Blueberry Fortress* for steep, technical, and powerful moves with small gear at the crux.

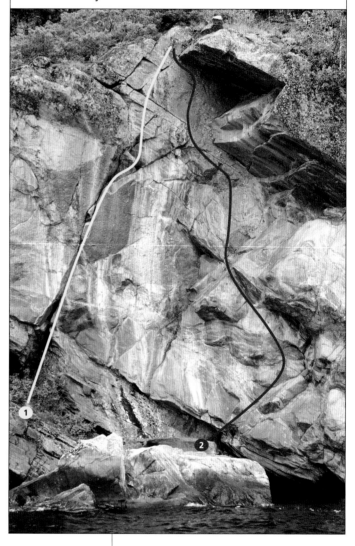

Government Bay-Left

2. Blueberry Fortress (5.11+) ★★★★ This route is the crown jewel of Crane Lake. Don't fall on the first move, or you and your belayer will fall in the water. Start over the water, then head through a thin section before pulling a lip without good holds and heading up to the roof. Instead of pulling the roof, traverse to the left to a horizontal finger crack. The whole climb together is long, heady, and a giant puzzle to unlock. **FA:** Sean Foster.

3. Pineapple Jazz (5.7) ★★★ The belayer can belay from dry land while the climber starts up on a ledge before heading up directly over the water for this exposed but great climb. 5 bolts. **FA:** Sean Foster.

4. Peach Wobbler (5.10) ★★ It's all about finding the holds and some fancy footwork as you boulder through crimps before a layback in the dihedral and pockets up to the roof. 6 bolts. **FA:** Sean Foster.

5. Over Easy Arête (5.9) ★★ Forty-five feet right of *Peach Wobbler*, climb up the arête, then move more on the face after the fourth bolt before heading to the anchors. 5 bolts. **FA:** Sean Foster.

6. Wundercling (5.9+) ★★ On the left of *Roktoberfest*, start in an undercling and continue interesting directional pulls that will test your balance and unused muscle groups. 6 bolts. **FA:** Jessica Goral.

7. Roktoberfest (5.10-) ★★ Farthest route on the right, head up the ramp where it leans to the right. **FA:** Martin Asao.

Katie Gielen on *Conflict Resolution* (5.11+) PHOTO: SETH IVERSON PHOTOGRAPHY

ONISHISHIN

Remote wilderness and pristine lakes. Boating to the crag. Hiking in all of your gear and equipment, miles from the nearest town. Encounters with moose and deer on the trail, and hearing the lingering echoes of wolf howls deep in the night. Onishishin, 10 miles north of the Minnesota border and deep in the Canadian wilderness, is the Midwest's best backcountry climbing, and words can't begin to capture the ruggedness, isolation, beauty, and quality of this area.

Initially developed over a period of fifteen years by Jeff Engel, Onishishin requires all the preparation of a backcountry climbing adventure but with the ease of clipping bolts. From slab 5.8 over a bog to a hard 5.13 dangling from a roof, there is a full variety of climbing that will test your technique as well as your brute strength.

The granite is beautifully textured, making the slabs feel just a little better than you would expect, and the jugs feel incredible. Three very different crags—Secret Lake, Swamp Wall, and Jeff's World, along with two smaller walls—make up the deep-woods experience that is Onishishin.

Spring season is beautiful but short. After ice-out there can be between two and four weeks of climbing (possibly encountering a snowbank or two) before the bugs invade and make climbing downright miserable. If you decide to attempt climbing during the summer, a bug head-net is almost a requirement. Once the bugs simmer down in August, it's beautiful climbing until the snow and ice set in, usually in October or November depending on the weather.

Note: When developing this area, Jeff originally referred to it as part of the "Crane Lake Area," then later it was more specifically

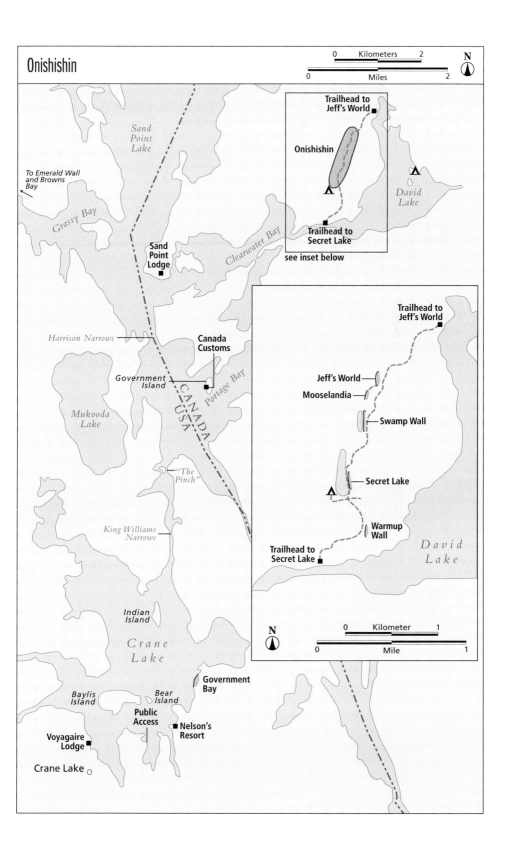

called "David Lake," then playfully dubbed "Jeff's World" by the early visitors who came here to climb. For this book, we decided to try to return to the area's indigenous roots, and so have given it the name Onishishin (accent on the second syllable). This word was given to us by a local in the nearby First Nation village on Lac LaCroix, and translates literally to "beautiful" or "pretty" but can also be more of a world view and refer to something that is "right and good." We discussed this with Jeff and all agree it's the perfect name for this special place.

Types of Climbing and Gear

Onishishin is a sport-climbing crag. Most routes have at most twelve bolts. A 60-meter rope works fine.

There are a couple trad routes and potential for more, so hauling your rack in wouldn't be in vain.

Land Acknowledgment

We acknowledge with respect and gratitude that this climbing area is on the traditional lands of the Anishinabewaki and Očhéthi Šakówiŋ people.

Permits, Local Ethics, and Regulations

Onishishin is in Canada, which means that you must have a passport to enter the country legally. You have two options: Option one is to obtain a **Remote Area Border Crossing Permit** for Canada. A quick search online will bring you to the official Canadian government page with the application and the most up-to-date information. Procedures have been known to change,

but the basics are that you will need a **passport** to apply, money for the application, and up to two months for the permit to get approved by mail. When you finally enter Canada, you need to have a physical copy of the permit in your possession, and you must cross the border at the place you identified in the application.

The second (and easier) option (still open at the time of publication but the customs office may close and you will want to check) is to boat to a **customs office** on Sand Point Lake on your way to Onishishin (see map for location). This is a Direct Reporting Site for marine private vessels. You will need your passport and must follow any rules for entering Canada as per the Canadian Customs website.

Upon return, you also will have to check back into the United States at one of the numerous US Customs kiosks sprinkled throughout the Crane Lake ports. Again, as procedures are changed and updated, be sure to research the most up-to-date protocol. Check out the **US Customs and Border Protection (CBP) Mobile App** called **CBP ROAM** (or the Reporting Offsite Arrival - Mobile) if you want to speed up the process for a remote location arrival. Plan ahead to make sure you're set up with everything you might need before crossing the border.

If you plan on camping or fishing, you'll need permits for those as well (see the "Camping and Amenities" section).

As far as local ethics concerning climbing are concerned, this area truly feels like wilderness. The woods take over the climbing areas pretty quickly up here, so bring wire brushes, chalk, and a five-in-one painter's tool for cleaning out crimps and the cracks. It's local etiquette to bring a wire brush and a small saw and clippers to maintain the trails on your way in (they overgrow fast). When you get to the crags, it's likely that you won't even see chalk on the walls, so it can be tough to find routes. After the first person climbs, feel free to clean the route as needed for the rest of your party and future users to make sure the woods don't envelop the area again.

Getting There and Parking

Getting to Onishishin requires planning and preparation.

The drive to the town of Crane Lake is pretty easy. For a map and more info on the climbing and amenities in that area, check out the Crane Lake chapter.

From Crane Lake, getting to Onishishin requires a boat. If you have your own boat and are a confident navigator, that's great! There are plenty of entry points along the lake. One of the best is the public boat launch located near Handberg's Marina, where there's also free overnight parking available.

If you don't have a boat, here are the services available at the time of publication for renting boats and/or getting a water taxi:

- **Anderson Canoe Outfitters:** Highly recommended by a lot of the climbing groups that helped to establish Onishishin. They offer shuttle services and rentals. For shuttles, their massive barge has a flat rate for the round-trip and can hold up to twelve people and six canoes (which you can also rent from them). If you need to stop at the Canada Customs office, they'll know how. They've heard of the David Lake campsite before and can drop you off right there or even at the Secret Lake

Trailhead! Just let them know where you want to be dropped off and your pickup time and place.

- **Voyagaire Lodge and Houseboats:** Another highly recommended option, they offer water taxi services and boats for renting for super-reasonable prices.
- **Cabins on Crane:** Boat rentals here are available all seasons, and they have a boat launch and places to stay on the US side of the border.
- **Handberg's Marina:** This marina rents boats by the day or week and also has a Service Department if you bring your own boat and need repairs or forgot something at home. The store includes a US Customs kiosk when you're coming back to Minnesota, and has lots of basic grocery goods.
- **Norway Lodge Resort & RV Park:** They offer boat rentals as well as cabins and RV sites if you want to stay on the US side of the border.

You can canoe in if you're really motivated, but it's about 10 miles on big windy lakes where storms crop up seemingly out of nowhere. Waves get big and cold fast. Having a motorized boat also means if someone gets hurt, you can get them out and back to civilization and help faster. We've provided some maps for you to see the lakes, the path, and the major landmarks for camping and climbing up in Onishishin.

Camping and Amenities

Before heading in, you can get gear and groceries in a few places:

- The town of **Virginia** is one of the last places that has a liquor store; it's about 45 minutes before Orr.

- Stop in the town of **Orr** for gas, groceries, etc. It's about 29 miles/40 minutes away from Crane Lake.
- Once on the water, you can stop at Handberg's Marina for boat and stove gas and last-minute snacks, or at **Sand Point Lodge**, in Canada, about 2 miles from Onishishin. Both have basics available.

There are two great options for backcountry camping when climbing at Onishishin. For both locations you'll need a **Canadian Crown Land Camping Permit** for Ontario (search online to obtain one).

A few important things for camping at either place:

- While the water looks pristine and it could be tempting to fill your water bottles straight from the lake, plan to purify drinking water, especially at Secret Lake.
- From spring until mid- to late summer, a bug head net will be a lifesaver.
- You're up in the northern wilderness and will probably still want fall-style warm gear, even in the middle of summer.
- Be ready to hear wolves howling. You might even encounter other—possibly bigger—wildlife. Be respectful and keep your distance.
- There is decent cell service at the top of Swamp Wall and Jeff's World, but it can be spotty or nonexistent at Secret Lake and the campsites.

If you've rented a boat or brought your own, you can camp on David Lake. The backcountry campsite has access to all of the climbing areas and is located on a scenic rock outcropping perfect for swimming and fishing. A bonus is the installed pit toilet down on the north side, about a 3-minute walk from camp (follow some ribbons along a trail).

You could grab a **Canadian Fishing License** (and a required, separate "Outdoors Card") online and catch some of your dinners. You can cast right off of the rocks where you dock your boat. The cold waters mean the smallmouth bass are big, plentiful, and put up a good fight.

If you're being shuttled in without a canoe or any way to paddle around, then plan to hike your gear into Secret Lake. A beautiful campsite about a mile inland is directly across the lake from the crag, right next to the water, and comes with stellar sunsets and sunrises. While the mile walk in can feel like a lot, especially since you have to pack in and pack out *everything*, it's worth it.

There is a stashed canoe that lives at Secret Lake to shuttle back and forth from the crag to the campsite instead of hiking the 15 minutes around the lake, and it allows you to climb the route *Bring Your Own Paddle*. The name tells you everything—you can't use the canoe unless you bring your own paddle.

Approach and Trailheads

Before heading out by boat, make sure you understand how to navigate the buoys along the international border as you will encounter several during this trip. There is also a very shallow section, so boat skills are a plus.

Starting from the public access on the south side of Crane Lake, head north, staying to the east of Bear and Baylis Islands, and continue past Indian Island into the King Williams Narrows. If you did not obtain an RABC, then as soon as you're through the KW Narrows, you're required to check in at Canada Customs on the west side of Government Island in Portage Bay.

After clearing customs go north through the Harrison Narrows, then northeast into Clearwater Bay, passing Sand Point on the left. Continue northeast, passing several islands, to the back side of the bay and around the south side of a peninsula, then turn east (left) and follow this narrow channel to David Lake. This channel is quite shallow and has some large rocks just below the surface, so go slow and keep the prop up.

Just before the channel widens out into David Lake is the trailhead to Secret Lake and its campsite.

To get to the David Lake campsite, go across David Lake to the peninsula on the other side of the island. Dock the boat on the south (right) side of the peninsula.

The trailhead to Jeff's World is on the far-north end of David Lake, on the west (left) side when the lake starts to narrow down. It starts at a birch tree with blue wrap around it.

Specific hiking instructions are in the sections that follow. All routes in the following sections are listed left to right.

Key GPS coordinates:
Trailhead to Secret Lake: N48.374' / W92.413'
Trailhead to Jeff's World: N48.2363' / W92.2403'
David Lake campsite: N48.23034' / W92.23207'
Secret Lake campsite: N48.22504' / W92.24498'
Secret Lake crag: N48.22528' / W92.24438'
Jeff's World: N48.23420' / W92.24036'
Swamp Wall: N48.23236' / W92.24313'

Hazards

You are climbing in a remote area. If you get hurt out there, it will take a while to get to any sort of medical facility. Depending on where you get hurt, you may or may not even have cell service to call for help. Having something like a SPOT beacon is a good "just in case" backup.

The sand flies and mosquitos can make you think plagues have hit the earth. If you're heading up in anything resembling nicer weather in spring and summer, bring bug shirts, bug head nets, bug spray, and bug everything if you want to survive.

Warm-Up Wall

There is no topo for these routes that are often dirty and covered with moss. They're good if you need to get a quick three climbs in, but there are better ones at Secret Lake if you're heading that way anyway.

Approach: From the Secret Lake trailhead, follow the trail through the woods as it meanders mostly uphill and trends east for about five minutes until you come to the wall on your right.

1. Family Affair (5.8+) No topo. Farthest left and the shortest line on the Warm-Up Wall, with a tiny overhang to end the route. **FA:** Jeff Engel.

2. Unnamed (Open project) No topo. The middle bolted line, 5.12-ish.

3. Ticks (5.10) ★ No topo. The first route you encounter on the far right and tallest side of the Warm-Up Wall. Pull on small edges before a thoughtful mantle to finish. **FA:** Jeff Engel.

Secret Lake

This area is on a secluded little lake about a mile inland. The climbs line the east side

Tyler Fast on *Mermar* (5.8) Photo: Taylor Krosbakken

of the lake and a campsite is on the west. The sunsets are spectacular, the Milky Way is bright at night, and when things get too warm while climbing, the lake is a great place to jump in.

Climbing at Secret Lake is fun, varied, and by far the most accessible for the variety of routes. Beginners can come here with people that climb 12s and 13s, and every route will be comfortably bolted and high quality. You will need to lead everything here, as access to the top is difficult (though in many places the top can be traversed once something is climbed).

Approach: From the Secret Lake trailhead, follow the trail through the woods as it meanders mostly uphill and trends east. Go past the Warm-Up Wall on your right, and eventually emerge onto a granite rib. Follow the cairns along the rib heading mostly north, then going back downhill via two Batman ropes. Eventually you'll see the lake up ahead and left. To get to the crag, stay on the main trail and follow it uphill, and you'll eventually come to the bolted route *Going Far Away Again*. Hiking time is 20 to 25 minutes. Before getting to the lake, there is a faint side trail that will take you around the south end of the lake to the camping area on the west side, which will likely involve some

Secret Lake-North End

AERIAL PHOTO: ADVENTURE MN FILMS AND PIXELBUZZ PRODUCTIONS

bushwhacking (about a 10-minute hike). The canoe is usually left parked somewhere on the east side of the lake, which makes it nice to shuttle your gear to the campsite.

Routes Not to Miss

Old Man Smoldering (5.10-), Qisma (5.10), Hotel Catahoula (5.11+), Lakota Son Rise (5.13-)

1. Bring Your Own Paddle (BYOP) (5.10) ★★★ TRAD No topo. Climb and belay directly out of the canoe stashed at Secret Lake in order to ascend the large crack in the corner at the north end of the wall. There's a fun variety of width, and at the top traverse a couple of feet to the left when you reach the roof before hitting the trees.

2. Nasubi (5.10-) ★★★ No topo. Around the corner from the rest and the farthest route climber's left down a path past *Gary Gnu*, look for a chimney that could maybe be an off-width. Climb the arête that forms the edge of this, and for full value, stay on the arête. For a more moderate variation, use the gap of the chimney/off-width to help yourself up. It's tougher on the face but fun to climb the crack. **FA:** Sean Foster.

3. Gary Gnu (5.8) ★★★ The easier of the two 5.8 warmups. The slab might seem intimidating, but the holds are all there if you take your time to find them. This route is the farthest left before heading down the path toward *Nasubi*. **FA:** Sean Foster.

4. Mermar (5.8) ★★★ Longer than *Gary Gnu*, this one is similar in style to a slab with good holds. The longer nature gives it a leg up over *Gary* for difficulty. **FA:** Marianne Bird.

5. Secret Hurl (5.7+) ★★★ TRAD This route is the crack line to the right of *Mermar*, heading up toward a roof. The anchor is bolted for ease, but the gear is great as the crack starts small and opens up before the roof. **FA:** Patrick Maun.

PHOTO: PATRICK MAUN

6. Old Man Smoldering (OMS) (5.10-)
★★★★ One of the other "best" 10s in the area, this route is a fun romp that has no particularly crazy moves, but at 75 feet is nice and long. **FA:** Jeff Engel.

7. Ryan 10a (5.10-) ★★★ Start on the angled block just to the right of *OMS*, and after a couple tricky moves at the start, head straight up the bolt line. **FA:** Ryan Angelo.

8. Afternoon Delight (5.11-) ★★★ Use good technique to carefully pull the roof before heading into the seam on the left as it eases up toward the top. **FA:** Patrick Maun.

9. Take Two (5.10+) ★★★ Head up to a kind of jug horn feature. Once you get over that, it's pretty easy to the top. **FA:** Jeff Engel.

10. Shake Hands With Bigger Things
(5.11+) ★★★ Think horizontally while still using crimps getting over the lip. It will make sense when you climb it. This one is tough. **FA:** Sean Foster.

11. Machine Gun Whiskey (5.11) ★★★ Start with some bouldery moves on overhanging jugs as you get up the wall to get into position. Once on the headwall, find the right sequence on itty-bitty crimps that stay sustained but eventually ease up near the top. **FA:** Tyler Hoffart.

12. Popcorn (5.11+) ★★★★ Look for the black-and-white streaked blocks on the left side of the main roof. Begin on the more chill slab past the first bolt to the no-hands ledge, clip the high clip, then turn into a heated popcorn kernel trying to POP your way up the route. Having parkour skills makes this route easier. **FA:** Tyler Hoffart.

13. Sean 10c (5.10) ★★★ Heady, exposed, and sequency, this technical climb gets you into the dihedral as you move up into a seam before heading left onto the face, up around the corner, and finishing on top of the roof. Don't worry about the roof—you'll find the biggest jugs you've ever held in your life to get through that section. Finish on the same top as *Jeff 10a* after the third bolt. **FA:** Sean Foster.

14. Jeff 10a (5.10-) ★★★ Some say this is a great warm-up, others just call the movement weird. The moves on the jugs through the roof are a little interesting as you try to essentially slide over the roof before joining up with *Sean 10c* to finish at the top. **FA:** Jeff Engel.

15. Reflections (5.12) ★★★★ This route has a boulder start through the streaked roof. Stellar dynamic movements and good clipping stances. **FA:** Tyler Hoffart.

16. Symbiosis (5.12+) ★★★ Start on *Reflections* before heading right at the second bolt, up through the roof for two more bolts to finish the route for a truly spectacular jaunt for the grade and area. **FA:** Tyler Thurmes.

Dan Brazil on *Machine Gun Whiskey* (5.11)

Rachelle Pass on *Lakota Son* (5.10)

18. Lakota Son Rise

(5.13-) ★★★★ This extension climbs *Lakota Son* before heading past the chains through a roof section that requires some creative heel hooking for an intense crux. **FA:** Nic Oklobzija.

19. Pele (5.12) ★★

This is the first route to the right of *Lakota Son* with a big roof. Head up the ledges to get the first bolt before climbing up the white rock and ending on the first roof. **FA:** Tyler Hoffart.

20. Jaguar Shark

(5.13) ★★★ Climb *Pele*, clip the anchors, and find a sit-down rest to the right so you can gather your wits and strength, and pray to the Canadian forest gods before heading into an insane roof section and into a slab and dihedral that require lots of balance after working hard. **FA:** Tyler Hoffart.

17. Lakota Son (5.10) ★★★ Look for some large rocks at the base of the route stacked into a chair near the middle of the main roof area. The crux really makes you think and feels intimidating, but once you go through them, it's not that bad. **FA:** Tyler Hoffart.

21. Suka (5.11) ★★ Climb the face up into the crack. A shorter route with unique movement, but the potential to flip and get the rope caught around your leg makes it a little more spicy. **FA:** Tyler Hoffart.

22. Suka Extension

(Open Project) ★★★ Climb *Suka*, clip the anchors, and figure out how to get through the roof. So far, no one has.

23. Jackknife (5.11+)

★★★★ Head up into a big roof traverse left before the slab/dihedral, another mini roof, and then end sharing the chains with *Jaguar Shark*. The technical details are what make this route truly fantastic. **FA:** Ryan Angelo.

24. Lost Soul (5.9+)

★★★ TRAD Find this route in the large right-facing dihedral— the crack is in the left wall. Follow that up to a thin seam for protection, and pull up onto a big ledge to breathe. The face holds get easier near the top. **FA:** Jeff Engel.

25. The Dogfather's First Rodeo (5.12-)

MIXED ★★ Start on *Lost Soul*, then where the hand crack heads left, follow the dihedral up to the bottom of the big roof. Bouldery moves follow the four bolts on the left side of the roof. **FA:** Kurt Hager and Alex Hager.

Secret Lake-Center

Kurt Hager on *The Dogfather's First Rodeo* (5.12-)
PHOTO: CRYSTEN NESSETH

26. Poison Ivy (5.9) ★★★ No topo. Watch out for the patch of poison ivy at the bottom of the route that gives it its name.

Hillary Waters rappelling on *Qisma* (5.10)

Climb fun vertical rock with a crux after clipping the first bolt. Bring a #2 cam if you don't want a serious runout on the top slab. **FA:** Jeff Engel.

27. Labor of Love (5.9) ★★★ Look for the horizontal flake halfway up the route. Climb the corner to the left of the pine tree up to the flake, then clip the two bolts at the flake for the crux to an overhanging corner before reaching the anchors. **FA:** Karen Schoenbauer.

28. Hotel Catahoula (5.11+) ★★★ This shares the first bolt with *Qisma*. Look for a giant pine tree growing from the cliff. A long and exposed route through the dihedral with multiple cruxes. The move at the arête up high makes you doubt everything. Don't think—just commit and do it, then think "OMG I can't believe that worked." **FA:** Tyler Hoffart.

29. Qisma (5.10) ★★★★ One of the best 5.10s for good reason. After the tree (optional to use), traverse right into thin crimps to a bulge. Head straight up with low-angle technical slab moves before continuing right toward the roof. Roof is choose-your-own-adventure. **Note:** Please leave the carabiner in the second bolt, as when cleaning it acts as a directional to avoid lowering over the sharp edges to the right. **FA:** Zaynab Alwan.

30. Nutella Sugarglider (5.11-)

★★★ Stick-clip the first bolt. The opening bouldery moves are a little intense as you pull through the roof. Trend to the left on classic low-angle slab before pulling a little roof with crimps and finishing in a dihedral. A fantastic climb with lots of different elements. *Note:* Please leave the carabiner in the second bolt, as when cleaning it acts as a directional to help avoid lowering over the sharp edges to the left. **FA:** Stan Lajoie.

31. Baby Come Home

(5.10-) ★★★★ As you hike into the Secret Lake Wall area, this is the second bolted route you encounter. A lower slab with a baby crux before climbing up into the corner and the roof. While the route looks intimidating, the roof has jugs and good feet. **FA:** Tyler Hoffart.

32. Going Far Away Again (5.11-) ★★★

Shares the first bolt of *Baby Come Home* before heading up the bolt line to the right. The whole slab is the crux; it eases after you're above it. Often wet. **FA:** Sean Foster.

Secret Lake-South End

Angie Jacobsen on *Baby Come Home* (5.10-) Photo: Sean Foster

33. Uncle Steve's Horrible Off-Width

(5.10-) ★★ Don't believe the name. Look for a wide crack in an inside corner 10 feet to the right of *Baby Come Home*. Encounter all types of crack climbing for about 60 feet before traversing left on the ledge below the roof for about 5 feet, then up another 5 feet to the bolted anchors. **FA:** Steve Mercer.

Bobby Omann on his Swamp Wall project PHOTO: SEVVE STEMBER

Swamp Wall

The Swamp Wall is located in a beautiful little jack pine bog (not really a swamp). Four people comfortably fit on the "Minnow" (the raft), but only one can climb at a time. It is possible to create a top-managed belay system off of the trees far back from the wall if you want to toprope, but half the fun of climbing here is climbing from the raft.

There is a handline set up along the wall for navigating the raft, so no need to bring a paddle. Put the *Minnow* back where you found her when you're done, and tie her up.

While people have deep-water soloed at the Swamp Wall, it's a bog with submerged trees that move. Hidden hazards could ruin your trip.

Approach from Secret Lake: Hike to the north end of the Secret Lake crag, past *Gary Gnu*, scramble down and around the route

Nasubi, and continue along the trail trending uphill. Once you're on higher ground, follow the cairns mostly north for about 20 minutes. Just before reaching the top of the Swamp Wall is a trail on the left—wind your way downhill—a bit scrambly in places—to where the raft is parked at the south end (climber's right) of the wall.

Approach from Jeff's World: From the top of the cliff at Jeff's World, hike south for about 10 minutes following the cairns. You'll emerge at the top of the Swamp Wall—keep walking south to find the trail to wind your way down as previously described.

Note: If you're heading directly to the Swamp Wall for the day, the Jeff's World trailhead will get you there faster.

Routes Not to Miss

Good Omann (5.8), Beach Party (5.9), Electric Stegosaurus (5.11+), Beast of the Bog (5.12+)

Swamp Wall

AERIAL PHOTO: ADVENTURE MN FILMS AND PIXELBUZZ PRODUCTIONS

1. Good Omann (5.8) ★★★★ Even people who don't like slab like this route. Pull the raft as far as you can before hitting the bog, and the route starts another 10 to 12 feet over from that. This means you have to get off the raft on the wall and traverse over to get that first clip. If you slip, you're going to fall in the squishy bog for some solid swamp butt. Once you're clipped, head up the slab on holds that are *just* good enough. **FA:** Matt Olson.

2. Swamp Foot (5.8) ★★ To the right of *Omann*, this route is good as long as it's clean. **FA:** Patrick Hertz.

3. Howlin' at the Moon (aka Waiting for Tyler, 5.8) ★★★ This route is about 20 to 30 feet left of *Dragonfly*, and you get to enjoy big holds as you fly up. **FA:** Brenda Piekarski.

4. Dreamt I Was a Dragonfly (5.12-) ★★★ On the overhanging section of the swamp wall, it's the leftmost climb. Enjoy juggy overhanging climbing to the fourth bolt, then turn the roof with some technical climbing before the vertical wall. **FA:** Tyler Hoffart.

5. Canadian Love Shield (5.11) ★★★ Follow some incredible jugs up some features that jut out of the wall before technical climbing at the lip. **FA:** Tyler Hoffart.

6. Electric Stegosaurus (5.11+) ★★★★ The premier route on this wall climbs straight up the center with good rests and two very different cruxes. Even after you get the big throw, it doesn't relent until you clip the anchors. **FA:** Tyler Hoffart.

7. Blinded by Psych (5.13-) ★★★ Begin climbing *Beast of the Bog* before following a left-angling seam to the triangle roof of *Stegosaurus*. Crimp through the roof before emptying your gas tank to clip the anchors of *Stegosaurus*. **FA:** Kurt Hager.

8. Beast of the Bog (5.12+) ★★★★ Scramble up 5.9 terrain to the first bolt at a standing rest. This route has both intricate sequencing and a full dyno. Delicately move up improbable thin granite plate jugs to the top, where you'll enjoy a tricky lip encounter. **FA:** Kurt Hager and Alex Hager.

9. Beach Party (5.9) ★★★★ This is the farthest route to the right and the first one you encounter floating in on the *Minnow*. It's vertical, but the bigger holds make you feel pretty good as you move around up the face. **FA:** Bobby Omann.

Kurt Hager on *Beast of the Bog* (5.12+) Photo: Sheila Novak

Jeff's World

Most of the best climbing here is the really hard stuff. The moderates are fun, but it's worth it to show up ready to project something at your limit. Because of the trees, even on sunny days you're going to be in the shade. The bugs hang out in swarms, ready to enjoy those who don't come prepared to fight them off.

Most of these climbs are bouldery with great rests on a ledge or kneebar. Unless you want to carry in a bunch of gear and long static line to sling trees, you'll need to lead these routes. You *can* set them up as TR. You truly feel isolated, enjoying this beautiful area with incredible rock.

Approach: From the Jeff's World trailhead, follow the trail as it meanders uphill trending west and south, eventually emerging on the granite rib. From here, cairns mark the faint trail as you continue along the rib until you start going downhill again. As you weave and drop down to the base, you're going to feel like you're heading into a hidden valley. When you get to the bottom using the Batman rope, turn north (climber's left—if you go climber's right, you'll hit *Mooselandia*). Hiking time is 25 to 30 minutes.

Routes Not to Miss

Gargoyle (5.10+), Cathedral (5.12+), Crown Land (5.13), The Wendigo (5.13)

1. Black Beta (5.12-) ★★★ This starts on the same big boulder as *Advanced Petting*. Open with some big moves before heading up the arête. **FA:** Brandon Busch.

2. Advanced Petting (5.10-) ★★ Head up the right side of the arête on the detached boulder for this short route. Using the wall doesn't help you. **FA:** Josh Helke.

Jeff's World–Left

PHOTO: SEVVE STEMBER

Kurt Hager on *Based on a True Story* (5.13) Photo: Bobby Omann

7. Sit Clip (5.9) ★★

This unique route feels more like a pitch of adventure climbing than sport climbing. On the left side under the big roof, begin on the slab about 5 feet right of the corner while heading to the left corner of the roof. Figure out your own beta to comfortably move and clip the fifth bolt. **FA:** Jim Klett.

8. FLR (5.10) ★★★

Start up *Sit Clip* before following the crack as it heads right after you clip the fifth bolt. The roof can feel intimidating, but once you hit the slab on top, things get easier. **FA:** Michael Endrizzi.

3. Contortion (5.11+) ★★

Head up sidepulls on a black streak. A tricky arête to a tricky move at the top. Short, but it makes you think.

4. Loud With the Lights Out (5.12+) ★★

This short route shares the anchors with *Quiet*. Powerful moves get you through the overhang. **FA:** Tyler Hoffart.

5. Quiet With the Lights On (5.12-) ★★

Though short, it's really fun for those who love technical climbing with a roof thrown in for good measure. Once you pull the roof, follow the cut "C" in the rock before heading to the anchors. **FA:** Kurt Hager.

6. Squeeze Jelly (5.10+) ★★★

This route is a fantastic compression line along the right to the left of *Sit Clip*. Stay on the arête for full 5.10 value fun. **FA:** Ryan Angelo.

9. Based on a True Story (5.13) ★★★★

One of the wildest routes in Jeff's World, knee pads are almost mandatory. Look for the flare feature to the left of *Gargoyle*. Open on some fun 5.12 moves before heading into what can only be described as 3-D roof climbing. The top is a little easier—but heady—on runout and lichen-covered rock. **FA:** Kurt Hager.

10. Crown Land (5.13) ★★★★

Offers the full package of boulders thrown together with no rests, making it a true power endurance test piece. The route starts down and left and moves up and to the right. Finish on the arête for *Cathedral* to the top. **FA:** Avery Turman.

Jeff's World-Center

PHOTO: SEVVE STEMBER

11. Gargoyle (5.10+) **★★★★** A fantastic climb with really big moves, big holds, and fun flakes moving right. Find the namesake rest on the ledge before weaving up and right and then back left toward the chains on holds worse than you'd hope. **FA:** Jeff Engel.

12. Cathedral (5.12+) **★★★★** Climb *Gargoyle* until the anchors, then keep going. Figure out how to pull the roof at the chains, then up an arête. The moves are hard, especially for taller folks, but it's a great weekend-warrior route. **FA:** Tyler Hoffart.

13. Notre Dame (5.12) Start on *Bloody Knuckles* before moving left at the roof through the *Gargoyle* anchors and finishing by topping out on *Cathedral*. Good linkup. **FA:** Randall Baum.

14. Bloody Knuckles (5.12-) **★★★** Start just right of *Gargoyle*, climbing a direct line up and sharing its chains. Crimps on the face with a hand in the flare. **Variation:** Climb inside the flare to downgrade this route to 12a. The crux is after the first bolt. Good route for knee-bars. **FA:** Chris Hirsch.

15. Action Satisfaction (5.13-) **★★★★** A cool route with a formidable crimp ladder in the crux. Start in the *Bloody Knuckles* flare, then traverse right after the first rest. **FA:** Tyler Thurmes.

PHOTO: SEVVE STEMBER

16. The Wendigo (5.13) ★★★★ Look for a bulge to open this route with amazing climbing, especially for taller climbers. Climb up through blank-looking rock with no intermediates. If you're 5 feet 10 inches or taller, it's one of the best routes in this guidebook. **FA:** Kurt Hager.

17. Chipmunk (5.12) ★★★★ Start with bouldery moves before getting to the top of the flake and moving up to the ledge. Head toward the giant horn and beware of the last move. Clip after the horn. **FA:** Noah Ridge.

18. Raptor (5.12-) TRAD ★★★ This route begins by placing gear up a ramp until a large ledge. Joins in with *Chipmunk* after the ledge. **FA:** Jeff Engel.

19. Nanook of the North (5.11-) ★★ No topo. The bolted route south of *Surfer Rosa*. Climb up the corner of a bit of a ramp on easy terrain before following the bolts. Fun underclings and liebacks. **FA:** Dan Brazil.

20. King of the North (Open Project) No topo. Right of *Chipmunk* and left of *Gorilla* on a beautiful white streak of rock, look for a lonely permadraw right after a small roof for this line. It's not bolted all the way to the ground, so the FA will have to add the starting bolt once they figure out the impossible: how to get off the ground. All the business is in that bottom 10 feet.

Jeff Engel with the gargoyle pose (required for the send) on *Gargoyle* (5.10+) Photo: Seth Iverson Photography

21. Gorilla (5.12-) ★★★ No topo. When looking at the streaked black-and-white "zebra wall," you'll see this route as it heads up easier climbing before moving left into the overhang, where the holds will become your best friends. **FA:** Ryan Angelo.

22. Conflict Resolution (5.11+) ★★★ No topo. Awkward opening moves get you under the roof. Clip the draw, then head over the lip. The draw placement allows for a cleaner fall. Once you pull the big roof, it's game over. **FA:** Sean Foster.

23. Surfer Rosa (5.10) ★★ No topo. Look for the "surfboard" jutting partway up the route. Opens with tough moves up the blunt arête—stay to the left of the bolt line if you want to make it easier. Stick-clipping those first two bolts is a good idea. After surfing there are some powerful moves to the top. **FA:** Jeff Engel.

24. Handicap Accessible (5.11) ★★ No topo. Good route, this is the farthest bolted route on the right. **FA:** Michael Endrizzi.

Mooselandia

Approach: From the bottom of the Jeff's World access gully, go south (climber's right) for about 100 yards and you'll find the little tiny crag known as Mooselandia, named as such for a moose antler found when the developers were working on this area. If you get to the swamp, you've gone too far.

1. Mooswu (Open Project) ★★★ No topo. This is the first bolted route climber's left. Follow some great balancey face moves to the giant ledge, then crank through an incredible roof that barely eases after you get to the lip. Note that the second bolt on the roof is really high up—an extended draw would help here.

2. My First Moose (aka Bosch Toss, 5.12-) ★★ No topo. This route heads straight up the center of the Mooselandia roof. Climb up the slab toward the roof, where you'll make the "Bosch Toss" move. **FA:** Bobby Omann.

3. Big Fish on the Rocks (5.9) ★★★ No topo. The line farthest climber's right—it's a great moderate addition to the area. Head toward the roof before making a couple spicy moves around the corner and finish straight up. **FA:** Angie Jacobsen.

MINNESOTA TOP 50 TICK LIST

The following list was compiled from surveys of climbers, comments and ratings from various online forums, interviews with local experts, heated discussions with friends over email and at the brewery, and personal bias. It was not voted on democratically, it is not scientific, and it is likely skewed toward the book creators' personal opinions. We invite you to write in all your favorites that we likely left off. Now go tick some routes.

Route	Grade	Page
☐ The Great Yawn	5.6	182
☐ Dislocation Overhang	5.6	141
☐ Piece of Cake	5.7	105
☐ Air Conditioned	5.7	121
☐ The Flake	5.7	140
☐ The Great Bird Chimney	5.7	164
☐ Lost Ego	5.8-	120
☐ Franklin's Direct	5.8	52
☐ The Future	5.8	74
☐ Jasper's Dihedral	5.8	27
☐ Good Omann	5.8	245
☐ Dance of the Sugar-Plump Faeries	5.7-5.10	178
☐ Bluebells	5.9	162
☐ Birch Flakes	5.9	200
☐ Rubble Trouble Direct	5.9	207
☐ The Bulge	5.10a	108
☐ Balcony Center	5.10a	30
☐ Compromises	5.10b	127
☐ Rapprochement	5.10b	161
☐ Gold Plated	5.10b	182
☐ Laceration Jam	5.10b	155
☐ Sentinel Crack	5.10b	119
☐ Jack Be Nimble	5.10b/c	191
☐ The Deputy	5.10	55
☐ Qisma	5.10	242
☐ Urge to Mate	5.10c	164
☐ Gargoyle	5.10+	249
☐ Digit Damage	5.11a	207
☐ Don't Bring a Knife to a Gunfight	5.11b	167
☐ Hidden Treasure	5.11b	162
☐ Driving in Duluth	5.11b	164
☐ The Poseidon Adventure	5.11d	173
☐ Mr. Lean	5.11d	165
☐ Narcoleptic Epic	5.11d	180
☐ Electric Stegosaurus	5.11+	245
☐ Blueberry Fortress	5.11+	228
☐ Chinese Freedom	5.12a	67
☐ Sunny and Sheer	5.12a	162
☐ Sigma	5.12b	130
☐ Oz	5.12b	159
☐ Soli Deo Gloria	5.12b	170
☐ Mississippi	5.12c	69
☐ Natural Selection	5.12c	89
☐ Femme Fatale	5.12c	73
☐ Cathedral	5.12+	249
☐ The Gales of November	5.13-	160
☐ Nexus	5.13a	130
☐ Palisaid	5.13a	162
☐ Paradigm Shift	5.13a	68
☐ Crown Land	5.13	248
☐ Dry Lightning	5.13c	92

Slavomír Tkáč on *Palisaid* (5.13a)
PHOTO: WILLIAM HOPKINS

ADDITIONAL RESOURCES

Previous Guidebooks

Barnyard Boogie (Nate Postma, 1990)

Climber's Guide to Blue Mounds State Park, A (Zumbro River Alpine Club and North Shore Climbers Group, undated)

Climber's Guide to Taylors Falls, The (Swenson, Roberts, and Schmidt, 1972)

Close to the Edge, Down by the River: A Climber's Guide to Interstate Park, 2nd ed. (Peter Von Grossman and Peter Scott, 1989)

Duluth's Urban Cragger: A Guide to Climbing and Bouldering in the City of Duluth (Laura Petersen and Josh Wiese, 2004)

Field Guide to Minnesota Bouldering, A (Cargill, Oklobzija, Craft, Marek, 2013)

Minnesota Rock: Selected Climbs (Mike Farris, 1995)

Minnesota/Wisconsin: Bouldering Guidebook (Cargill, Oklobzija, Vongsavanthong, Horn, Marek, 2017)

North Shore Adventures: The Best Hiking, Biking, and Paddling from Duluth to Grand Portage (Katie Berg, 2018)

Peter's Guide to Duluth Bouldering (Peter Dodge, 2011)

Prairie Walls: A Climber's Guide to Minnesota's Blue Mounds State Park (Eric Landmann and Don Hynek, 1989)

Rock Climbing Guidebook to Blue Mounds State Park, A (Scott Wurdinger, 1989)

Rock Climbing: Minnesota and Wisconsin, 1st ed. (Mike Farris, 2000)

Rock Climbing: Minnesota and Wisconsin, 2nd ed. (Mike Farris, 2012)

Superior Climbs: A Climber's Guide to the North Shore, 1st ed. (David Pagel, 1984)

Superior Climbs: A Climber's Guide to the North Shore, 2nd ed. (David Pagel and Richard Kollath, 1991)

Willow Climbing Guide (Jeff Engel and Anthony Vicino, 2011)

Other Sources

Climb Duluth: climbduluth.com

Duluth Climbers Coalition: duluthclimbers.org

Jeff's World—Full Film (Adventure MN Films, available at www.adventuremnfilms.com/jeffs-world, 2017)

Minnesota Climbers Association: mnclimbers.org

"Minnesota Climbing" page on mountainproject.com

Minnesota Department of Natural Resources: dnr.state.mn.us (Parking permits, route closures, state "I Can Climb" programs, etc.)

North Shore Vertigals: northshorevertigals.wordpress.com

Vertical Jones: The Midwest's Climbing Magazine (Stephen Regenold, editor/publisher, Volumes 1–11, Mar 1998–Jan/Feb 2002)

INDEX

ABOUT THE AUTHORS

Katie Berg moved to Duluth, Minnesota, for college, and while working her way through undergrad and graduate school at UMD, she served as a rock-climbing instructor for a local climbing gym while spending months of her summers climbing in Yosemite, the Grand Tetons, the Wind River Range, Devil's Tower, the Red River Gorge, Greece, the Dolomites in Italy, and, of course, all of her favorite local crags. She is a college writing professor and a dance competition coach and choreographer, as well as a climbing guide in the summers for Midwest Mountain Guides.

Angie Jacobsen is a mother of two, scientist, storyteller, and angler based in St. Paul, Minnesota. She has been climbing since 2008, and she is a lead guide for Devils Lake Climbing Guides, as well as a freelance photographer.

About The Cover

In the summer of 2020, two women set a goal to lead the route Oz, an iconic test piece on the intimidating cliffs of Palisade Head. Despite being accomplished boulderers and sport climbers, they were novices to trad climbing. If successful, they would be the first (known) women to send Oz on gear. I knew immediately that *this* had to be my cover shot. Other women joined #TeamLadyOz and we belayed, provided tech support with anchors and gear, critiqued placements, and provided tons of psyche and snacks. I hung on a rope a hundred feet down over the side of that cliff for countless hours, took thousands of images, tested different heights, angles, and lighting, learned where the moves were that would make the best picture, and hauled myself back up. And I made them wear bright colors. In the end, both Liz Horn (on the cover) and Rachelle Pass sent Oz. And I got my shot.

#TeamLadyOz: Liz Horn, Sarah Vanderheiden, Rachelle Pass, and Angie Jacobsen Photo: Pi